T0236460

Lecture Notes in Computer Science   8603

Commenced Publication in 1973
Founding and Former Series Editors:
Gerhard Goos, Juris Hartmanis, and Jan van Leeuwen

More information about this series at http://www.springer.com/series/7407

Lucio Grandinetti · Thomas Lippert
Nicolai Petkov (Eds.)

Brain-Inspired Computing

International Workshop, BrainComp 2013
Cetraro, Italy, July 8–11, 2013
Revised Selected Papers

 Springer

Editors
Lucio Grandinetti
Faculty of Engineering
University of Calabria
Arcavacada di Rende
Italy

Thomas Lippert
Jülich Supercomputing Centre
Jülich
Germany

Nicolai Petkov
Institute for Mathematics
and Computer Science
University of Groningen
Groningen
The Netherlands

ISSN 0302-9743   ISSN 1611-3349   (electronic)
ISBN 978-3-319-12083-6   ISBN 978-3-319-12084-3   (eBook)
DOI 10.1007/978-3-319-12084-3

Library of Congress Control Number: 2014953214

Springer Cham Heidelberg New York Dordrecht London

Printed on acid-free paper

Springer is part of Springer Science+Business Media (www.springer.com)

Preface

Brain-inspired computing is a fast developing research topic. On one hand, it relates to fundamental neuroscience research that leads to insights into the information processing function of the brain. On the other hand, it is aimed at utilizing these insights in new methods and technologies for information processing and might even initiate a paradigm change in this area. Brain-inspired computing creates opportunities for collaboration of scientists from various disciplines: neuroscience, computer science, engineering, natural sciences, and mathematics. The understanding of the importance of this area led to the initiation of the EU flagship project 'Human Brain' in the framework of the EU program for future and emerging technologies (FET). The current book includes contributions from renowned scientists who participated in the International Workshop on Brain-Inspired Computing in Cetraro, Italy, July 8–11, 2013. It contains contributions that concern brain structure and function, computational models and brain-inspired computing methods with practical applications, high-performance computing, and visualization for brain simulations.

August 2014

Lucio Grandinetti
Thomas Lippert
Nicolai Petkov

Organization

BrainComp2013 is organized by the Department of Electronics, Informatics, and Systems, University of Calabria, Italy, Forschungszentrum Juelich, Germany, and Johann Bernoulli Institute for Mathematics and Computer Science, University of Groningen.

Program Committee

Nicolai Petkov, Chair	University of Groningen, Netherlands
Thomas Lippert, Chair	Forschungzentrum Juelich, GmbH, Germany
Lucio Grandinetti	University of Calabria, Italy
Jack Dongarra	University of Tennessee Knoxville, USA

Speakers

K. Amunts
G. Azzopardi
F. Baetke
A. Bandera
U. Beierholm
G. Bhanot
M. Biehl
Y. Botros
M. Diesmann
L. Grandinetti

S. Gruen
B. ter Haar Romeny
T. Kuhlen
J. Labarta
A. Leonardis
T. Lippert
R. Marfil
V. Martin
K. Meier
A. Morrison

M. Okadan
L. Pastor
N. Petkov
N. Ramsey
A. Rodriguez-Sanchez
T. Schulthess
F. Schürmann
T. Sterling
R. Visvanathan

Sponsoring Institutions

IBM
Jülich Supercomputing Centre, Germany
ParTec Cluster Competence Center, Germany
Intel
University of Calabria, Italy

Contents

HPC and Visualization for Human Brain Simulations

Brain Structure and Function - A Neuroscience Perspective

Towards a Multiscale, High-Resolution Model of the Human Brain

Katrin Amunts[1,2(✉)], Oliver Bücker[3], and Markus Axer[1]

[1] Research Centre Juelich, Institute of Neuroscience and Medicine (INM-1),
Juelich, Germany
{k.amunts,m.axer}@fz-juelich.de
[2] Cecile and Oskar Vogt Institute for Brain Research,
Heinrich Heine University Düsseldorf, Düsseldorf, Germany
katrin.amunts@uni-duesseldorf.de
[3] Juelich Supercomputing Centre (JSC), Research Centre Juelich,
Juelich, Germany
o.buecker@fz-juelich.de

Abstract. To understand the microscopical organization including cellular and fiber architecture it is a necessary prerequisite to build models of the human brain on a sound biological basis. We have recently pushed the limits of current technology by creating the first ultra-high resolution 3D-model of the human brain at nearly cellular resolution of 20 microns, the BigBrain model. At the same time, 3D Polarized Light Imaging provides a window to analyze the fiber architecture, i.e., the way, how brain regions are inter-connected, with unprecedented spatial resolution at the micrometer level. Considering the complexity and the pure size of the human brain with its nearly 86 billion nerve cells, both approaches are most challenging with respect to data handling and analysis in the TeraByte to PetaByte range, and require supercomputers. Parallelization and automation of image processing steps open up new perspectives to speed up the generation of new, ultra-high resolution models of the human brain, to provide new insights into the three-dimensional micro architecture of the human brain.

Keywords: Ultra-high resolution brain models · BigBrain · Cytoarchitecture · Microstructure · Fiber architecture · UNICORE · Workflows

1 Introduction

The cerebral cortex of the human brain is a highly heterogeneous structure. Since the beginning of the 20th century it is well known that the cortex consists of organ-like units, which Brodmann and others have called cortical areas [1]. Using a light microscope, Brodmann observed that every cortical area showed a characteristic cytoarchitecture. Cytoarchitectonic features include the distribution of neurons, the presence of particular cell types such as giant Betz cells, which are characteristic for the primary motor area 4 [2–4], clustering of cell bodies, and the formation of cortical layers (thickness, density, etc.), which run in parallel to the cortical surface (Fig. 1). Based on such differences, Brodmann published his famous monograph and a map, which displayed 43 cytoarchitectonic areas. Most of the areas of the cerebral cortex

© Springer International Publishing Switzerland 2014
L. Grandinetti et al. (Eds.): BrainComp 2013, LNCS 8603, pp. 3–14, 2014.
DOI: 10.1007/978-3-319-12084-3_1

show 6 layers (isocortex or neocortex, because it is developed late during brain evolution) with the notable exception of the motor cortex, which looses its fourth layer during postnatal development [1, 5]. The different regions of the isocortex subserve sensory (e.g., visual, auditory, somatosensory, gustatory, vestibular, pain), motor, and multimodal associative (e.g., working memory, attention, goal-directed behaviour) functions. Non-isocortical regions have more (e.g., entorhinal cortex) or less (e.g., hippocampus) layers than the isocortex. Therefore, these regions are called allocortex. It is known, that this laminar pattern is related to the connectivity of neurons, and reflects the prevailing inputs and outputs of the layers. For example, Layer I contains many axons, which establish short and long-range intracortical connections. Layers II and III have ipsilateral and commissural connections with cortical areas in the same and the other hemisphere. Layer IV is the major target of the ascending thalamo-cortical input, whereas the neurons of layers V and VI project to subcortical targets (e.g., basal ganglia, thalamus, brain stem and spinal cord). It is estimated that each neuron of the cerebral cortex has approximately 7.000 synapses [6], i.e., contacts to other neurons; the precise number of synapses differs between layers [7].

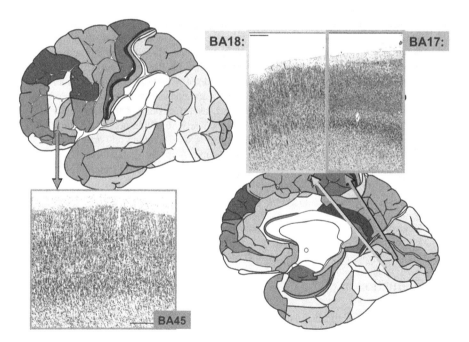

Fig. 1. Cytoarchitecture of the human cerebral cortex as basis of Brodmann's map from 1909. Each area of the cerebral cortex in Brodmann's map is labeled by a different color. The cytoarchitecture is illustrated in three cortical areas, BA 45, 17 and 18, belonging to different functional systems. Cell bodies are stained in black, and show a different distribution and density from the surface of the brain (top) to the cortex/white matter border. The space between the cell bodies is called neuropil. It contains synapses, dendrites and axons as major structures, which are relevant for connectivity between brain regions (Color figure online).

Using image analysis in combination with statistical tools of analysis, we have developed an approach to map cytoarchitectonic areas of the cerebral cortex in samples of (ten) human postmortem brains [8], and to register these maps in standard references space. Therefore, we have created probabilistic cytoarchitectonic maps in 3D. These maps can then be used, for example, as microstructural references for functional imaging studies of the living human brain. To allow comparisons between in vivo MR findings and postmortem cytoarchitectonic maps, the cytoarchitectonic maps have been made available in different software packages such as SPM toolbox (http://www.fz-juelich.de/inm/inm-1/DE/Forschung/_docs/SPMAnatomyToolbox/SPMAnatomyToolbox_node.html; [9–11]) and FSL (http://fsl.fmrib.ox.ac.uk/fsl/fslwiki/Atlases?highlight=%28probabilistic%29|%28maps%29). Or, they can be directly downloaded from the JuBrain website (https://www.jubrain.fz-juelich.de/apps/cytoviewer/cytoviewer-main.php).

The analysis of in vivo imaging studies based on cytoarchitectonic maps contributes to our knowledge of the relationship of the microstructural segregation of the human brain and the involvement of cortical areas and subcortical nuclei into a certain mental process (e.g., [12–14]), or they can be used as an atlas to guide or to interpret studies on connectivity and functional segregation as obtained during in vivo neuroimaging studies [15, 16]. The spatial resolution, which is necessary to address this type of structure-functional relationships is determined by the resolution of in vivo neuroimaging studies, which is in the range of 1 millimetre, i.e., at the mesoscopic level.

The highly complex organization of the human cerebral cortex at the level of single cells and their connections can be achieved only with a resolution at a few micrometres. It requires postmortem methods for the analysis, in most cases. As compared to investigations of the brains of non-human primates and rodents, the human brain is highly challenging due to the pure size of the whole human brain and the number of nerve cells (nearly 86 billion) in combination with the same number of glial cells [17, 18]. Neurons have a size of a several micrometers; the largest of them, the giant Betz cells of the primary motor cortex, can reach a height of 120 μm [19]. To address the microscopical organization of the human brain is not only challenging from the neuroscientific perspective, but also with respect to computational demands.

We have recently pushed the limits of existing three-dimensional brain data sets to a microscopical scale, and developed the BigBrain model [20]. The model is based on 7404 cell-body stained histological sections, which were corrected for artifacts, and reconstructed as a volume with 20-micrometre spatial resolution isotropic. This model provides a basis for extracting morphometric parameters characterizing the cortical folding, cell densities or cortical thickness, which can be used, e.g., for modelling and simulation. Moreover, it will serve as a new reference brain at a microscopical level, where structural and activity data from other researchers can be integrated while keeping the functionally relevant topography of the brain at the level of cortical layers and below [21]. In order to generate this model, methods of high performance computing were necessary – the total size of the data set was 1 TByte, and for the automated repair, 2D- and 3D alignment, and intensity correction 295,000 h were necessary for 100 iterations, measured on an AMD Opteron 2.1 GHz system. I/O operations hereby required a significant amount of time [20].

The architecture of cells in different brain areas and nuclei represents an important aspect of brain organization. It reflects differences in brain connectivity between brain areas, and cortical layers. E.g. thalamic projections from the lateral geniculate body terminate in layer IVB of the primary visual cortex, whereas layer III pyramidal cells project to other cortical areas including those in the contralateral hemisphere [22], and layer V Meynert cells of the primary visual cortex form T-shape projections to higher associative visual areas [23]. The fiber architecture is functionally highly relevant, because the connectivity within a cortical area and between brain regions determines, to a high degree, the role that an area has in a certain network.

Diffusion imaging has been successfully used in visualizing the course of fiber tracts based on mathematical models. It takes advantage of the fact, that the diffusion of water molecules along nerve fibres is different from that across fibres [24–29]. Due to short acquisition times, diffusion imaging becomes more and more applied in order to analyse the connectome of healthy human subjects and patients [30–33]. Single axons and fibre bundles with a diameter of a few micrometres cannot be detected by diffusion imaging because of limitations in the spatial resolution.

Other techniques for analysing nerve fibres include macroscopical dissection techniques, myelin staining in histological sections and sensitive optical coherence tomography (PS-OCT) [34, 35], while tracing techniques, which are highly successful in determining the projections at the axonal level in brains of experimental animals (e.g., [23, 36, 37]), and which provide the "gold standard" are largely excluded for approaching human brain connectivity with a few exceptions [38]. As a consequence, human brain connectivity is less well analyzed than that of non-human primates, other mammals and invertebrates, although a profound understanding of connectivity would not only be crucial to approach human brain organization in the healthy brain, but also in a clinical context, to develop better diagnosis and therapies.

2   3D Polarized Light Imaging (3D-PLI) as a New Tool to Analyze Human Brain Fiber Architecture

3D-PLI is a neuroimaging technique that has opened up new avenues to study the complex nerve fiber architecture across the entire human brain at the micrometer level [39, 40]. Whole brain analysis in combination with high spatial resolution is a prerequisite to demonstrate both long-range fiber pathways and termination fields of single fibers emanating from the cortical layers. The method is based on unstained histological sections of postmortem brains, their analysis using a polarimeter, the calculation of fiber directions based on mathematical models, and the 3D-reconstruction of the data. In short:

Brain Preparation. The technique is applicable to unstained 60–100 micron thick histological sections of postmortem human brains generated with a cryostat microtome. The brain tissue is being fixed in 4 % of buffered formalin for at least three months before it undergoes the sectioning process. Depending on the section thickness and the sectioning plane (coronal, sagittal, or horizontal), about 1,500–3,000 sections are prepared per brain. These sections need to be imaged and analyzed in a complex workflow.

Basic Principles. It is the optical anisotropy of brain tissue that gives rise to pass polarized light through the unstained brain sections (i) to render microstructural details within the sample and (ii) to derive their spatial orientations. The anisotropy is mainly caused by the nerve fibers, i.e. the long projections of neurons. Each fiber has distinct optical axes and interacts with light in a manner that is dependent on its three-dimensional orientation with respect to the incident light. This physical effect widely known as birefringence has been shown to be strongest for myelinated fibers [41]. This is mainly due to the radially arranged lipid bilayers largely consolidating the myelin sheath. Non-myelinated axons, however, also exhibit birefringence though with a much smaller detectable effect. In this case the macromolecular arrays of large molecules (i.e. neurofilaments) in the axon are likely to cause the birefringence.

Image Acquisition. In 3D-PLI, circularly polarized light is passed through the brain section and the local changes in the polarization state of light are measured using a dedicated polarimetric setup. Hence, the setup is equipped with a circular polarizer unit, a rotating linear polarizer and a specimen stage sandwiched in-between. Since these elements are built in a microscopic device with a Köhler illumination, each brain section can be scanned with a resolution at the level of nerve fiber diameters, thus, providing images with pixel sizes of $1.3 \times 1.3 \ \mu m^2$. Due to the restricted field of view of this polarizing microscope ($2.7 \times 2.7 \ mm^2$), to image an entire brain section, it is digitized tile-wise with overlapping contents. This leads to about 3,500 images or $140,000 \times 100,000$ pixels, respectively, for one coronal human brain section covering an area of $14 \times 10 \ cm^2$. A typical 3D-PLI measurement includes eighteen complete scans per section rather than one, during the linear polarizer rotates between $0°$ and $170°$ around the stationary section. The acquired raw data set of the coronal section described above, therefore, requires 500 GB of storage space in total.

Core Image Analysis. Based on the eighteen measurements, a sinusoidal variation of the measured light intensity, referred to as light intensity profile, can usually be observed for each image pixel. The individual course of a light intensity profile essentially depends on the locally prevailing 3D fiber orientation. Deviations from the sinusoidal shape might indicate crossing fiber constellations, fibers pointing straight out of the sectioning plane, or simply no detectable birefringence. Basic principles of optics (Snell's law and Huygens-Fresnel principle) and the Jones calculus [42] mathematically link the measured light intensity profile to the fiber orientation described by a pair of angles (φ, α) or, alternatively, by a unit vector. The phase of the light intensity profile defines the in-section direction angle φ and its amplitude reflects the out-of-section inclination angle α. The image of all derived fiber orientations covering an entire brain section represents the fiber orientation map (FOM). An example of a FOM derived from 3D-PLI applied to a coronal section through the medial human brain is shown in Fig. 2.

Workflow. Collection and storage of the vast amount of data obtained with high-resolution 3D-PLI are not the only challenges we have to face. The core image analysis as described above is complemented by (i) image pre-processing approaches for artifact and noise removal (by means of image calibration and independent component analysis [43]) and by image post-processing approaches finally enabling the reconstruction of the entire series of sections into a coherent virtual fiber model of the human brain (e.g., segmentation of tissue and background, stitching of the tiles, non-linear image

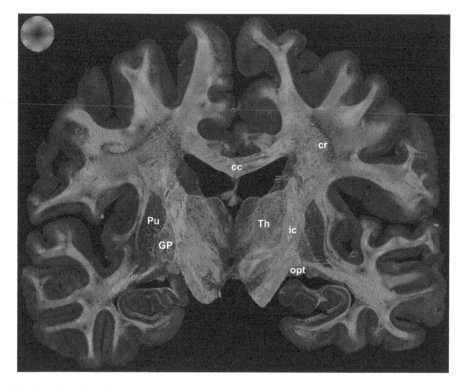

Fig. 2. Fiber orientation map of a coronal human brain section. Fiber orientations are encoded in HSV color space as indicated by the color sphere on the top left. The color encodes the direction angle φ and the saturation defines the inclination angle α (from saturated color for $\alpha = 0°$ to black for $\alpha = 90°$). To give an example, transversal in-plane fibers are colored in red. Legend: cc = corpus callosum, cr = corona radiata, ic = capsula interna, Th = thalamus, Pu = putamen, GP = globus pallidus, opt = optic tract (Color figure online).

registration [44], fiber tractography [40]). Each of these steps is computationally intensive and needs to be compiled into an efficient and applicable workflow.

3   Automation and Parallelization of the 3D PLI Workflow

A first approach towards a fully automated and parallelized 3D-PLI workflow is being set up to utilize advanced supercomputing infrastructures efficiently. The main goal is to combine fast data access, complex (partially already developed) data analyses and high-performance computing in an easy-to-use manner, thus, cumulating in an automated workflow.

Supercomputing Environment. The Jülich Supercomputing Centre provides resources of the supercomputer JuDGE (Juelich Dedicated GPU Environment) for neuroscientific research. JuDGE is an IBM iDataPlex Cluster with 206 compute nodes. Each compute node has 2 Intel Xeon X5650 (Westmere) 6-core 2.66 GHz processors,

2 NVIDIA Tesla M2050 or M2070 (Fermi) GPUs and 96 GB main memory. This leads to a complete system of 2472 cores, 412 graphic processors, 19.8 TB main memory and 239 Teraflops peak performance [45]. In addition, access to the JuRoPA (Jülich Research on Petaflop Architectures) system is granted. This system has 3288 compute nodes each with 2 Intel Xeon X5570 (Nehalem-EP) 2.93 GHz quad-core processors and 24 GB main memory. This leads to complete system of 26304 cores, 79 TB main memory and a peak performance of 308 Teraflops. The system has a Linpack performance of 274.8 Teraflops and is placed since June 2009 in the Top500 list (actual: rank 136 [Nov 2013]) [46].

Platform. To assemble and streamline the 3D-PLI workflow, the UNICORE platform (Uniform Interface to Computing Resources) is used. This framework offers a ready-to-run grid system including client and server software. UNICORE enables distributed computing and makes data resources available in a seamless and secure way in intranets and the internet. [47] The implementation of UNICORE entails benefit for developers as well as for users. In the stage of developing a new software package for the workflow, for example, careful parameter optimization has to be performed. A structured call of the software with an iterating set of parameters can be managed easily with UNICORE.

Furthermore, even an untrained neuroscientist can do complex data analysis and routine data production without knowing all details about the different inputs, calls and requirements of individual software packages of the workflow. The number of variables to be declared by the user can be reduced to a minimum and the conversion of the raw data set into a FOM is done automatically. This clearly minimizes operation failures as compared to manual calls of individual software packages.

Optimized Workflow. In general, the parallelization is being realized at the level of the implemented algorithms, the processing strategies, and the workflow itself. While the individual parallelization of the algorithms is a developer specific task, the latter two types of parallelization can be done by UNICORE without having deep knowledge in using supercomputers.

Individual applications such as image segmentation and stitching as well as the determination of the fiber orientations are optimized in terms of internal usage of CPUs or GPUs or a hybrid usage of both units. In addition, some of the applications enable to process images or even image pixels independently from each other and can, therefore, be treated in parallel. The calibration procedure is an adequate candidate to be applied pixel-wise by farming. Applications in the workflow that are independent from each other are performed in parallel. This is the case for the image segmentation and image stitching, for example. In order to take advantage of specific features of different supercomputers (e.g., GPU vs. faster CPU), both systems JuDGE and JuRoPA are addressed within the workflow. It turns out to be an asset to utilize the faster CPUs of the JuRoPA system for the stitching application and the core image analysis. It is important to take into account that a better speedup can be used up by the data transfer between the systems. In our constellation it is possible to copy the data from the GPFS file system of JuDGE to the Lustre Storage of JuRoPA instead of transferring the data by uftp [48]. A schematic of the optimized workflow is shown in Fig. 3.

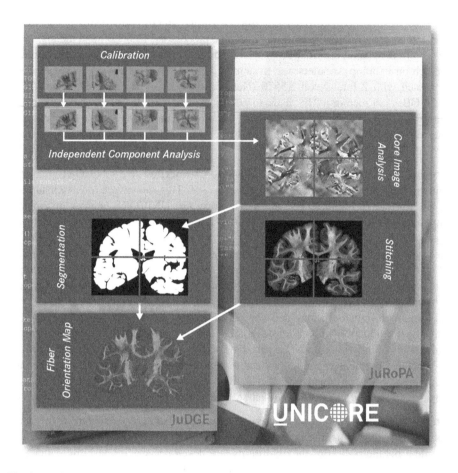

Fig. 3. Optimized workflow for 3D-PLI. UNICORE builds the framework to manage software package calls with input parameters and to organize the distributed calculation using JuDGE or JuRoPA.

The optimized 3D-PLI workflow for an individual high-resolution brain section can be reduced to a few hours as compared to several days or even weeks. As a consequence from the gained speedup, images with sizes far above 4 GB can now be processed at reasonable time scales, however, at the expense of the used data format. The file format NIfTI format (Neuroimaging Informatics Technology Initiative) [49], commonly used in neuroscience has to be exchanged by a container format, which is able to handle images substantially larger than 4 GB. Since this amount of data cannot be handled in a useful manner with sequential IO, parallel HDF5 [50] is the format of choice. Clearly, only the described workflow approach with the appropriate file format will allow an effective and fast processing of thousands of brain sections with 3D-PLI in the near future.

4   Conclusions

In future, we have to face several PetaBytes of data originating from postmortem studies (including 3D-PLI) to be collected, archived, analyzed, and finally integrated into a joint virtual model of the human brain. Specific challenges are posed by the multi-modal and multi-scale features of the obtained structural data, which characterize individual voxels in individual brains at different levels of detail and abstraction. Scalars, vectors or even more advanced mathematical objects are typically used to describe brain characteristics at the nanometer scale up to the millimeter scale. Comparison and visualization of such data, therefore, require common data access, and standardized scientific data formats and reference systems.

For 3D-PLI we have started to set up a customized e-infrastructure to parallelize and automatize the complex workflow, which was demonstrated to be beneficial in many aspects. The user can initiate a workflow calculation without knowing all tools and supercomputers used in the entire process, for example. Clearly, the computation time is speeded up significantly while the reproducibility of results is much better.

Acknowledgement. The authors thank Janine Klapper for help in preparing the manuscript, and Thomas Lippert for scientific discussion and support. Daniel Mallmann and André Giesler from the "Federated Systems and Data" group at the Jülich Supercomputing Centre generously assisted with the adaptation of UNICORE to the specific workflow requirements.

References

1. Brodmann, K.: Vergleichende Lokalisationslehre der Großhirnrinde in ihren Prinzipien dargestellt auf Grund des Zellenbaues. Barth JA, Leipzig (1909)
2. Brodmann, K.: Beiträge zur histologischen Lokalisation der Grosshirnrinde. I: Die Regio Rolandica. Beiträge zur Lokalisation der Grosshirnrinde II, 79–107 (1903)
3. Sherwood, C.C., Lee, P.W.H., Rivara, C.B., Holloway, R.L., Gilissen, E.P.E., Simmons, R. M.T., Hakeem, A., Allman, J.M., Erwin, J.M., Hof, P.R.: Evolution of specialized pyramidal neurons in primate visual and motor cortex. Brain Behav. Evol. **61**, 28–44 (2003)
4. Braak, H., Braak, E.: Pyramidal cells of Betz within cingulate and precentral gigantopyramidal field in human-brain - Golgi and pigment architectonic study. Cell Tissue Res. **172**, 103–119 (1976)
5. Amunts, K., Schmidt-Passos, F., Schleicher, A., Zilles, K.: Postnatal development of interhemispheric asymmetry in the cytoarchitecture of human area 4. Anat. Embryol. (Berl.) **196**, 393–402 (1997)
6. Pakkenberg, B., Pelvig, D., Marner, L., Bundgaard, M.J., Gundersen, H.J., Nyengaard, J.R., Regeur, L.: Aging and the human neocortex. Exp. Gerontol. **38**, 95–99 (2003)
7. DeFelipe, J., Marco, P., Busturia, I., Merchan-Perez, A.: Estimation of the number of synapses in the cerebral cortex: methodological considerations. Cereb. Cortex **9**, 722–732 (1999)
8. Schleicher, A., Palomero-Gallagher, N., Morosan, P., Eickhoff, S., Kowalski, T., de Vos, K., Amunts, K., Zilles, K.: Quantitative architectonic analysis: a new approach to cortical mapping. Anat. Embryol. (Berl.) **210**, 373–386 (2005)

9. Eickhoff, S.B., Paus, T., Caspers, S., Grosbas, M.H., Evans, A.C., Zilles, K., Amunts, K.: Assignment of functional activations to probabilistic cytoarchitectonic areas revisited. Neuroimage **36**, 511–521 (2007)

10. Eickhoff, S., Stephan, K.E., Mohlberg, H., Grefkes, C., Fink, G.R., Amunts, K., Zilles, K.: A new SPM toolbox for combining probabilistic cytoarchitectonic maps and functional imaging data. Neuroimage **25**, 1325–1335 (2005)

11. Eickhoff, S.B., Heim, S., Zilles, K., Amunts, K.: Testing anatomically specified hypotheses in functional imaging using cytoarchitectonic maps. Neuroimage **32**, 570–582 (2006)

12. Amunts, K., Weiss, P.H., Mohlberg, H., Pieperhoff, P., Gurd, J., Shah, J.N., Marshall, C.J., Fink, G.R., Zilles, K.: Analysis of the neural mechanisms underlying verbal fluency in cytoarchitectonically defined stereotaxic space - the role of Brodmann,s areas 44 and 45. Neuroimage **22**, 42–56 (2004)

13. Makuuchi, M., Grodzinsky, Y., Amunts, K., Santi, A., Friederici, A.D.: Processing non-canonical sentences in Broca's region: reflections of movement distance and type. Cereb. Cortex **23**(3), 694–702 (2013)

14. Grothe, M., Zaborszky, L., Atienza, M., Gil-Neciga, E., Rodriguez-Romero, R., Teipel, S.J., Amunts, K., Suarez-Gonzalez, A., Cantero, J.L.: Reduction of basal forebrain cholinergic system parallels cognitive impairment in patients at high-risk of developing Alzheimer's Disease. Cereb. Cortex **20**, 1685–1695 (2010)

15. Clos, M., Amunts, K., Laird, A., Fox, P.T., Eickhoff, S.B.: Tackling the multifunctional nature of Broca's region meta-analytically: connectivity-based parcellation of area 44. Neuroimage **83**, 174–188 (2013)

16. Caspers, S., Eickhoff, S.B., Zilles, K., Amunts, K.: Microstructural grey matter parcellation and its relevance for connectome analyses. Neuroimage **80**, 18–26 (2013)

17. Herculano-Houzel, S.: The remarkable, yet not extraordinary, human brain as a scaled-up primate brain and its associated cost. Proc. Natl. Acad. Sci. U.S.A. **109**(Suppl 1), 10661–10668 (2012)

18. Hilgetag, C., Barbas, H.: Are there ten times more glia than neurons in the brain? Brain Struct. Funct. **213**, 365–366 (2009)

19. Blinkov, S.M., Glezer, I.I.: The Human Brain in Figures and Tables: A Quantitative Handbook. Basic Books, New York (1986)

20. Amunts, K., Lepage, C., Borgeat, L., Mohlberg, H., Dickscheid, T., Rousseau, M.E., Bludau, S., Bazin, P.L., Lewis, L.B., Oros-Peusquens, A.M., Shah, N.J., Lippert, T., Zilles, K., Evans, A.C.: BigBrain: an ultrahigh-resolution 3D human brain model. Science **340**, 1472–1475 (2013)

21. Amunts, K., Hawrylycz, M., Van Essen, D., Van Horn, J.D., Harel, N., Poline, J.B., De Martino, F., Bjaalie, J.G., Dehaene-Lambertz, G., Dehaene, S., Valdes-Sosa, P., Thirion, B., Zilles, K., Hill, S.L., Abrams, M.B., Tass, P.A., Vanduffel, W., Evans, A.C., Eickhoff, S. B.: Interoperable atlases of the human brain. Neuroimage (2014, in press)

22. Clarke, S.: Callosal connections and functional subdivision of the human occipital lobe. In: Gulyas, B., Ottoson, D., Roland, P.E. (eds.) Functional organization of the human visual cortex, pp. 137–149. Pergamon Press, Oxford (1993)

23. Rockland, K.S.: Visual cortical organization at the single axon level: a beginning. Neurosci. Res. **42**, 155–166 (2002)

24. Le Bihan, D., Mangin, J.F., Poupon, C., Clark, C.A., Pappata, S., Molko, N., Chabriat, H.: Diffusion tensor imaging: concepts and applications. J. Magn. Reson. Imaging **13**, 534–546 (2001)

25. Pierpaoli, C., Jezzard, P., Basser, P.J., Barnett, A., Di Chiro, G.: Diffusion tensor MR imaging of the human brain. Radiology **201**, 637–648 (1996)

26. Wedeen, V.J., Rosene, D.L., Wang, R., Dai, G., Mortazavi, F., Hagmann, P., Kaas, J.H., Tseng, W.Y.I.: The geometric structure of the brain fiber pathways: a continous orthogonal grid. Science **335**, 1628–1634 (2012)
27. Basser, P.J., Jones, D.K.: Diffusion-tensor MRI: theory, experimental design and data analysis - a technical review. NMR Biomed. **15**, 456–467 (2002)
28. Mori, S., van Zijl, P.C.: Fibre tracking: principles and strategies - a technical review. NMR Biomed. **15**, 468–480 (2002)
29. Johansen-Berg, H., Rushworth, M.F.: Using diffusion imaging to study human connectional anatomy. Annu. Rev. Neurosci. **32**, 75–94 (2009)
30. Fornito, A., Bullmore, E.T.: Connectomics: a new paradigm for understanding brain disease. Eur. Neuropsychopharmacol. (2014, in press)
31. Jbabdi, S., Behrens, T.E.: Long-range connectomics. Ann. N. Y. Acad. Sci. **1305**, 83–93 (2013)
32. Van Essen, D.C.: Cartography and connectomes. Neuron **80**, 775–790 (2013)
33. Grefkes, C., Fink, G.R.: Connectivity-based approaches in stroke and recovery of function. Lancet Neurol. **13**, 206–216 (2014)
34. Wang, H., Black, A.J., Zhu, J., Stigen, T.W., Al-Qaisi, M.K., Netoff, T.I., Abosch, A., Akkin, T.: Reconstructing micrometer-scale fiber pathways in the brain: multi-contrast optical coherence tomography based tractography. Neuroimage **58**, 984–992 (2011)
35. de Boer, J.F., Milner, T.E., van Gemert, M.J., Nelson, J.S.: Two-dimensional birefringence imaging in biological tissue by polarization-sensitive optical coherence tomography. Opt. Lett. **22**, 934–936 (1997)
36. Petrides, M., Pandya, D.N.: Distinct parietal and temporal pathways to the homologues of Broca's area in the monkey. PLoS Biol. **7**(8), e1000170 (2009). Epub, 11 Aug 2009
37. Schmahmann, J.D., Pandya, D.N.: Fiber Pathways of the Brain. Oxford University Press, New York (2006)
38. Galuske, R.A., Schlote, W., Bratzke, H., Singer, W.: Interhemispheric asymmetries of the modular structure in human temoral cortex. Science **289**, 1946–1949 (2000)
39. Axer, M., Grässel, D., Kleiner, M., Dammers, J., Dickscheid, T., Reckfort, J., Hütz, T., Eiben, B., Pietrzyk, U., Zilles, K., Amunts, K.: High-resolution fiber tract reconstruction in the human brain by means of three-dimensional polarized light imaging. Front. Neuroinform. **5**, 1–13 (2011)
40. Axer, M., Amunts, K., Gräßel, D., Palm, C., Dammers, J., Axer, H., Pietrzyk, U., Zilles, K.: A novel approach to the human connectome: Ultra-high resolution mapping of fiber tracts in the brain. Neuroimage **54**, 1091–1101 (2011)
41. Vidal, B.C., Mello, M.L.S., Caseiro-Filho, A.C., Godo, C.: Anisotropic properties of the myelin sheath. Acta Histochem. **66**, 32–39 (1980)
42. Jones, C.J.: A new calculus for the treatment of optical systems. J. Opt. Soc. Am. **31**, 488–493 (1941)
43. Breuer, L., Axer, M., Dammers, J.: A new constrained ICA approach for optimal signal decomposition in polarized light imaging. J. Neurosci. Methods **220**, 30–38 (2013)
44. Palm, C., Axer, M., Gräßel, D., Dammers, J., Lindemeyer, J., Zilles, K., Pietrzyk, U., Amunts, K.: Toward ultra-high resolution fiber tract mapping of the human brain - registration of polairization light images and reorientation of fiber vectors. Front. Hum. Neurosci. **4**, 1–16 (2010)
45. Sitt, J.D., King, J.R., Naccache, L., Dehaene, S.: Ripples of consciousness. TINS **17**, 552–554 (2013)

46. http://www.fz-juelich.de/ias/jsc/EN/Expertise/Supercomputers/JUROPA/JUROPA_node.html
47. http://unicore.eu
48. http://uftp-multicast.sourceforge.net/
49. http://nifti.nimh.nih.gov/
50. http://www.hdfgroup.org/HDF5/

From RNA Replicators to Genes to Survival Machines with Brains

Gyan Bhanot[1,2(✉)]

[1] Department of Physics, Department of Molecular Biology and Biochemistry,
Rutgers, The State University of New Jersey, Piscataway, NJ, USA
gbhanot@rci.rutgers.edu
[2] Institute for Advanced Simulation (IAS) and Jülich Supercomputing Centre
(JSC), Jülich, Germany

Abstract. I describe the evolution of life and the evolution of complex
dynamical systems such as the brain as an emergent phenomenon, which allow a
subset of multicellular life to learn its environment and adapt to it, enabling it to
survive and replicate. Its ultimate purpose is to allow organisms to project their
genetic materials into subsequent generations. It can only be understood in the
context of its function.

> *"If superior creatures from*
> *space ever visit earth, the first question*
> *they will ask, in order to assess the level*
> *of our civilization is*
> *'Have they discovered evolution yet?'"*
>
> Richard Dawkins in *"The Selfish Gene"*

1 The Origins of the Earth and the Appearance of Life

The solar system was formed approximately 5 billion years ago from the gravitational
collapse of a dust cloud due to perturbations. This collapse created a proto-star, with an
accretion disk around it. The proto-star evolved into the sun and the accretion disk into
the planets. Using radiometric dating of terrestrial and lunar rocks and meteorites, the
age of the earth is estimated to be 4.54 ± 0.05 billion years [1]. There is evidence that
life began on earth around 3.6–4 billion years ago [2, 3], after the formation of a
sufficiently thick crust on its molten core. The most convincing scientific theory about
life's origins is its emergence from a soup of inorganic molecules under the action of
heat and light in the early earth. These theories have as their underpinnings the
experiments in the 1950's by Miller and Urey [4, 5], who showed that organic molecules could be synthesized out of inorganic molecules. In this experiment, they
showed that when water, methane and ammonia, which were abundant on earth before

---

Invited talk given at the "International Workshop on Brain Inspired Computing: Computational
models, algorithms, applications, and implementations", Cetraro, Italy, July 8–11, 2013.

© Springer International Publishing Switzerland 2014
L. Grandinetti et al. (Eds.): BrainComp 2013, LNCS 8603, pp. 15–21, 2014.
DOI: 10.1007/978-3-319-12084-3_2

the appearance of oxygen, were subjected to electrical discharges (lightening), they could form hydrocarbons, sugars and 11 out of the 20 amino acids which form the proteins that are the basis of all life on earth.

Early life: the RNA world: Amino acids can form long chains (RNA) with the ability to store genetic information and catalyze enzymes. The universality of the genetic code and the ubiquitous RNA/Protein Ribosome machinery that is used by all life to translate the DNA message into proteins, suggests that an RNA world preceded cellular life. Several other ribosome enzymes (ribozymes) such as the Hammerhead ribozyme, which can self-cleave [6], and RNA polymerase, with the ability to auto-catalyze [7], suggests that the RNA World is embedded in fossilized form in life today.

What was the RNA world like [8]? RNA is composed of sequences of nucleotides, which are formed from amino acids with their nitrogenous base attached to a sugar-phosphate backbone. The RNA world was likely a primordial soup of strands of RNA "living" in a sea of free-floating nucleotides. The bond between most nucleotides break easily, but some nucleotide sequences have lower energies, which may have allowed them to remain attached for a longer time. This may have created long chains of specific nucleotides that remained attached long enough to attain auto-catalysis, allowing them to self-synthesize their own sequence by harvesting the appropriate nucleotides from their surroundings. The RNA world consisted of many varieties of

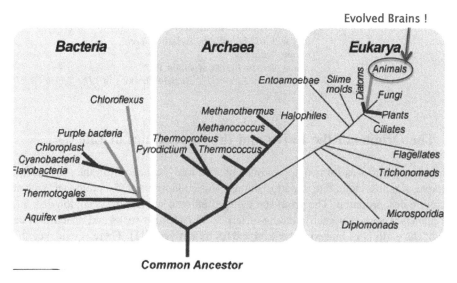

Fig. 1. The tree of life. The tree consists of three major branches, bacteria, archaea and eukarya, all evolved from a common ancestor, which was most likely evolved from an Eventually, stable varieties of replicator molecules appeared, which continued to compete for survival. Some may have built enclosures (cell walls) to protect themselves. Inside these walls, replicators became complex, and evolved methods to store (DNA), retrieve (Polymerase, Ribosomes) and process (signaling pathways) information. They invented ways of increasing stability and eliminating rivals. Eventually, they built "survival machines" (Fig. 1) which are the organisms we see in the world today (image from: http://www.astrobio.net/topic/origins/origin-and-evolution-of-life/worlds-smallest-power-station/).

"replicator" molecules, which competed electro-chemically and mechanically with each other for resources. The fitness of such replicators depended on their longevity, fecundity and accuracy of replication. The most successful ones survived, consumed or subverted the rest through their ability to outcompete the rest [8].

Brains are simulating machines: The leaves the tree of life represent extant life forms, most of which did not bother to evolve brains. Most of cellular life that exists today is single celled (unicellular). In a minority, cooperative systems of specialized cells emerged, which could outcompete their rivals. In these systems, complex, multicellular life forms arose, which abandoned the clonal immortality of unicellular life to become mortal, lumbering survival machines (SMs). They invented methods to regulate energy within cells [9], and invented suicide, death and sex [10], mechanisms, which made them fitter in projecting their RNA, DNA, genes and genomes from one generation to the next. This small minority of "animal" life, which includes humans, eventually evolved brains.

Brains are "simulating machines", which process, reduce and translate sensory cues and send appropriate instructions to sets of cells (organs) to make them perform specific actions. The goal of this processing is to increase the likelihood that the organism will not be eaten, will get sufficient nutrition to mature into an adult, find a mate and reproduce. Survival Machines who learn by "Trial and Error" get hurt. So SMs evolved brains, allowing them to distinguish friend from foe, react quickly to danger signals, retain memory of past events and seek food and mates. The reason why we have brains is that SMs with "Brains" are fitter. SMs who process sensory data and "simulate" the world better can anticipate danger, eat better, live longer, and leave more progeny.

How did neurons evolve? Neurons may have evolved in cooperative cell systems to allow specialized groups of cells to process input signals from other cells and transmit instructions to affect the behavior of distant cells in the collection. A selectively permeable membrane separates the cell interior from the exterior. Almost all eukaryotic cells maintain a small trans-membrane electric potential of between 40 and 80 millivolts between the interior (the cathode or - terminal) and the exterior (the anode or + terminal). When the cell membrane is disturbed, it gets locally depolarized, and this depolarization can spread to affect other regions of the cell and the surrounding medium. A passive or active exchange of ions across the membrane can also change the potential, and these signals can also travel into the extracellular medium and change the potential on other cells. In specialized groups of cells (neurons), the shape and relative arrangement of cells, and specific chemically or voltage gated ion-channels, permit the depolarization to propagate in a directed way, much like the signals in an electrical transmission system. In these cells, the depolarization can be sudden (within 1–100 ms) and can create an "action potential", a depolarization spike which can rapidly transmit to neighboring cells. The depolarization spike signal travelling from cell to cell can be used to send as a signal to distant groups of cells.

The evolution of the brain: Using such neural circuits, SMs evolved specialized "brains" to perform specific functions. For example, the Jellyfish "brain" is an undifferentiated nerve network, the so- called "nerve net [10]". Using this network, jellyfish detect the presence of other animals and transmit the information to other nerve cells using a circular nerve ring. Another key function of the system is to coordinate the jellyfish swimming motion by opening and contracting its skirt in a coordinated manner.

In contrast, worms have a well defined CNS (Central Nervous System) whose architecture defines a basic design which has remained unchanged from worms to humans. It consists of an anterior brain connected to a nerve cord (shown in Fig. 2 for the earthworm *Lumbricus terrestris*). Impulses of light, moisture, tough are detected by skin cells and transmitted by a pair of nerve cells in each segment to small ganglia (collection of nerve cells) in the segment as well as to the brain, where the signals are analyzed. The ganglia and the brain then send impulses to muscles to make them respond appropriately. However, the worm "brain" is not the sole "commander" of its nervous system. With its brain removed, worms are able to move, mate, burrow, feed, and learn mazes.

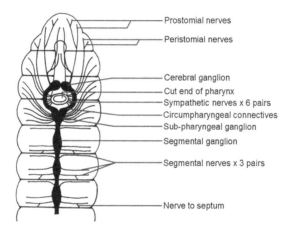

Nervous system of *Lumbricus* (dorsal dissection)

Fig. 2. From http://cronodon.com/files/earthworm_CNS_lateral.gif: The earthworm central nervous system.

Insect brains have a similar pattern. They are giant fiber systems of nerve cells connecting ganglia with a nerve cord running down the body (Fig. 3). The function of the system is to allow rapid conduction of impulses to leg/wing muscles. With more sensory receptors than vertebrates, they are sensitive to odors, sounds, light, texture, pressure, humidity, temperature, and chemicals.

Vertebrates have the most complex brain system. The spinal cord, protected by vertebrae, is now a servant of the brain. The brain itself is a series of swellings, consisting of the hindbrain, the midbrain, and the forebrain. From the hindbrain sprouts a distinctive structure, the "cerebellum" or little brain. Figure 4 shows the basic architecture of the vertebrate brain, which has remained unchanged from fish to humans [11]. The detailed changes in the architecture reflect the changes due to the organism's evolutionary history and the need to perform specific functions in its lifecycle.

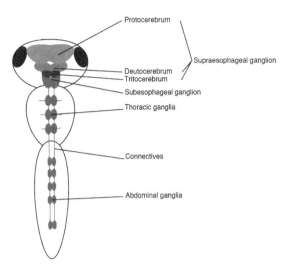

Fig. 3. From: http://bioteaching.files.wordpress.com/2010/05/overall_anatomy.jpg: A prototype of the insect brain.

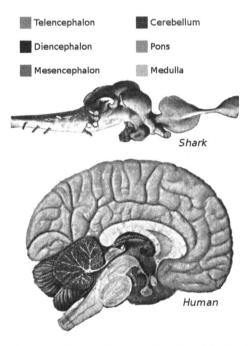

Fig. 4. The vertebrate brain topology is the same in all vertebrates (image from http://en.wikipedia.org/wiki/Brain).

The ancestral cerebrum was two small swellings for smell. In amphibians, there was more gray matter (cell bodies and synapses) between neurons and the cerebrum processed impulses from sensory areas. Gray matter moved outward to the surface to form the cerebral cortex. In some reptiles, the neocortex arose. Mammals, which evolved from reptiles of this type, have the most developed neocortex.

Vertebrate brains have four characteristic features. They have a *centralized architecture,* consisting of a network of structures of nerve cells in the anterior brain, connected to a spinal column. The neuron and sense organ bodies are all located at one end of the organism *(encephalization).* The brain structures are *specialized,* with a greatly increased size and variety of elements compared to invertebrates. Finally, the vertebrate brain has a high degree of *plasticity,* which allows it to learn perceptual and motor tasks and reassign tasks to subunits in response to catastrophic events such as stroke or injury.

The mammalian brain is a simulator [12], which creates a time evolution of events using the sensory inputs from olfaction, sight, touch, hearing, taste and pain stimuli. It regulates posture and locomotion by using a map of the body. It is responsible for our *instincts* and emotions, such as hunger, love/lust/sex, anger, hate/fear, territoriality, possessiveness, dominance/submissiveness, irritability/serenity, parenting etc. It also gives mammals *cognitive capabilities,* such as arousal, attention, thinking, evaluating, insight, abstraction, creativity, choice, purpose, seeking, planning, generalization, judgment, introspection, programming, interest, preference, discrimination, learning, habituation, memory, recognition, retention, knowledge etc.

Consciousness: Although "consciousness" is often believed to be unique to humans and is usually discussed in hushed, reverential tones, it may have appeared in the mammalian brain quite simply, when the brain's "simulation" of the world included a model of itself. This model then allows us to represent the world as a collection of other individuals, some more similar to us than others. Over time, *the representation becomes the reality,* because all of the organism's experiences are tied to the model. The organism is then unable to disentangle itself from the representation and identifies itself as having a "conscience" or "soul" [13].

What needs to be modeled: What does it mean to "understand" how the brain works? Any "model" of the brain should begin by elucidating the architectural, molecular, functional and signaling mechanisms and their evolutionary origins for the following six properties of the brain: 1. Fidelity in entering and exiting states; 2. Ability to interpret sensory input and create appropriate triggers; 3. Ability to recover from error; 4. Robustness to perturbations of sensory inputs; 5. Ability to retain memory of past events; and 6. Plasticity, which gives its subunits the capacity to reassign function [14].

A study of the brain is the ultimate frontier. The brain is an adaptive, dynamic, adaptive system, which simulates the world to allow organisms to learn, survive and replicate. It can only be understood in the context of evolution, as an emergent phenomenon, which uses the underlying architecture bequeathed to it by evolution to create robust, stable, controllable states.

Acknowledgement. None of the work described here is original. In the process of preparing this manuscript, I learned a lot. I am grateful to the Juelich Supercomputing Centre (JSC) at the

Forschungszentrum Juelich for the opportunity to learn from the talks and discussions at the workshop, and for their hospitality and support, which enabled me to attend this workshop. This work was also supported by Grant Nos. NSF PHY11-25915 and NSF Grant #1066293 from the National Science Foundation, the Kavli Institute of Theoretical Physics at UCSB. I thank the Aspen Center for Physics for their hospitality during the writing of this manuscript.

References

1. Dalrymple, G.Brent: The age of the Earth in the twentieth century: a problem (mostly) solved. Spec. Publ. Geol. Soc. Lond. **190**(1), 205–221 (2001). doi:10.1144/GSL.SP.2001. 190.01.14
2. Schopf, J.W., Kudryavtsev, A.B., Czaja, A.D., Tripathi, A.B.: Evidence of Archean life: stromatolites and microfossils. Precambrian Res. **158**, 141–155 (2007)
3. Schopf, J.W.: Fossil evidence of Archaean life. Philos. Trans. Roy. Soc. Lond. B Biol. Sci. **361**(1470), 869–885 (2006)
4. Miller, S.L.: Production of amino acids under possible primitive earth conditions. Science **117**(3046), 528–529 (1953). doi:10.1126/science.117.3046.528. PMID 13056598
5. Miller, S.L., Urey, H.C.: Organic compound synthesis on the primitive earth. Science **130** (3370), 245–251 (1959). doi:10.1126/science.130.3370.245. PMID 13668555
6. Forster, A.C., Symons, R.H.: Self-cleavage of plus and minus RNAs of a virusoid and a structural model for the active sites. Cell **49**(2), 211–220 (1987). doi:10.1016/0092-8674(87) 90562-9. PMID 2436805
7. Johnston, W., Unrau, P., Lawrence, M., Glasner, M., Bartel, D.: RNA-catalyzed RNA polymerization: accurate and general RNA-templated primer extension. Science **292**(5520), 1319–1325 (2001). doi:10.1126/science.1060786. PMID 11358999
8. Dawkins, R.: The Selfish Gene, 30th Anniversary Edition. Oxford University Press, Oxford (2006). ISBN-10: 0199291152; ISBN-13: 978-0199291151
9. Lane, N.: Power, Sex, Suicide: Mitochondria and the Meaning of Life. ISBN-10: 0199205647; ISBN-13: 978-0199205646. ibid. Life Ascending: The Ten Great Inventions of Evolution. ISBN-10: 0393338665; ISBN-13: 978-0393338669
10. Satterlie, R.A.: Neuronal control of swimming in jellyfish: a comparative story. Can. J. Zool. **80**, 1654–1669 (2002). doi:10.1139/z02-138
11. Shepherd, G.M.: Neurobiology. Oxford University Press, New York (1994). ISBN: 9780195088434
12. Eagelman, D.: Incognito: The Secret Lives of the Brain. Pantheon Books, New York (2011). ISBN-10: 0307389928 | ISBN-13: 978-0307389923
13. Harris, S.: The End of Faith: Religion, Terror, and the Future of Reason. W. W. Norton, New York (2004). ISBN-10: 0393327655; ISBN-13: 978-0393327656
14. Doidge, N.: The Brain That Changes Itself: Stories of Personal Triumph from the Frontiers of Brain Science. Penguin Books, New York (2008). ISBN-10: 0143113100; ISBN-13: 978-0143113102

Integrating Brain Structure and Dynamics on Supercomputers

S.J. van Albada[1]([✉]), S. Kunkel[2], A. Morrison[1,2,3], and M. Diesmann[1,4]

[1] Institute of Neuroscience and Medicine (INM-6) and Institute for Advanced Simulation (IAS-6), Jülich Research Centre and JARA, Jülich, Germany
s.van.albada@fz-juelich.de
[2] Simulation Laboratory Neuroscience – Bernstein Facility for Simulation and Database Technology, Institute for Advanced Simulation, Jülich Research Centre and JARA, Jülich, Germany
[3] Faculty of Psychology, Institute of Cognitive Neuroscience, Ruhr-University Bochum, Bochum, Germany
[4] Medical Faculty, RWTH Aachen University, Aachen, Germany

Abstract. Large-scale simulations of neuronal networks provide a unique view onto brain dynamics, complementing experiments, small-scale simulations, and theory. They enable the investigation of integrative models to arrive at a multi-scale picture of brain dynamics relating macroscopic imaging measures to the microscopic dynamics. Recent years have seen rapid development of the necessary simulation technology. We give an overview of design features of the NEural Simulation Tool (NEST) that enable simulations of spiking point neurons to be scaled to hundreds of thousands of processors. The performance of supercomputing applications is traditionally assessed using scalability plots. We discuss reasons why such measures should be interpreted with care in the context of neural network simulations. The scalability of neural network simulations on available supercomputers is limited by memory constraints rather than computational speed. This calls for future generations of supercomputers that are more attuned to the requirements of memory-intensive neuroscientific applications.

Keywords: Computational neuroscience · Neural networks · Scalability · Simulation technology

1 Introduction

Neuroscience is a new player in the field of supercomputing applications compared to longtimers like particle and plasma physics, meteorology, and cryptography. The requirements for the successful and efficient implementation of neuroscientific models on supercomputers are just being identified, and therefore present applications likely only scratch the surface of what will ultimately be possible.

© Springer International Publishing Switzerland 2014
L. Grandinetti et al. (Eds.): BrainComp 2013, LNCS 8603, pp. 22–32, 2014.
DOI: 10.1007/978-3-319-12084-3_3

This chapter provides an overview over the current status and recent developments in the area of large-scale neuronal network simulations on supercomputers. We start by arguing for the need for such large-scale models as a complement to other modeling approaches. This is followed by a view into the inner workings of the neural network simulator NEST [1], elucidating features that enable simulations to make efficient and comprehensive use of modern supercomputers. Evaluating simulator performance is not entirely straightforward, due to an interplay between factors including scalability, computational speed, and memory consumption. We argue for more emphasis on accuracy as well as absolute runtime and memory usage next to traditional scalability. Finally, we discuss limitations to network scaling, which point to the need for supercomputers with large amounts of memory, particularly to accommodate synaptic infrastructure. This contrasts with the main line of supercomputer development, which tends to emphasize floating point performance.

2   The Need for Large-Scale Models

The success of many existing neuroscientific models is in no small part attributable to their simplicity. Nevertheless, if we are to obtain an integrated understanding of brain structure, dynamics, and function, it will be necessary to move to larger and more complex models. One reason is that brain regions and cortical[1] layers and areas are specialized for certain operations, yet achieve their function through extensive recurrent interactions. In the cerebral cortex, for instance, higher-order functions are thought to arise through successive transformations of signals in an approximate hierarchy of mutually connected areas.

Another ground for developing large-scale models is to establish links between microscopic dynamics and meso- and macroscopic measures such as voltage-sensitive dye (VSD) images, local field potentials (LFP), functional magnetic resonance images (fMRI), the electroencephalogram (EEG), and the magnetoencephalogram (MEG). Reaching the relevant spatial scales will be doubly advantageous: The comparison with a richer diversity of experimental results will enable models to be better constrained, and models will contribute to the understanding of meso- and macroscopic measures as their underlying mechanisms become accessible.

One might argue that each region, layer, or area can be represented by a lower-dimensional system through coarse-graining or subsampling. However, certain characteristics of the network are inevitably lost under such simplifications. Coarse-graning may deprive the model of its complex network-of-networks architecture. An argument against subsampling is as follows: Neurons in mammalian cortex on average receive on the order of 10^4 inputs, and are connected to approximately 10 % of the neurons in their local neighborhood. The smallest network that combines physiological connection probabilities with realistic

---

[1] The cerebral cortex is the thin layer of cells on the outer surface of the vertebrate brain, responsible for high-level sensory, cognitive, and motor functions. We here refer to the cerebral cortex also simply as 'cortex'.

in-degrees therefore consists of around 10^5 neurons [2]. In a smaller network, some of the inputs need to be replaced by external drives that are not self-consistently determined. This remains true in larger networks, albeit to a lesser extent. Even if a network could be reduced without losing essential characteristics, full-scale simulations are needed to verify the validity of the reduction.

Large model size does not stand in direct contradiction to simplicity: Low-dimensional single-neuron dynamics can be used, and the number of parameters can be restricted for instance by giving populations of neurons identical properties. Large-scale models can, however, become more complex due to the inclusion of multiple disparate neural populations, brain regions, or areas with source- and target-specific connectivity. The added complexity of such highly structured models becomes increasingly manageable as comprehensive anatomical data sets are being made available [3,4].

How large is 'large' in the context of neuronal network models? A single area of primate cortex comprises on the order of 10^7–10^8 neurons, the combined vision-related areas of the macaque cortex contain on the order of 10^9 neurons [5], the number of neurons in human cortex is approximately 2×10^{10}, and the total number of neurons in the human brain is roughly 10^{11} [6]. Figure 1 illustrates the architecture of the primate cortex. Since interconnections outnumber neurons by a factor of 10^3–10^5, they dominate the memory consumption of neuronal network models that are faithful to physiology, and their representation in particular should be optimized for the efficient use of supercomputers.

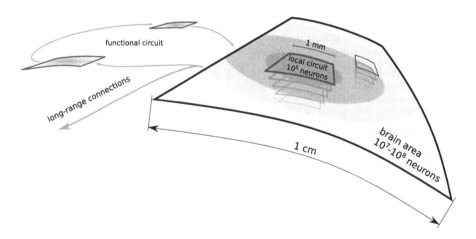

Fig. 1. Sketch of the organization of primate cortex. The cortex is structured into layers and areas, each containing smaller local circuits with distance-dependent connectivity (schematically shown by the concentric disks). The areas combine to form functional circuits via long-range connections. While areas are highly heterogeneous both within and between species, rough sizes are indicated.

3   Neural Network Simulation Technology

The basic elements of neuronal network models are neurons and their inter-connections, which normally occur at synapses: close appositions of the membranes of sending and receiving neurons, where neurotransmitters are exchanged. Neurons integrate their inputs from other neurons, which may be excitatory or inhibitory, respectively causing positive and negative excursions of the voltage across the neuronal membrane. The combined voltage excursion is compared to a threshold, and an all-or-none electrical event called a spike or action potential is produced when the threshold is exceeded. This signal is then transmitted to target neurons with a delay on the order of 1–10 ms. Average spike rates of cortical neurons in the awake state have been estimated to lie somewhere between 0.05 and 30 spikes per second, depending on the species, area, behavioral state, and recording method [7–9]. Synapses are plastic on both short and long time scales, changing their strengths for instance according to the activity level or relative spike timing of pre- and post-synaptic neurons.

The dynamics of such networks can be investigated using various simulators that are specialized for different levels of description, of which we mention the most prominent ones. NEURON [10] and GENESIS [11] focus on detailed models where each neuron is represented using multiple cellular compartments. Nengo [12] takes a more top-down approach, emphasizing functional aspects of neural groups. Finally, Brian [13] and the NEural Simulation Tool (NEST) specialize in few-compartment and point neuron models.

The design features of NEST are optimized for efficiency and accuracy. It is globally time-driven, yet enables the calculation of precise spike times at lower computational cost than globally event-driven schemes [14,15]. The equations for neurons with linear subthreshold dynamics are integrated exactly, while standard numerical solvers are used for nonlinear neuron models. Since neurons are effectively decoupled for the duration of the minimal propagation delay in the network, spikes are buffered locally over this delay, after which all processes exchange the local buffers in a collective communication phase. As the minimal delay tends to be larger than the integration time step of typically 0.1 ms, this reduces the frequency of inter-process communication and thus enhances computational efficiency.

Neural simulators differ in their degree of parallellizability. PGENESIS, the parallel version of GENESIS, runs on systems including shared-memory machines, networked workstations, and supercomputers, and has been used for instance to simulate a large-scale model of cerebellar cortex on 128 processors of a Cray T3E [16,17]. Scaling of NEURON on the IBM Blue Gene architecture has been demonstrated up to $128,000$ cores [18,19]. The SPLIT simulator was found to scale well up to $8,192$ processors on a Blue Gene/L supercomputer, enabling a simulation of 22×10^6 neurons with 11×10^9 synapses [20]. Other parallelizable simulators include NCS [21], C2 [22], and Compass [23]. The latter two are among the most scalable tools, but are not publicly available, and the simulations described use constraints on network architecture.

NEST displays particularly good scalability, running on systems ranging from a single processor to hundreds of thousands of cores. It enables the use of hybrid MPI and OpenMP parallelism to limit communication costs which increase with the number of MPI processes. Communication is performed by collective MPI functions, which is the most efficient option for randomly connected networks in which neurons can have targets on any process. For networks with some degree of modularity, more efficient schemes may be found. Networks of 10^8 neurons with 10^{12} synapses and up have been successfully simulated on the JUGENE BlueGene/P system and the K supercomputer by Fujitsu [24]. The largest neuronal network simulation to date was achieved using NEST on K, and involved 1.73×10^9 neurons connected via 10.4×10^{12} synapses with spike-timing-dependent plasticity [25].

The use of NEST on supercomputers has been facilitated by its native simulation language interpreter which avoids dependence on the installation of external packages. A more intuitive Python interface called PyNEST also exists [26], as well as a recently added interface based on Cython, an extension of Python that also supports C/C++ constructs [27]. The latter bindings are more compact and maintainable than PyNEST, and can be cross-compiled on supercomputers, exploiting the increased availability of Python.

Scaling NEST to massively parallel computing architectures has been made possible by the optimization of its neuronal and connection infrastructure [28]. This optimization was supported by a theoretical model which quantified the contributions of various memory components depending on the network size and the number of cores. The design choices were made with a randomly connected, or at least not perfectly modular network in mind, which is a biologically reasonable assumption. As the number of cores grows, the number of neurons per core decreases, and the number of non-local neurons to be represented increases. Moreover, a larger machine implies a larger number of cores on which any given neuron has no targets. The third generation kernel of NEST exploits this sparseness of both neurons and synapses by the use of sparse tables which combine low memory consumption with fast look-up.

4   Assessing the Performance of Neural Simulators

In traditional scalability plots, runtime is plotted against the number of cores for either a proportional increase in network size (weak scaling), or for constant network size (strong scaling). The application is considered to scale perfectly when runtime is constant for the case of weak scaling, assuming that not only the number of neurons but also the number of synapses increases in proportion to the number of cores (i.e., the mean in-degree of the neurons is unchanged), or when runtime is inversely proportional to the number of cores for the case of strong scaling. On a double logarithmic scale, this amounts to a straight line with slope -1. This way of displaying the performance of simulators can be misleading, as a faster update of the neuronal state leads to communication dominating runtime already at fewer cores, causing the scaling to appear worse.

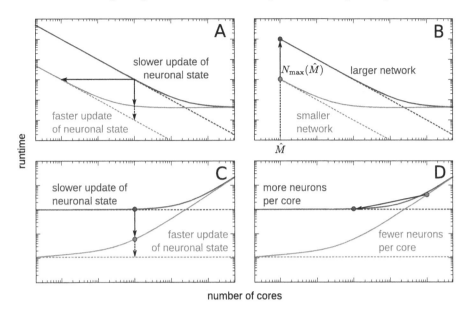

Fig. 2. Scaling plots can be counterintuitive. (A) Optimizing solvers can lead to apparently worse strong scaling, as the runtime approaches the time taken up by communication already at a smaller number of cores. (B) Simulating a larger network improves strong scaling results. (C) In weak scaling, communication increases with the number of cores. A faster update of the neuronal state can lead to either a constant negative offset or, if computation and communication overlap temporally, to a convergence of the two lines as runtime becomes purely determined by communication. In both cases, the quality of scaling appears to have been diminished. (D) Memory optimization can allow the same network to be simulated faster on fewer cores, as indicated by the dots and arrow.

Figures 2A,C schematically show this respectively for strong and weak scaling. Apparent scaling performance also depends on the size of the networks simulated, as shown in Figs. 2B,D. Optimizing memory consumption allows larger networks to be simulated, simultaneously improving scalability, since communication only dominates at a larger number of cores.

This suggests a few approaches for correctly assessing simulator performance. The first, general point is that care should be taken in interpreting scalability results. For instance, the slope of a strong scaling graph is a good indicator of the degree to which it pays to increase machine size. However, for most practical purposes the absolute runtime and memory consumption are more important than this slope or the range over which scaling is linear. Next to scaling, simulation codes are often evaluated on the basis of the fraction of peak floating point performance they achieve. However, floating point operations constitute only a minor fraction of the operations in the simulation of a network model as described by NEST, placing a structural limit on this performance measure. False conclusions can also be avoided by evaluating scalability in a comparative fashion, by juxtaposing the results of two or more different implementations of a given benchmark network. Finally, simulator performance encompasses more than just runtime, memory consumption, and scalability: the results should of course be accurate as well. Accuracy can be evaluated in a deterministic manner for single-neuron simulations or non-chaotic networks, or in a statistical manner for chaotic networks [29].

5   Neuronal Network Simulations are Limited by the Available Memory

Simulations of highly connected neuronal networks require large amounts of working memory, which for brain-scale networks is only provided by supercomputers. The maximum-filling NEST simulation of nearly two billion neurons on the K supercomputer is still about two orders of magnitude away from the full scale of the human brain. Although a substantial amount of time can be spent on neuronal updates especially for plastic synapses, large-scale neuronal network simulations are thus nevertheless mainly constrained by memory rather than CPU power, as opposed for instance to molecular dynamics simulations. This bears directly on turn-around times, as memory-intensive simulations often spend substantial amounts of time in the queue, and queuing time tends to exceed the time taken by the simulation itself.

The infrastructure that enables efficient access to local neuron and synapse objects represents the limiting factor for the scalability of NEST in terms of memory usage. It causes a memory overhead proportional to the total number of neurons, since each MPI process maintains two sparse tables indicating for *all* neurons both their locality and that of their targets. In fact, when using hybrid parallelization, the latter of the two sparse tables is required per thread. Thus, if the number of synapses per neuron is constant, the maximal number of neurons per core decreases somewhat with machine size, implying an upper limit on the number of cores that can be efficiently used [24]. This means that increasing the available memory by adding cores does not suffice unless alternative neuron and synapse infrastructures can be found: more local memory is needed in order to be able to represent larger networks.

The large degree of convergence of biological neural networks and their lack of perfect modularity lead to frequent random memory access, implying that a high memory bandwidth and cache efficiency are needed for the delivery of spikes to local targets, and a high communication bandwidth for the delivery of spikes across nodes. In fact, these factors are more important for neuronal network simulations than floating point performance, which is the primary focus in the development of supercomputer architectures. Thus, there is a potential for optimizing computer architectures for the performance of neural network simulation codes.

6   Conclusions

Developments in the simulation technology of NEST have enabled simulations of neuronal networks to be scaled to the full complement of cores provided by the peta-scale supercomputers available today. This scalability was achieved with the help of a mathematical model of memory consumption [28]. The influence of the different components of a simulation engine for spiking neuronal networks on computing time, however, is still a largely unexplored territory. One of the reasons, next to the lack of human resources, is that in recent years the NEST code has undergone major redesign with respect to the organization of memory, providing little stability for systematic profiling. Previous studies have looked at the functional completeness [30] and the numerical accuracy [15, 29] of simulation codes. Clearly, function and accuracy deserved priority: a simulation can be arbitrarily fast if accuracy is uncontrolled. The time seems ripe now to look at computing time with a modeling approach similar to the one used for memory consumption.

Other factors are of the same importance as the ability to scale simulations to very large networks. Such simulations only advance science if they are reliable and reproducible. The computational neuroscience community has not yet reached the point where simulation results published in peer-reviewed papers can be routinely reproduced, for reasons that are beyond the scope of this chapter.

The existence of standardized simulators enhances both reliability and reproducibility by avoiding user-specific code that undergoes little testing. The fact that NEST is open source makes the code more reliable by exposing it to elaborate testing by the user community, and supporting a long-term development model of iterative refinement. The existence of a formal software development workflow including a bug tracker, a test suite, and a continuous integration framework also contributes to reliability, as documented in [31]. Reproducibility is aided by versioning and the publication of simulation scripts. However, executing the identical script with the same simulation code in a different laboratory is only the weakest form of reproducibility. If there is a semantic error in the model specification or a bug in the simulation code, a false result will be reproduced. Compact human-readable model description languages adapted to the problem domain need to be developed to facilitate the detection of semantic errors, and results need to be cross-checked with different solvers, random number generators, or even complete simulation engines. The meta-simulation language PyNN [32] takes a step in this direction by striving to provide both a model specification language with a high degree of expressiveness, and the ability to instantiate and run the model with different simulation engines. The developer community of NEST maintains the NEST backend of PyNN and contributes to the improvement of the model specification language.

Full-scale simulations of the human brain at the resolution of neurons and synapses addressed by NEST require the use of exa-scale supercomputers. Major work on the simulation technology will be required to find memory and communication architectures suitable for this class of systems. The Next-generation Supercomputing Project of MEXT, which led to the construction of the peta-scale supercomputer K in Kobe, is an example where members of the NEST community were funded in a co-development scheme [33]. This ensured that an instrument useful for basic science was constructed, and appropriate simulation software was available when the computer went online. It is our hope that this success story of peta-scale systems based on a continuous dialogue between hardware developers, system-level developers, and application developers can be repeated for the upcoming exa-scale era. The time spent on basic development work at an instrument that is already online should be reduced to a minimum. Scientists are eager to use the short and costly lifespan of a supercomputer to address neuroscience challenges.

Acknowledgements. This work was supported by JUQUEEN grant JINB33 of the Jülich Supercomputing Centre, EU grants 269921 (BrainScaleS) and 604102 (Human Brain Project), the Helmholtz Alliance on Systems Biology, the Next-Generation Supercomputing Project of MEXT, and the Helmholtz Association in the Portfolio Theme Supercomputing and Modeling for the Human Brain.

References

1. Gewaltig, M.-O., Diesmann, M.: NEST (NEural Simulation Tool). Scholarpedia **2**(4), 1430 (2007)
2. Potjans, T.C., Diesmann, M.: The cell-type specific cortical microcircuit: relating structure and activity in a full-scale spiking network model. Cereb. Cortex **24**, 785–806 (2014)
3. Markov, N.T., Ercsey-Ravasz, M.M., Ribeiro Gomes, A.R., Lamy, C., Magrou, L., Vezoli, J., Misery, P., Falchier, A., Quilodran, R., Gariel, M.A., Sallet, J., Gamanut, R., Huissoud, C., Clavagnier, S., Giroud, P., Sappey-Marinier, D., Barone, P., Dehay, C., Toroczkai, Z., Knoblauchi, K., Van Essen, D.C.: A weighted and directed interareal connectivity matrix for macaque cerebral cortex. Cereb. Cortex **24**, 17–36 (2014)
4. Meyer, H.S., Egger, R., Guest, J.M., Foerster, R., Reissl, S., Oberlaender, M.: Cellular organization of cortical barrel columns is whisker-specific. PNAS **110**, 19113–19118 (2013)
5. Collins, C.E., Airey, D.C., Young, N.A., Leitch, D.B., Kaas, J.H.: Neuron densities vary across and within cortical areas in primates. PNAS **107**, 15927–15932 (2010)
6. Herculano-Houzel, S.: The human brain in numbers: a linearly scaled-up primate brain. Front. Hum. Neurosci. **3**, 31 (2009)
7. Kerr, J.N.D., Greenberg, D., Helmchen, F.: Imaging input and output of neocortical networks in vivo. PNAS **102**, 14063–14068 (2005)
8. Greenberg, D.S., Houweling, A.R., Kerr, J.N.D.: Population imaging of ongoing neuronal activity in the visual cortex of awake rats. Nat. Neurosci. **11**, 749–751 (2008)
9. Shinomoto, S., Kim, H., Shimokawa, T., Matsuno, N., Funahashi, S., Shima, K., Fujita, I., Tamura, H., Doi, T., Kawano, K., Inaba, N., Fukushima, K., Kurkin, S., Kurata, K., Taira, M., Tsutsui, K.-I., Komatsu, H., Ogawa, T., Koida, K., Tanji, J., Toyama, K.: Relating neuronal firing patterns to functional differentiation of cerebral cortex. PLoS Comput. Biol. **5**, e1000433 (2009)

10. Hines, M., Carnevale, N.T.: The NEURON simulation environment. Neural Comput. **9**, 1179–1209 (1997)
11. Bower, J.M., Beeman, D.: The Book of GENESIS: Exploring realistic neural models with the GEneral NEural SImulation System. Springer, New York (1995)
12. Stewart, T.C., Tripp, B., Eliasmith, C.: Python scripting in the Nengo simulator. Front. Neuroinf. **3**, 7 (2009)
13. Goodman, D.F.M., Brette, R.: The Brian simulator. Front. Neurosci. **3**, 192–197 (2009)
14. Morrison, A., Straube, S., Plesser, H.E., Diesmann, M.: Exact subthreshold integration with continuous spike times in discrete time neural network simulations. Neural Comput. **19**, 47–79 (2007)
15. Hanuschkin, A., Kunkel, S., Helias, M., Morrison, A., Diesmann, M.: A general and efficient method for incorporating precise spike times in globally time-driven simulations. Front. Neuroinform. **4**, 113 (2010)
16. Goddard, N.H., Hood, G.: Parallel GENESIS for large-scale modeling. In: Computational Neuroscience, pp. 911–917. Springer, New York (1997)
17. Howell, F.W., Dyhrfjeld-Johnsen, J., Maex, R., Goddard, N., de Schutter, E.: A large-scale model of the cerebellar cortex using PGENESIS. Neurocomputing **32**, 1041–1046 (2000)
18. Migliore, M., Cannia, C., Lytton, W.W., Markram, H., Hines, M.: Parallel network simulations with NEURON. J. Comput. Neurosci. **21**, 119–223 (2006)
19. Hines, M., Kumar, S., Schürmann, F.: Comparison of neuronal spike exchange methods on a Blue Gene/P supercomputer. Front. Comput. Neurosci. **5**, 49 (2011)
20. Djurfeldt, M., Lundqvist, M., Johansson, C., Rehn, M., Ekeberg, O., Lansner, A.: Brain-scale simulation of the neocortex on the IBM Blue Gene/L supercomputer. IBM J. Res. Dev. **52**, 31–41 (2008)
21. Hoang, R.V., Tanna, D., Bray, L.C.J., Dascalu, S.M., Harris Jr., F.C.: A novel CPU/GPU simulation environment for large-scale biologically realistic neural modeling. Front. Neuroinf. **7**, 19 (2013)
22. Ananthanarayanan, R., Esser, S.K., Simon, H.D., Modha, D.S.: The cat is out of the bag: Cortical simulations with 10^9 neurons and 10^{13} synapses. In: Supercomputing 09: Proceedings of the ACM/IEEE SC2009 Conference on High Performance Networking and Computing, pp. 1–12. IEEE, Portland (2009)
23. Preissl, R., Wong, T.M., Datta, P., Flickner, M., Singh, R., Esser, S.K., Risk, W.P., Simon, H.D., Modha, D.S.: Compass: a scalable simulator for an architecture for cognitive computing. In: Proceedings of the International Conference on High Performance Computing, Networking, Storage and Analysis, pp. 54:1–54:11. IEEE Computer Society Press, Los Alamitos (2012)
24. Helias, M., Kunkel, S., Masumoto, G., Igarashi, J., Eppler, J.M., Ishii, S., Fukai, T., Morrison, A., Diesmann, M.: Supercomputers ready for use as discovery machines for neuroscience. Front. Neuroinform. **6**, 26 (2012)
25. RIKEN BSI: Largest neuronal network simulation achieved using K computer. Press release, 2 August 2013
26. Eppler, J.M., Helias, M., Muller, E., Diesmann, M., Gewaltig, M.-O.: PyNEST: a convenient interface to the NEST simulator. Front. Neuroinf. **2**, 12 (2009)
27. Zaytsev, Y.V., Morrison, A.: CyNEST: a maintainable Cython-based interface for the NEST simulator. Front. Neuroinf. **8**, 23 (2014)
28. Kunkel, S., Potjans, T.C., Eppler, J.M., Plesser, H.E., Morrison, A., Diesmann, M.: Meeting the memory challenges of brain-scale simulation. Front. Neuroinform. **5**, 35 (2012)

29. Henker, S., Partzsch, J., Schüffny, R.: Accuracy evaluation of numerical methods used in state-of-the-art simulators for spiking neural networks. J. Comput. Neurosci. **32**, 309–326 (2012)
30. Brette, R., Rudolph, M., Carnevale, T., Hines, M., Beeman, D., Bower, J.M., Diesmann, M., Morrison, A., Goodman, P.H., Harris Jr., F.C., Zirpe, M., Natschläger, T., Pecevski, D., Ermentrout, B., Djurfeldt, M., Lansner, A., Rochel, O., Vieville, T., Muller, E., Davison, A.P., El Boustani, S., Destexhe, A.: Simulation of networks of spiking neurons: a review of tools and strategies. J. Comput. Neurosci. **23**, 349–398 (2007)
31. Zaytsev, Y.V., Morrison, A.: Increasing quality and managing complexity in neuroinformatics software development with continuous integration. Front. Neuroinf. **6**, 31 (2012)
32. Davison, A., Brüderle, D., Eppler, J.M., Kremkow, J., Muller, E., Pecevski, D., Perrinet, L., Yger, P.: PyNN: a common interface for neuronal network simulators. Front. Neuroinf. **2**, 11 (2008)
33. Diesmann, M.: The road to brain-scale simulations on K. BioSupercomputing Newsl. **8**, 8 (2013)

Computational Models
and Brain-Inspired Computing

A Geometric Model for the Functional Circuits of the Visual Front-End

Bart M. ter Haar Romeny[(✉)]

Department of Biomedical Engineering, Eindhoven University of Technology,
Eindhoven, The Netherlands
B.M.terHaarRomeny@tue.nl

Abstract. This paper reviews a biologically-inspired geometric model
for the functional circuits of the visual front-end. An axiomatic approach is taken towards the filters and their tasks in early vision. A high-
dimensional Lie-group based approach models the convolutions of the
receptive fields in a multi-scale, multi-orientation, multi-velocity, multi-
spatial frequency, multi-disparity and multi-color framework. In these
new, and essentially invertible, extra-dimensional expansions new geometric reasoning can be developed. They give a feasible approach to the
understanding of context, Gestalt, and association fields and enable full
exploitation of adaptive, geometry-driven strategies, such as for contour
completion and convection. The high-dimensionality leads to high computational costs, but, just as in human vision, this can be solved by
massively parallel implementations, which is one of the goals of the EU
Human brain project.

1 Introduction - A Lie Group Model for Early Vision

Decades of neural recordings and optical imaging methods, like voltage sensitive
dyes [2,14] and calcium intrinsic imaging, have revealed a highly precise organization of the visual front-end. The receptive fields on the retina, increasing in
size with eccentricity in a sunflower arrangement, have inspired to a multi-scale
model sampling of the incoming image, well known in the computer vision community as scale-space theory. The image is transformed into a higher dimensional
stack, the 'deep structure', in which new geometric reasoning possibilities emerge
for image analysis, such as edge focusing and topological analysis. The sensitivity
profiles of the simple cells of V1 in the primary visual cortex have been modeled
as Gabor functions and multi-scale and regularized Gaussian derivatives, which
enable the robust extraction of differential structure up to high order [12]. The
pinwheel structure of the cortical columns has inspired to a multi-orientation
representation, in so-called orientation scores [8], a stack of all responses of the
oriented filters of the pinwheel on the image. The disentangling of orientations
now enables the analysis of crossing structures, and the linking of similarly oriented filters between columns gives rise to new theories for the understanding
of Gestalt and perceptual grouping. The processing of velocities is modeled by
monocular pairs of receptive fields, by dedicated retinal parasol ganglion cells,

© Springer International Publishing Switzerland 2014
L. Grandinetti et al. (Eds.): BrainComp 2013, LNCS 8603, pp. 35–50, 2014.
DOI: 10.1007/978-3-319-12084-3_4

coupled by a small time delay (presumably the amacrine cells). Such a pair is a tuned detector for a specific velocity in a specific direction. These local detectors can be modeled as a multi-velocity, multi-scale and multi-orientation stack. They project to a specific set of layers in the lateral geniculate nucleus, the magnocellular layers. Similarly, the processing of disparities is modeled by binocular pairs of receptive fields, spatially shifted by a small distance, giving rise to far and near disparity detecting cells in V1. Again a stack of disparity values is modeled to be available at each spacial position. To measure local spatial frequencies, receptive fields with a sensitivity profile modeled by a Gabor function with varying spatial frequencies are needed. And lastly, at each position the three basic colors need to be extracted, as well as the differential structure of color.

The notion emerges that the formation of higher dimensional structures is a key paradigm in early vision. The extra dimensions give ample space for pluriform data analysis by higher levels. However, such representations are constrained, in the sense that no information should get lost. This leads to the mathematical formulation that such new spaces should be invertible. We will show that this requirement leads to only specific kernels allowed. This leads to interesting questions if these math-inspired kernels are also used by biology.

The plasticity of the visual system in the first three months after birth forms many of the receptive fields and connections. We explore the possibility to describe these processes of self-organization from a mathematical point of view with an axiomatic, first principles approach for two cases: the notion of best aperture, and the self-emergence of Gaussian derivative kernels from eigenpatches.

It seems counter-intuitive to create these high-dimensional and thus computationally expensive data representations. The model for the huge arrays of filter banks encountered in early vision needs a generic mathematical framework. However, we like to show in this paper the benefits of such a representation, and propose a common mathematical framework. As all extra dimensions are continuous group actions, we propose a generic geometric model based on Lie groups.

The model is inspired by the pioneering geometric modeling work of Koenderink [21], Young [41,42], Lindeberg [22], Petitot [29], Citti and Sarti [5], Weickert [38], Duits [7], Florack [12] ter Haar Romeny [37], Nielsen [26] and many others. The Lie group model for early vision is currently further developed in an ERC program by Duits, and a EU program MANET, lead by Citti.

2   Multi-scale Sampling by the Retina

The retina holds about 150 million receptors, and 1 million ganglion cells, whose axons form the optic nerve. The ganglion cells collect information from the receptors in a so-called receptive field (RF) structure, which has a center-surround Mexican hat (Laplacian of Gaussian) sensitivity profile on the retina. The retina has a high-resolution central fovea, and decreasing resolution with eccentricity. Rodieck [32] analyzed the retinal size distribution and layout meticulously, and found a linear relation with eccentricity, for the two groups of retinal ganglion

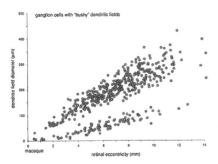 

Fig. 1. Left: The retina is a multi-scale sampling device. Retinal RF size increases with eccentricity [32]. Upper dots: parasol ganglion cells. Lower dots: midget ganglion cells. Right: Spurious resolution in the face of the first author. Typically pixels are measured with the wrong aperture function, such as squares, giving rise to spurious resolution, i.e. sharp edges and corners that are not in the original scene [21]. Blurring (squeeze your eye lashes) reduces these artefacts.

cells, the small midget cells (for shape), and the larger parasol cells (for motion), see Fig. 1. Visual acuity and velocity perception acuity decrease linearly with eccentricity.

2.1   Optimal Aperture Kernels - Optimal Receptive Fields

The optimal shape can be derived from *first principles*. The task of the retina is a first observation of visual space. Image sampling needs to be done with a finite aperture, i.e. the receptive field, connected to the retinal ganglion cell. The typical aperture shape in today's man-made image acquisition equipment is square, as it is easy to fabricate on a detector chip. Koenderink [21] already noted in the eighties that such a representation gives rise to 'spurious resolution', the appearance of non-existing edges and corners. The effect appears clearly when we zoom in to pixel level (Fig. 1): the face of the author certainly has no square corners all over and sharp edge discontinuities.

The axiomatic derivation below is based on Nielsen [26].

- A measurement is done with a finite aperture. When the aperture is too small, no photons come in anymore;
- All locations are treated similarly; this leads to translation invariance;
- The measurement should be linear, so the superposition principle holds.

These first principles imply that the observation must be a convolution (the example below is for simplicity in 1D):

$$h(x) = \int_{-\infty}^{\infty} L(y)g(x-y)dy \tag{1}$$

$L(x)$ is the luminance in the outside world, at infinite resolution, $g(x)$ is the unknown aperture, $h(x)$ the result of the measurement. The following constraints apply:

A. The aperture function $g(x)$ should be a normalized filter: $\int_{-\infty}^{\infty} g(x)\,dx = 1$.
B. The mean (first moment) of the filter g(x) is arbitrary (and is taken 0 for convenience): $\int_{-\infty}^{\infty} xg(x)dx = x_0 = 0$.
C. The width is the variance (second moment), set to σ^2: $\int_{-\infty}^{\infty} x^2 g(x)dx = \sigma^2$.

The entropy H of our filter is a measure for the amount of the maximal 'disorder', i.e. spurous extra's when the filter is applied, and is given by: $H = \int_{-\infty}^{\infty} -g(x)\ln g(x)dx$. A minimization problem with given constraints is typically solved with an Euler-Lagrange approach, from the calculus of variations. We look for the $g(x)$, for which the entropy is minimal given the constraints:

$$\int_{-\infty}^{\infty} g(x)\,dx = 1 \quad \text{and} \quad \int_{-\infty}^{\infty} xg(x)dx = 0 \quad \text{and} \quad \int_{-\infty}^{\infty} x^2 g(x)dx = \sigma^2.$$

The entropy under these constraints with the Lagrange multipliers λ_1, λ_2 and λ_3 is:

$$\tilde{H} = \int_{-\infty}^{\infty} -g(x)\ln g(x)dx + \lambda_1 \int_{-\infty}^{\infty} g(x)\,dx + \lambda_2 \int_{-\infty}^{\infty} xg(x)dx + \lambda_3 \int_{-\infty}^{\infty} x^2 g(x)dx$$

and is minimum when $\frac{\partial \tilde{H}}{\partial g} = 0$. This gives

$$-1 - \text{Log}[g(x)] + \lambda_1 + x\lambda_2 + x^2\lambda_3$$

from which follows

$$g(x) = e^{-1+\lambda_1+x\lambda_2+x^2\lambda_3}. \tag{2}$$

λ_3 must be negative, otherwise the function explodes, which is physically unrealistic. The three constraint equations are now:

$$\int_{-\infty}^{\infty} g(x)\,dx = 1, \lambda_3 < 0 \quad \rightarrow \quad e\sqrt{-\lambda_3} = e^{\lambda_1 - \frac{\lambda_2^2}{4\lambda_3}}\sqrt{\pi}$$

$$\int_{-\infty}^{\infty} xg(x)dx = 0, \lambda_3 < 0 \quad \rightarrow \quad e^{\lambda_1 - \frac{\lambda_2^2}{4\lambda_3}}\lambda_2 = 0$$

$$\int_{-\infty}^{\infty} x^2 g(x)dx = \sigma^2, \lambda_3 < 0 \quad \rightarrow \quad \frac{e^{-1+\lambda_1 - \frac{\lambda_2^2}{4\lambda_3}}\sqrt{\pi}\left(\lambda_2^2 - 2\lambda_3\right)}{4\left(-\lambda_3\right)^{5/2}} = \sigma^2$$

The three λ's can be solved from these three equations:

$$\left\{ \lambda_1 = \frac{1}{4}\text{Log}\left[\frac{e^4}{4\pi^2\sigma^4}\right], \lambda_2 = 0, \lambda_3 = -\frac{1}{2\sigma^2} \right\}$$

Indeed λ_3 is negative. These λs now specify the aperture function $g(x;\sigma)$ (Eq. 2):

$$g(x;\sigma) = \frac{1}{\sqrt{2\pi}\sigma}e^{-\frac{x^2}{2\sigma^2}}, \tag{3}$$

which is the Gaussian kernel.

The Gaussian kernel has all the required properties. It is smooth, does not generate spurious resolution, is circular, and is the *unique* solution of this basic set of constraints. It blurs the image, but that is the natural consequence of an observation with a finite aperture. We cannot see molecules with our naked eye. The Gaussian kernel is the Green's function of the famous diffusion equation:

$$\frac{\partial L}{\partial s} = \vec{\nabla}.\vec{\nabla}L \text{ or } \frac{\partial L}{\partial s} = \frac{\partial^2 L}{\partial x^2} + \frac{\partial^2 L}{\partial y^2} \tag{4}$$

where $\vec{\nabla} = \{\frac{\partial}{\partial x}, \frac{\partial}{\partial y}\}$ is the nabla or gradient operator. Blurring can thus also be interpreted as local diffusion of intensity.

The Gaussian kernel as optimal observation aperture has also been derived with other axiomatic approaches (no spurious resolution, no extra extrema, maintaining causality, etc.), reviewed by Weickert [39].

The diffusion Eq. (4) leads to an interesting model for the center-surround receptive field structure. Typically, this shape is modeled by a difference-of-Gaussians model, or a Gabor filter. The center-surround shape is also well modeled by the Laplacian of a Gaussian kernel, the 'Mexican Hat' function. The diffusion equation equates this to $\frac{\partial L}{\partial s}$. Thus such an RF may measure the change of output when the size σ of the observing kernel changes, i.e. when there is interesting local structure. In homogeneous areas there is no signal (also implied by the second order derivatives). But how do we perceive then homogeneous areas? From experiments with stabilized retinal images [31] we know that vision disappears within seconds after stabilization, filling in foreground homogeneous areas (color and luminance) with the background color growing from the contours. This must be an effect in higher levels of the visual system.

3   Regularized Multi-scale Derivative Operators and Invariants

When measuring (i.e. the process of observation) with the Gaussian kernel as the optimal sampling aperture, we obtain a discrete sampled dataset in 2D or higher dimensionality. It is a classical problem to take derivatives of discrete data [17], as we cannot apply the famous definition

$$\frac{df(x)}{dx} = \lim_{h \downarrow 0} \frac{f(x+h) - f(x)}{h}$$

as h cannot go to zero; it is the finite pixel distance. It was solved by Laurent Schwartz [33], for which he received the Field Medal: The derivative of such a series of samples is obtained by smoothing ('regularizing') it with a smooth so-called 'test function', which in our case is a convolution with a Gaussian function. The derivative operator and the convolution operator may be interchanged, as they are linear operators (this can be easily proven in the Fourier domain where a convolution becomes a product). So we finally convolve with the derivative of a Gaussian function to obtain robust multi-scale derivatives (to any order):

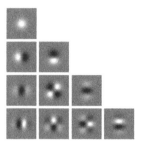

Fig. 2. Multi-scale Gaussian derivatives of order zero (top, just blurring) to order 3 (bottom). This set is known as the N-jet of Gaussian derivatives.

$$\frac{\partial}{\partial x}\{L_0(x,y) \otimes G(x,y;\sigma)\} = L_0(x,y) \otimes \frac{\partial}{\partial x}G(x,y;\sigma). \tag{5}$$

In fact, we find all multi-scale derivatives (see Fig. 2 for 2D examples), the so-called N-jet of Gaussian derivatives [36].

A Gaussian derivative is a *regularized* derivative. It has been shown that Gaussian blurring is equivalent to Tikhonov regularization [16]. Note that differentiation is now done by integration, i.e. by the convolution integral. It may be counterintuitive to perform a blurring operation when differentiating, but there is no way out: differentiation always involves some blurring by necessity. The scale σ of the differential operator cannot be taken arbitrarily small. There is a fundamental limit to the upper and lower bound of the scale σ given the order of differentiation, accuracy and scale [16]. A good rule of thumb is to not go smaller than $\sigma = 0.7\sqrt{n}$ pixels for n-th order derivatives.

The parameter σ is a free parameter, we can choose it as we like. However, the selection of the proper scale depends on the task: e.g. do we want to detect the edges of the tree or the edges of the leaves or the tree? Fig. 3 shows the contours of a city scene, calculated by the gradient magnitude, at different scales. Clearly the larger edges define larger (and often more 'important') contours.

Derivatives with respect to x or y do not make much sense, as the position and direction of the man-made coordinate system is completely arbitrary. We need to be invariant with respect to translations and rotations of the coordinate

   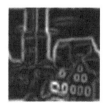

Fig. 3. Edges at different scales give different sized details. Left: original scene of Utrecht, the Netherlands. Gradients at $\sigma = 1, 3$ and 7 pixels. Image resolution 512×512.

system [12,24]. There are several ways to accomplish this. In this section we discuss two methods (for 2D images): intrinsic geometry with gauge coordinates and tensor index contraction.

An classical way is to take derivatives with respect to a coordinate system which is intrinsic, i.e. attached to the local image structure, in our case to the isophotes. Such local coordinates are called 'gauge coordinates'. People on different locations on the earth perceive the orientation of their world locally as the same. In the same way we choose in every pixel a new coordinate system $\{v, w\}$, fixed to the normal and tangential direction of the intensity landscape (isophotes).

Isophotes (i.e. lines of constant intensity) fully describe the image. We define a first order gauge frame in 2D as the local pair of unit vectors $\{v, w\}$, where v points in the tangential direction of the isophote, and w in the orthogonal direction, i.e. in the direction of the image gradient. So in every pixel a differently oriented $\{v,w\}$ frame is attached to the image. Any derivative with respect to v and w is invariant under translation and rotation, and so any combination of such gauge derivatives. So, $\frac{\partial L}{\partial w}$ is the gradient magnitude. And $\frac{\partial L}{\partial v} \equiv 0$, as there is no change in the luminance as we move tangentially along the isophote, and we have chosen this direction by definition. However, we can only measure derivatives in our pixel grid along the x-axis and the y-axis (by convolution with the proper Gaussian derivatives), so we need a mechanism to go from gauge coordinates to Cartesian coordinates. This is derived as follows:

Writing derivatives as subscripts ($L_x = \frac{\partial L}{\partial x}$), the unit vectors in the gradient and tangential direction are

$$\mathbf{w} = \frac{1}{\sqrt{L_x^2 + L_y^2}} \begin{pmatrix} L_x \\ L_y \end{pmatrix} \qquad \mathbf{v} = \begin{pmatrix} 0 & 1 \\ -1 & 0 \end{pmatrix}.\mathbf{w}$$

as $\mathbf{v}$ is perpendicular to $\mathbf{w}$. The directional differential operators in the directions $\mathbf{v}$ and $\mathbf{w}$ are defined as $\mathbf{v}.\nabla = \mathbf{v}.\left(\frac{\partial}{\partial x}, \frac{\partial}{\partial y}\right)$ and $\mathbf{w}.\nabla = \mathbf{w}.\left(\frac{\partial}{\partial x}, \frac{\partial}{\partial y}\right)$.

Higher order derivatives are constructed[1] through applying multiple first order derivatives, as many as needed. So L_{vv}, the second order derivative with respect to V is now $\left(\left(\begin{pmatrix} 0 & 1 \\ -1 & 0 \end{pmatrix} \frac{1}{\sqrt{L_x^2+L_y^2}} \begin{pmatrix} L_x \\ L_y \end{pmatrix} \cdot \left(\frac{\partial}{\partial x}, \frac{\partial}{\partial y}\right)\right)\right)^2 f(x,y)$

Here is a table of the lowest order differential invariants:

L_v	0
L_w	$\sqrt{L_x^2 + L_y^2}$
L_{vv}	$\frac{-2L_x L_{xy} L_y + L_{xx} L_y^2 + L_x^2 L_{yy}}{L_x^2 + L_y^2}$
L_{vw}	$\frac{-L_x^2 L_{xy} + L_{xy} L_y^2 + L_x L_y (L_{xx} - L_{yy})}{L_x^2 + L_y^2}$
L_{ww}	$\frac{L_x^2 L_{xx} + 2L_x L_{xy} L_y + L_y^2 L_{yy}}{L_x^2 + L_y^2}$

---

[1] See for most *Mathematica* code of the formulas in this chapter the book: [16].

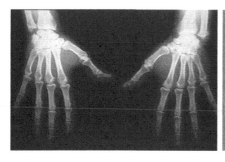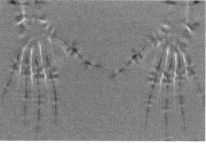

Fig. 4. Ridges of the fingers of a hand. Resolution 703×467 pixels, scale of the ridge operator L_{vv} is 3 pixels.

The second order gauge derivative L_{vv} is a well-known ridge detector. In Fig. 4 the ridges (centerlines) are extracted of the fingers of an X-ray of a hand.

3.1 Invariants from Tensor Contraction

In differential geometry, general derivatives are often denoted as (lower-script) indices, where the index runs over the dimensions, e.g. in 2D:

$$L_i = \begin{pmatrix} L_x \\ L_y \end{pmatrix}$$

When two similar indices occur in the same formula, they are summed over. The so-called Einstein convention means that in such a case the summation sign is left out:

$$L_i L_i \equiv \sum_{i=x}^{y} L_i L_i = \sum_{i=x}^{y} L_x L_x + L_y L_y$$

Famous examples are:

L	L	intensity
$L_i L_i$	$L_x^2 + L_y^2$	gradient magnitude square
L_{ii}	$L_{xx} + L_{yy}$	Laplacian
$L_i L_{ij} L_j$	$L_x^2 L_{xx} + 2 L_x L_y L_{xy} + L_y^2 L_{yy}$	ridge strength
$L_{ij} L_{ij}$	$L_{xx}^2 + 2 L_{xy}^2 + L_{yy}^2$	deviation from flatness

A neat and effective way to visualize such complex tensor contractions are the Feynman diagrams [20]. Special interest points in images, formed by invariant singularity points in scale-space such as top-points, SIFT, SURF), have received much attention for efficient image registration [23] and content-based image retrieval [30].

The invariants have by definition a translation and rotation invariant shape, i.e. are circular. Complex receptive fields in V1 exhibit a similar structure. Could they represent geometrically invariant scalar properties?

Fig. 5. Image of a disk with a very low signal to noise ratio. Right: gradient magnitude extraction with scales of $\sigma = 1, 2, 3, 4$ pixels. The signal to noise ratio increases, the localization accuracy decreases. Left: intensity profile of the middle row of the noisy disk image (as indicated by the red line) (Color figure online).

4 Multi-scale Structure

The multi-scale structure (the 'deep structure') of images is rich in information. It contains the information of the *scale* of features, which can be exploited to establish their importance. Stated differently, it contains the *hierarchy* of the structures in the image. Let us consider the extraction of larger edges from a noisy background. How can we combine the effects of reducing noise but giving up on localization accuracy when we go to coarser scales, with the finer spatial accuracy but higher noise when we consider finer scales? This is done by edge focusing [4]. Blurring an image to reduce the noise destroys the localization, as can be seen in Fig. 5.

The steepest point of an edge is given by the maximum of the gradient, which can easily be found by the zero crossing of the second order derivative in the gradient direction. In Fig. 6 the zero crossings (black for downgoing, white for upgoing edges) are plotted along the image line profile as a function of scale. This is the *signature function*. The edges follow geodesic tracks. Some edges survive the blurring for a long time, and they form the 'important' edges. Note that a black geodesic annihilates with a white geodesic in a singularity, a so-called top-point. Note also, that the up- and downgoing edges of the disk come together, indicating their intrinsic relation. From this we see important cues emerging from the deep structure analysis for the notion of symmetry and long-range contextual connections ('Gestalt').

In the nineties an influential paper by Perona and Malik [28] focused attention on adaptive mechanisms for the differential geometric extraction of information: e.g. the powerful notion of edge preserving smoothing by adapting the scale of the operator to the local edge strength. This field, known as geometry-driven diffusion, saw an influx of attention by mathematicians, and has now developed into a mature framework, incorporating non-linear geometry-driven diffusion equations and energy minimization variational approaches [15]. Edge preserving smoothing is now implemented widely, in both professional as consumer imaging applications. It is interesting, and its role largely still unclear, that the lateral geniculate nucleus receives 75 % of its input from retrograde, corticofugal connections from the primary visual cortex. The fact that there the differential structure is extracted makes it an interesting possible adaptive feedback mechanism model in early vision.

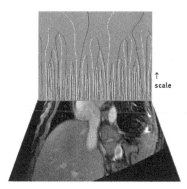

Fig. 6. Multi-scale signature function of a noisy row of pixels in an MRI image of the liver. The zerocrossings of the second order derivatives are indicated as white (upgoing edges) or black (downgoing edges) dots, as a function of exponential scale (vertical). Vertical is the scale direction, horizontal is the x-direction. Note how the most important edges survive the blurring the longest. The signature function generates the intrinsic hierarchy of structure.

5   Multi-orientation Operators

The Gaussian derivative kernels have many interesting properties, as being steerable, separable (extensively used for efficient computer implementations) and they come at all orientations in the visual cortex. The Nobel laureates Hubel and Wiesel were the first to discover that certain visual cells in the striate cortex of cats have a directional preference [18,19]. It has turned out that the majority of neurons in the primary visual cortex exhibits such an orientation preference, and, moreover, that there exists an intriguing spatial and directional organization into so-called cortical hypercolumns, see Fig. 7.

The layout is precise and characteristic, with a now famous pinwheel structure of spokes, forming radial iso-orientation lines of the tuning curves of the receptive cells of the cells involved. The discovery and development of voltage sensitive dyes by Grinvald et al. [34] made it possible to make high resolution and real-time optical recordings of many cells in action simultaneously. Today many additional powerful in-vivo optical imaging techniques have been developed [13], among which functional optical imaging at cellular level of intrinsic cellular signals by calcium fluorescence two-photon microscopy.

It has been found recently with this technique that the pinwheels are extremely well organized [6], and that the singularities in the center are really singularities (see Fig. 6) [27]. The cells along the spokes in the pinwheel exhibit receptive fields with a similar orientation of the tuning curve, while there are indications that the size of the receptive fields decreases with distance from the pinwheel center [35]. The cortical columns form a regular array on the cortical surface, organized in the binocular bands. The rotation direction reverses between neighboring columns. The columnar organization seems to solve the problem of mapping multiple parameters on a 2D cortical surface. A hypercolumn can be interpreted as a

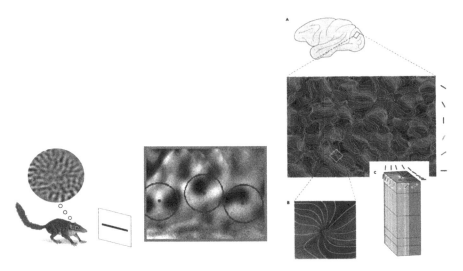

Fig. 7. Left: Voltage sensitive dyes revealed a precise organization of the visual cortex into cortical hypercolumns, with a characteristic pinwheel structure. Right: Cortical hypercolumns.

Fig. 8. Precise organization of cells around the pinwheel singularity, which is in the center of the image. Calcium fluorescence two-photon microscopy intrinsic imaging. Upper right: stimulus direction. From Ohki et al. [27].

"visual pixel", representing the optical world at a single location, neatly decomposed into a complete set of orientations. This neat organization can be modeled as multi-orientation structure, explained below (Fig. 8).

5.1 Long-Range Connections Between Pinwheels

Non-random horizontal connections within the cortical circuitry have been long identified. Early synaptic physiological studies of the horizontal pathway in cat striate cortex showed that neurons in layer II and III of the primary visual cortex with aligned receptive field sites and similar orientation preferences excite each other [20–22]. Apparently the visual system not only constructs a score of local orientations, it also accounts for spatial context and alignment by excitation and inhibition a priori. The spatial layout of these connections was convincingly shown by Bosking et al., who combined voltage-sensitive dye optical imaging with local injections of biocitin [40]. The connections run parallel to the brain's

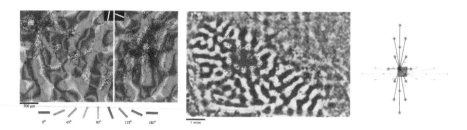

Fig. 9. Left: Long range connections between pinwheels, voltage sensitive dye optical recording, combined with local biocitin injections (black dots). From Bosking et al. [40]. Middle: Long range interactions between pinwheels over relatively large distances on the visual cortex of the tree shrew. The black-and-white areas indicate the left and right eye dominance stripes. From Bosking et al. [40]. Right: Model of contextual long-range connections between cortical hyper-columns. From Alexander et al. [1].

surface, linking columns across the spatial visual field with a shared orientation preference even over relatively large distances [25], allowing cells to integrate visual information from spatially separated receptive fields ('contextual connections'), see Fig. 9.

6 Orientation Scores

The multi-orientation 'deep structure' can be described by adding orientation as an extra dimension to the image, just as a 'scale-space'. As the physical unit is not meters but dimensionless, it is coined an 'orientation score'. An orientation score is $U_f := W_\psi f$ of a function f is constructed by means of a convolution with an anisotropic wavelet ψ via

$$U_f(\mathbf{x}, \theta) = (\widetilde{\psi_\theta} * \mathbf{f})(\mathbf{x}) = \int_{\mathbb{R}^2} \overline{\psi(\mathbf{R}_\theta^{-1}(\mathbf{y} - \mathbf{x})} \mathbf{f}(\mathbf{y}) d\mathbf{y} \qquad (6)$$

where $\psi \in \mathbb{L}_2(\mathbb{R}^2)$ is the con volution kernel with orientation $\theta = 0$, i.e. aligned with the vertical axis, and W_ψ denotes the transformation between inage f and orientation score U_f. The overline denotes complex conjugate, $\tilde{\psi}_\theta(\mathbf{x}) = \psi_\theta(-\mathbf{x})$ and $\mathbf{R}_\theta$ is the 2D rotation matrix. Exact reconstruction from the orientation scores constructed by 6 is given by

$$f = \mathcal{F}^{-1} \left[M_\psi^{-1} \mathcal{F} \left[\mathbf{x} \mapsto \frac{1}{2\pi} \int_0^{2\pi} (\tilde{\psi}_\theta * \mathbf{U_f}(., \theta))(\mathbf{x}) d\theta \right] \right] \qquad (7)$$

where $\mathcal{F}$ is the unitary Fourier transform on $\mathbb{R}$, and

$$M_\psi = 2\pi \int_0^{2\pi} \overline{\mathcal{F}[\psi^\theta]} \mathcal{F}[\psi^\theta] d\theta = \int_0^{2\pi} |\mathcal{F}[\psi^\theta]|^2 d\theta \qquad (8)$$

is the stability measure of the inverse transformation. The wavelets are defined in the polar Fourier domain as a wedge of the pie, a so-called 'cake kernel'

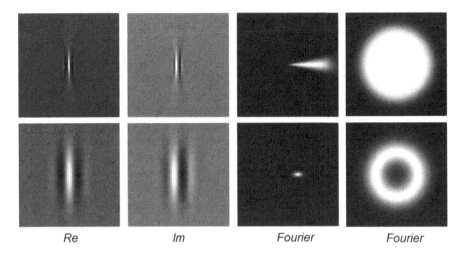

| Re | Im | Fourier | Fourier |

Fig. 10. Top row: Re and Im representations of the 'cake'kernels, with the domain in Fourier space. Bottom row: same for Gabor kernels. Images from [3].

[9,10]. The sum of all wavelets integrates to the full domain, therefor enabling invertibility. The spatial representation of the kernel is our convolution kernel. It resembles the Gabor filter, but the Gabor kernel is not invertible, it only samples a small section of the radial (spatial frequency) dimension. Figure 10 shows the 'cake' and Gabor kernels in the spatial and Fourier domain. The Gabor kernels need to sample the Fourier space over several scales (frequency bands), making them far less efficient. The cake kernels show outstanding performance in e.g. retinal vessel tracking [3].

The long-range connections are distributed over an elongated area, with the long axis in the direction of the connected orientations. This gives a nice model for a contextual voting system, where neighboring columns all contribute to the central column by voting for neighbor, we are all on the same contour or line as you are. Field et al. [11] showed evidence for a local 'association field'. Duits and Franken [9,10] and Citti and Sarti [5] developed interesting theory for contour enhancement and completion by left-invariant parabolic diffusion equations in the orientation scores.

7   Lie Vision

An exciting development, proposed by R. Duits (now exploring this in an ERC grant 2014–2017), is the possible extension of scores to the domains of:

- multi-scale
- multi-orientation
- multi-velocity (Heisenberg group)

- multi-spatial frequency (Gabor transform)
- multi-disparity
- multi-color

Motion analysis is a separate channel (parasol retinal ganglia magnocellular layers in LGN) in early vision. Essentially pairs of receptive fields are formed, separated by a time-delay, very likely by the amacrine cells. Because of the common framework, a model for long range connections may be developed, giving rise to new notions for dealing with occlusion and transparent motion, depth segmentation and local deformation analysis, e.g. from MR tagging data (Gabor). It is essential to couple the Lie group spaces, such as location and orientation. A pilot experiment, where dMRI data was filtered with location-only, or orientation-only, and location-orientation simultaneously, clearly showed the superiority of the combination. See Fig. 23.

The Lie group model of early visual functional circuits introduces mathematically an explosion of dimensions. This is supported by the findings of the huge numbers of filterbanks we encouter in early vision [18]. Massively parallel implementation is needed, and this is just what the EU Human Brain Project is aiming at. The advances in optical imaging, like intrinsic calcium fluorescence imaging at cellular levels, may give us new clues is this mathematically elegant model is also an elegant model for human vision functional circuits.

References

1. Alexander, D., van Leeuwen, C.: Mapping of contextual modulation in the population response of primary visual cortex. Cogn. Neurodyn. **4**, 124 (2012)
2. Bartfeld, E., Grinvald, A.: Relationships between orientation-preference pinwheels, cytochrome oxidase blobs, and ocular-dominance columns in primate striate cortex. Proc. Nat. Acad. Sci. U.S.A. **89**(24), 11905–11909 (1992)
3. Bekkers, E.J., Duits, R., ter Haar Romeny, B.M., Berendschot, T.J.: A new retinal vessel tracking method based on orientation scores. arXiv:1212.3530v4, Computer Vision and Pattern Recognition, pp. 1–28 (2012)
4. Bergholm, F.: Edge focusing. IEEE Trans. Pattern Anal. Mach. Intell. **9**, 726–741 (1987)
5. Citti, A., Sarti, G.: A cortical based model of perceptual completion in the roto-translation space. JMIV **24**(3), 307–326 (2006)
6. Crair, M.C., Ruthazer, E.S., Gillespie, D.C., Stryker, M.P.: Relationship between the ocular dominance and orientation maps in visual cortex of monocularly deprived cats. Neuron **19**, 307–318 (1997)
7. Duits, R., Felsberg, M., Granlund, G., ter Haar Romeny, B.: Image analysis and reconstruction using a wavelet transform constructed from a reducible representation of the Euclidean motion group. Int. J. Comput. Vis. **72**(1), 79–102 (2007)
8. Duits, R., Franken, E.: Left-invariant diffusions on the space of positions and orientations and their application to crossing-preserving smoothing of HARDI images. Int. J. Comput. Vis., **40** (2010)
9. Duits, R., Franken, E.M.: Left invariant parabolic evolution equations on SE(2) and contour enhancement via invertible orientation scores, Part I: Linear left-invariant diffusion equations on SE(2). Q. Appl. Math. AMS **68**, 255–292 (2010)

10. Duits, R., Franken, E.M.: Left invariant parabolic evolution equations on SE(2) and contour enhancement via invertible orientation scores, Part II: Nonlinear left-invariant diffusion equations on invertible orientation scores. Q. Appl. Math. AMS **68**, 293–331 (2010)

11. Field, D., Hayes, A., Hess, R.F.: Contour integration by the human visual system: evidence for a local 'association field'. Vis. Res. **33**–2, 173–193 (1993)

12. Florack, L.M.J., ter Haar Romeny, B.M., Koenderink, J.J., Viergever, M.A.: Scale and the differential structure of images. Image Vis. Comput. **10**(6), 376–388 (1992)

13. Frostig, R.D.: In vivo optical imaging of brain function. CRC Press, Boca Raton (2009)

14. Grinvald, A.: Imaging input and output dynamics of neocortical networks in vivo: exciting times ahead. Proc. Nat. Acad. Sci. U.S.A. **102**(40), 14125–14126 (2005)

15. ter Haar Romeny, B.M. (ed.): Geometry-Driven Diffusion in Computer Vision. Computational Imaging and Vision Series, vol. 1. Kluwer Academic Publishers, Dordrecht (1994)

16. ter Haar Romeny, B.M. (ed.): Front-End Vision and Multi-Scale Image Analysis: Multi-Scale Computer Vision Theory and Applications, written in Mathematica. Computational Imaging and Vision Series, vol. 27. Springer, Berlin (2003)

17. Hadamard, J.: Sur les problèmes aux dérivées partielles et leur signification physique. Bul. Univ. Princeton **13**, 49–62 (1902)

18. Hubel, D.H.: Eye, Brain and Vision. Scientific American Library, vol. 22. Scientific American Press, New York (1988)

19. Hubel, D.H., Wiesel, T.N.: Receptive fields, binocular interaction and functional architecture in the cat's visual cortex. J. Physiol. **160**, 106–154 (1962)

20. Kaiser, D.: Physics and Feynman's diagrams. Am. Sci. **93**, 156–165 (2005)

21. Koenderink, J.J.: The structure of images. Biol. Cybern. **50**, 363–370 (1984)

22. Lindeberg, T.: Scale-Space Theory in Computer Vision. The Kluwer International Series in Engineering and Computer Science. Kluwer Academic Publishers, Dordrecht (1994)

23. Lindeberg, T.: Image matching using generalized scale-space interest points. In: Kuijper, A., Bredies, K., Pock, T., Bischof, H. (eds.) ssvm 2013. LNCS, vol. 7893, pp. 355–367. Springer, Heidelberg (2013)

24. Misner, C.W., Thorne, K.S., Wheeler, J.A.: Gravitation. Freeman, San Francisco (1973)

25. Mooser, F., Bosking, W.H., Fitzpatrick, D.: A morphological basis for orientation tuning in primary visual cortex. Nature Neurosci. **7**, 872–879 (2004)

26. Nielsen, M.: From paradigm to algorithms in computer vision. Master's thesis, Department of Computer Science, University of Copenhagen, March 1995

27. Ohki, K., Chung, S., Chng, Y.H., Kara, P., Reid, R.C.: Functional imaging with cellular resolution reveals precise micro-architecture in visual cortex. Nature **433**, 597–603 (2005)

28. Perona, P., Malik, J.: Scale-space and edge detection using anisotropic diffusion. IEEE Trans. Pattern Anal. Mach. Intell. **12**(7), 629–639 (1990)

29. Petitot, J.: Neurogéometrie de la vision-Modeles mathématiques et physiques des architectures fonctionelles. Les Éditions de l'École Polytechnique (2008)

30. Crandall, D.J., Huttenlocher, D.P.: Weakly supervised learning of part-based spatial models for visual object recognition. In: Leonardis, A., Bischof, H., Pinz, A. (eds.) ECCV 2006, Part I. LNCS, vol. 3951, pp. 16–29. Springer, Heidelberg (2006)

31. Riggs, L.A., Ratliff, F.: The effects of counteracting the normal movements of the eye. J. Opt. Soc. Am. **42**, 872–873 (1952)

32. Rodieck, R.W.: The First Steps in Seeing. Sinauer Associates Inc, Sunderland (1998)
33. Schwartz, L.: Théorie des Distributions. Publications de l'Institut Mathématique de l'Université de Strasbourg, Paris (1950–1951)
34. Shmuel, A., Grinvald, A.: Coexistence of linear zones and pinwheels within orientation maps in cat visual cortex. Proc. Nat. Acad. Sci. **97**(10), 5568–5573 (2000)
35. Swindale, N.V., Matsubara, J.A., Cynader, M.S.: Surface organization of orientation and direction selectivity in cat area 18. J. Neurosci. **7**, 1414–1427 (1987)
36. ter Haar Romeny, B.M.: The Differential Structure of Images, pp. 565–582. CRC Press, Boca Raton (2012)
37. ter Haar Romeny, B.M.: Front-End Vision and Multi-scale Image Analysis. Springer Verlag, Berlin (2003)
38. Weickert, J.A.: Anisotropic diffusion in image processing. Ph.D. thesis, University of slautern, Department of Mathematics, Kaiserslautern, Germany, 29 January 1996
39. Weickert, J.A., Ishikawa, S., Imiya, A.: On the history of Gaussian scale-space axiomatics. In: Sporring, J., Nielsen, M., Florack, L.M.J., Johansen, P. (eds.) Gaussian Scale-Space Theory. Computational Imaging and Vision Series, Chap. 4, vol. 8, pp. 45–59. Kluwer Academic Publishers, Dordrecht (1997)
40. Weliky, M., Bosking, W.H., Fitzpatrick, D.: A systematic map of direction preference in primary visual cortex. Nature **379**, 725–728 (1996)
41. Young, R.A.: The Gaussian derivative model for machine vision: visual cortex simulation. J. Opt. Soc. Am. (1986)
42. Young, R.A.: The Gaussian derivative model for machine vision: I. retinal mechanisms. Spat. Vis. **2**(4), 273–293 (1987)

Models of the Visual Cortex for Object Representation: Learning and Wired Approaches

Antonio J. Rodríguez-Sánchez$^{(\boxtimes)}$ and Justus Piater

Intelligent and Interactive Systems, University of Innsbruck,
Technikerstr. 21A, Innsbruck 6020, Austria
{Antonio.Rodriguez-Sanchez,justus.piater}@uibk.ac.at
http://iis.uibk.ac.at/public/antonio

Abstract. Computational modeling now spans more than three decades. Biologically-plausible models are usually organized into a hierarchy that models the brain in primates after carefully examining neurophysiological and psychophysical studies. Currently, these models extract some values (corners, edges, textures, contours) from images and then apply machine learning algorithms to learn objects or shapes. Are they really that different from classical, non-biologically-inspired, computer vision methods? What facts can we learn from the primate visual system other than the extensively used edge extraction by means of Gabor filters? Should we work more on the representation along this hierarchy before applying a learning strategy? We review the status of computational modeling for object recognition and propose what can be the next challenges to solve.

Keywords: Computational neuroscience · Computer modeling · Biological plausibility · Machine learning

1 Introduction

In the century after the detailed descriptions of the nervous system by Ramón y Cajal [1–3], there has been great progress. A specially important moment for vision were the discoveries of Hubel and Wiesel [4,5] about neurons in area V1 of the visual cortex.

Computational models of visual processes are of interest in fields such as cybernetics, robotics, computer vision and others. Biological inspiration - and even biological realism - is currently of great interest in the computer vision community. There has been much emphasis in dividing computer models between bottom-up and top-down models [6]. This is an important characteristic of a model: On a bottom-up model the flow of information only proceeds from the lower - closer to the image, smaller neuronal receptive fields and more neuronally populated - to higher areas (that are more abstract in terms of representation and neuron receptive fields analyze a big portion of the visual field). Top-down models

© Springer International Publishing Switzerland 2014
L. Grandinetti et al. (Eds.): BrainComp 2013, LNCS 8603, pp. 51–62, 2014.
DOI: 10.1007/978-3-319-12084-3_5

contain a mechanism that incorporates some filtering or selection from neurons at the top that will influence neurons at the bottom, usually that mechanism follows on the visual system, such as attention [7]. In some cases, bottom-up models may evolve into top-down models like the Neocognitron [8].

We analyze here models from another perspective which has not been considered this far: that of hard-wired models or models that incorporate learning. We want to analyze if learning is necessary. In neurophysiology this is an old debate and one that was solved long ago, experiments support that a learning phase in the early years of mammals is necessary for a proper environment adaptation [9]. Another question is how much is genetic (learnt and incorporated across generations) and how much is acquired by the individual. Even though there is no question regarding the need of learning in evolved biological systems, we comment on the problems that are intrinsic to learning and some others on how machine learning is used for computer vision. We raise the following question: Do we want to develop models that are infants in the sense that they need a learning phase (a task that takes the first years of their life in humans) to be fully functional? Or is it more effective to focus on modeling the neurons in the adult brain?

2   Computational Models of the Visual Cortex for Object Representation

Computer models of the Visual Cortex may be considered as neural networks, although not in the classical sense. These models try to emulate biological neurons by means of mathematical equations. To come up with these mathematical equations, these models are typically influenced by studies in neuroscience. Not much time had passed since Hubel and Wiesel [5,10,11] presented the influential work about simple neurons in area V1 that would lead to their Nobel prize in 1982, that the first theories regarding neural networks incorporating mathematical formalities for biological-inspired terms - such as *excitatory connection, lateral inhibition, learning* or *attention* - were presented [12–14].

In the early 80 s we have three fundamental contributions: That of Marr's Vision [15], Zucker's essay [16] and Fukushima's neocognitron. Marr's theory consists of three stages for deriving shape information from the intensity values of the image. The first stage is the Primal Sketch that corresponds to the properties of the 2-D image, mainly intensity changes (following the main function of simple neurons) and geometry (blobs, edges, virtual lines, etc.). The second stage is the 2.5-D sketch that accounts for the properties of the image in a viewer-centred frame (distance from the viewer, discontinuities in depth, surface orientation, etc.). Finally, the 3-D representation is an object-centred representation and its spatial organization by means of a hierarchical representation with volumetric primitives (spatial configurations of sticks or axes) and surface properties. Zucker's essay proposes a number of constraints to achieve vision, these constraints were classified as *computational, behavioural and implementational.*

In this essay, Zucker states the machinery that is available to the visual system and thus, defines its restrictions. More importantly, he proposes the need of multiple levels of description, evolving from the concrete to the abstract. Among Zucker's contraints, we can find lateral inhibition, edges, contours and grouping, which appear at a higher or lower level in most current models. The Neocognitron [17–19] is a network hierarchically organized into several layers inspired by the simple and complex cells in area V1. By means of a learning algorithm, it can learn different patterns. It is robust to deformation, size and changes in location.

In those years, there were conflicting theories over synchronous [20–22] and control models [23–25]. One of the best representatives of the later - and one that was tested with patterns of letters - is the control-based network model of Olshausen and colleagues [25]. This model performs a transformation from the retinal reference frame to an object-centred frame. This is accomplished by means of shifting circuits and control neurons. The control neurons dynamically conduct information from lower levels of a hierarchical network to higher levels of the network. Thanks to the shifting circuits and the control neurons, the window of attention changes in size for scale invariance and position. This model was extended to the later SIAM [26].

Current models try to mimick the areas of the visual cortex involved in the object recognition or the motion pathways (Fig. 1). Explaining the areas of the visual cortex is beyond the scope of this work. The reader may find details regarding later discoveries on the visual cortex in recent summary papers [27,28]. Following that strategy, Visnet [29] consists of a four layer network that emulates

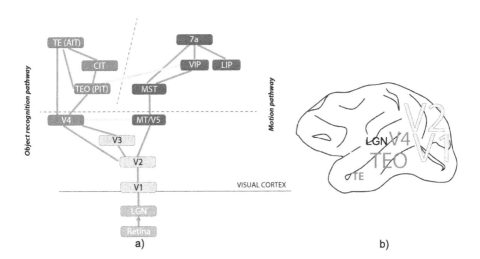

Fig. 1. Simplification of the visual cortex. (a) Connections from bottom to top. Left path is the object recognition pathway, right path is the motion pathway. (b) Approximate locations of the areas involved in object recognition in the macaque's brain. Letter font is related to area size

V1, V2, V4 and TEO/TE (Fig. 1) and achieves invariant object recognition. The fundamental blocks of Visnet are a (1) series of hierarchical layered networks that inhibit each other, (2) convergent connections from a population of cells from a layer to the next and (3) a trace learning rule that is Hebbian based. Lateral inhibition is performed following [30], and competition is applied by means of a soft winner take-all. The convergent connections aim is to achieve representations of increasing complexity and includes spatial local information in the competitve network layers. The Hebbian rule allows for a temporal trace of cells previous activity, thus previous cellular activity affects learning.

Widely popularized is the hierarchy of neuronal layers proposed by Riesenhuber and Poggio [31,32] whose main inspiration comes from Fukushima's Neocognitron [17–19]. As with the Neocognitron, there are two types of layers: one consist of simple units (S layers) and another of complex neurons (C layers). Simple and complex layers are interleaved in the hierarchy. A simple unit receives inputs from the complex units from the layer below in a Gaussian-weighting fashion. A complex unit is fed from simple units at the layer below and at different scales and positions to achieve some level of 2D invariance, from this set of simple units the strongest is selected through max selection. The original model was later extended to seven layers and the inclusion of a Support Vector Machine for object classification [33,34]. A summary of this later work is as follows: S1 contains a pool of edge detectors (Gabor filters) at 4 orientations, 17 sizes and 2 phases. C1 receives inputs from S1 at the same orientation and slightly different positions and sizes. A pool of 10 C1 units at different preferred orientations feed S2 units, the selection of S2 unit parameters is achieved through a learning process from natural images. Then C2 - as before on C1 - select the strongest S2 units at slightly different positions and scales. This process is further iterated in the two new layers (S3 and C3) in order to achieve a higher degree of invariance according to the authors. Finally, S4 is composed of view-tuned cells whose input are C3 units.

Amit [35] presented a parallel neural network for visual selection. Objects are represented as composed of features localized at different locations with respect to an object centre. Simple features (edges and conjunctions) are detected in lower levels, while higher levels carry out disjunctions over regions. Detection is accomplished by first constructing a graph of features and finding the candidate regions on the image through a Hough transform. The Hough transform also accounts for size and rotation invariance.

Suzuki and colleagues [36] construct a model of the form pathway based on predictive coding [37,38]. Predictive coding hypothesizes that feedback connections from high to lower-order cortical areas carry predictions of lower-level neural activities. Fidler, Leonardis and colleages [39] compositional hierarchies advantages include less storage needs, processing demands, robustness to clutter and expressive power. Compositionality is a property of hierarchical representations that define internal nodes in terms of simple constituent components according to the Gestalt laws of grouping. In this hierarchical representation at higher levels of the hierarchy we obtain parts that form objects. And these parts are shared among objects.

Some models focus their work on modeling areas or connections between two or three areas with a higher degree of complexity that what is present in the classical hierarchical methods. One example is the work of Weidenbacher and Neumann [40] that models contours and surface junctions in a feedforward and feedback recurrent network. This model is inspired by work in lateral connections [41] and is successful at detecting occlusions. Lately, cells in area V4 have been the source of inspiration for much work. One example is Murphy and Finkel [42], where V4 cells are modeled as a set of feature vectors of contours: mean polar angle, mean curvature of region, mean curvature of adjacent clockwise region, mean curvature of counter-clockwise region, mean direction of curvature region, mean distance from center of mass and indication of inner or outter contour. COSFIRE [43] is also about modeling units close to neurons in area V4. In this model, orientation-selective cells are combined into an AND-gate-like model. V4-like units are trained for a specific task of recognition.

Computer models have evolved from the theories of the first years to real applications that can compete with state-of-the-art computer vision systems. To mention some applications, the Neocognitron was successfully tested with character recognition, Visnet with faces, Serre and Poggio's or 2DSIL [44] were successfully compared with at the time current computer vision systems in tasks of object recognition. COSFIRE was applied to a clinical application, that of finding retinal vascular bifurcations.

3   Is Learning Really Necessary?

The short answer is Yes. In fact, learning is a fundamental part of most evolved biological systems. This fact has been quite well established in neuroscience for some time, many works which were summarized by Barlow [9] came to that conclusion. Kittens and young monkeys *learned* disparity or öther fine-tuned characteristics in their first months of life. In the case of orientation selectivity, Leventhal and Hirsch [45] showed that kittens would discriminate diagonal contours only if they were exposed to diagonal lines early in their life. This was not so dramatic for the case of horizontal/vertical lines. To summarize, there is hard-wired representation for lines (horizontal vs vertical), but experience was required for diagonal contours. Regarding object recognition in monkeys, familiar objects seem to activate less neurons than unfamiliar ones, and these neurons are more narrowly tuned [46]. It is clear then, that learning is required at the first months/years of a mammal, but from a computer modeling approach: Why do we want to learn? Do we want to model an infant visual cortex or an adult one? We also have to consider at what stage in the hierarchy we want to apply learning and more importantly what combination of *features* should be learned.

There are a number of problems when we consider a pure learning approach. The first one is that learning is time consuming, the second is the dependency on the learning data. Still most models presented in Sect. 2 apply learning on datasets. In Computer Vision, after using several types of image datasets that were used to compare a method to other methods, scientists are warning about

the problems of using these image datasets, which is called the *dataset bias*.
A recent work [47] shows the dangers of using image datasets the classical way,
that is, learning with a subset of the dataset and then evaluating within the
same dataset. Even when obtaining high classification rates in the evaluation
phase, it is questionable that the system has done a proper object generalization.
This, as that work shows, can be readily seen by evaluating against a different
image dataset containing the same type of objects than the former one. Results
showed those cross-database results to be very dissapointing. Thus, by using
datasets, be either one or a combination of some, there is no class or object
being learnt, but specific feature setups. We can avoid this by combinig different
datasets, or adding more and more images that include more variabilty. But how
many images/variability are enough? There is no clear answer to that, in fact,
that would depend on the classes or objects being learnt.

Related to that work is the interesting study of Pinto and collaborators [48].
They constructed a simple V1-like model (edge detectors) that was a simple
thresholded Gabor function over 16 different orientations and 6 spatial frequencies combined with a Support Vector Machine. The model did not contain a
representation of shape and no mechanisms for recognition under position, size
or pose variation. As it was expected, such a simple system performed poorly
when tested on an easy task of differentiating just two categories (planes from
cars) that introduced real-world variability (position, scale, in-plane rotation and
depth rotation). But surprisingly this system performed better than five state of
the art systems [49–53] when using the popular Caltech 101 database [54] that
included those two categories among the 102 categories in that database. The
reason behind this is that even though such a database contains pictures taken
from real-world scenarios, it does not include the random variability found in
the real world, while the former and basic two-category test did. The authors,
again, warn us about the risks of such biased datasets when performing tests on
real-world images.

We argue that one of the sources of these problems may be the result of
learning features that are too close to the image, instead of learning generalized concepts regarding the object. Thus, the classical learning stage over edges,
corners, textures, colors, etc. as most models do, comes too early for a proper
object generalization. Learning is necessary and is a fundamental part of any
biological visual information processing, but we argue that we need to work
more on a more elaborated, complex, effective and abstract object representation. All of this would bring us then to the question of at what level to apply
learning?. Studies have shown [55, 56] that by applying a learning algorithm over
a set of natural images, the features being extracted is a similar set of localized,
oriented and bandpass filters equvalent to the properties of simple cells in area
V1 of the visual cortex. A similar study showed this case also for complex cells
[57]. But models presented in Sect. 2 did not apply learning to obtain Gabor-like
features since we have a mathematical model for such filters and thus we can
avoid the learning at the visual cortex V1 level. Learning is then left for later
levels. For example in [58] thousands of images are used in order for layer S2

(the equivlent to V4 in the model) to become selective to boundary conformations. According to [59–61], neurons in area V4 are selective to shapes, and their data from neuronal recording was best fit with a function depending on the curvature and angular position of their boundary conformations. As a popular example, the model of Riesenhuber, Serre, Poggio and colleagues does not achieve a shape representation through any explicit form of curvature computation. Rather, the shape representation is obtained through the learning of repeated convergences layer by layer of approximate straight-line fits to boundaries beginning with edge elements. We argue that what is missing in most models is a *true* modeling of intermediate areas, thus avoiding a learning stage that is still too early in the hierarchy. Can we substitute the learning of curvatures and shape by a hard-wired mathematical formulation? This would be the equivalent to the fact that we do not apply learning to images in order to learn Gabor-like filters, but use the well known Gabor filter formulation. That is, can we *postpone* the application of learning for later in the hierarchy and thus, to learn a more abstract and efficient object representation?

4   2DSIL: A Hard-Wired Model of Shape

Models presented in Sect. 2 apply learning very early in their hierarchies. The problem is that the representations to which learning is applied is still too close to the images: They are mostly combinations of edges, corners, colors and similar features. Before applying machine learning, computational neuroscientists and computer vision scientists alike should work more at the representation level. We should obtain a representation that is more abstract than edges, corners or colors. The idea is to learn objects as such not as a result of the combination of low-level features, not even after a successive combination of those features in a hierarchy. A chair certainly has some visual qualities that make it a chair, but it is not its edges and corners but its parts and the general shapes of those parts, that is, a higher level representation than the ones we directly extract from images. On top of this, the *chair-ness* characteristic of a chair is that is something where you can sit on. We advocate for machine learning, but its application should be on a sufficiently abstract representation of an object that at the same time possesses the right structure for the task. Thus, we should make efforts also on the representation part of object recognition. To summarize, there are two important elements that are still missing on computer models: (1) The addition of intermediate representations, such as shape, color constancy or parts and (2) the attachment of semantic information to objects. This cannot be done overnight, but we can take steps towards it.

The strategy of most models up to date, does not explicitly include either curvature or end-stopped units, both well-known to exist in the visual cortex. Units that may appear similar may be learned; however, this is not necessarily so and depends on the training data selection as commented in the previous section. We have presented a model - known as 2DSIL [44, 62, 63] - that contributes a direct representation of curvatures and shapes by creating mathematical models for those units.

58   A.J. Rodríguez-Sánchez and J. Piater

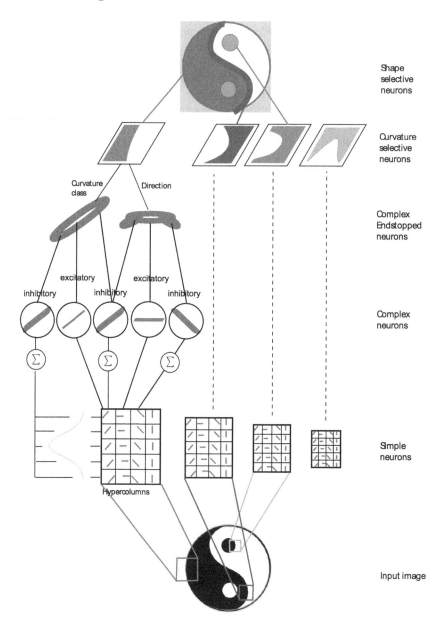

Fig. 2. Architecture of 2DSIL. Model simple neurons perform edge analysis. Responses from model simple neurons are integrated into model complex neurons receptive fields. By combining model simple and complex neurons we achieve endstopping. Responses of model endstopped cells are used to get different curvature classes. The main element in this architecture is that of Shape-selective neurons, they represent curvature parts in a curvature × position (radial and angular) domain following neurophysiology studies [59–61]. More details about the model can be found in Rodrıguez-Sánchez and Tsotsos [62]

A summary of the architecture of 2DSIL is presented in Fig. 2: Simple neurons are modeled as difference of Gaussians and organized in hypercolumns at four scales. Complex neurons are the combination of five displaced neurons relative to their prefered orientation. Complex endstopped neurons are the result of combining excitatory (from simple neurons) and inhibitory inputs (from complex neurons). If the excitatory an inhibitory components are at the same orientation, we obtain neurons that respond to different degrees of curvature. If they are at different orientations, we obtain neurons selective to the orientation of the curvature. By combining these two types of curvature selectors, we obtain curvature neurons. A shape neuron is a population of the different curvature-selective neurons at different locations. The possible number of shapes that may be represented by our model Shape neurons is very large, given the limited type of neurons at each level of the architecture. A Shape neuron has a response depending on the position and curvature of the stimulus component parts. Details regarding the model as well as how these intermediate representations are achieved through mathematical formulation at the neuronal level can be found in [62].

5   Conclusions

Computer vision systems use features extracted from images that are fed into a learning algorithm. These computer vision systems fail when compared to the efficiency, accuracy or robustness to changes of the mammalian visual system. Some scientists then proposed to overcome these problems by looking at biological visual systems and modeling neurons in the brain. A new field in computational neuroscience was born inspired in the advances from neurophysiology, and with it biologically-plausible or inspired models. Unfortunately, models do not exploit the complexity and representation richness of the mammalian visual system, but we find ourselves doing what has been the classical ways to attack the problem in computer vision: Extract edges, corners, contours and use machine learning.

We propose that we need to work on the representation before resorting to learning. We need to learn an object at its highest level of abstraction, not as a conjunction of lines and corners. Representations up to now are still too close to the image and too far from an abstract representation of an object. 2DSIL has taken some steps in evolving in that path and showed that it can be successfully applied to a computer vision task [44]. The model has also mimicked neurons in area V4 [62] with a high degree of fidelity, thus showing that by selecting the appropiate representation, there is no learning required for obtaining neurons selective to shapes as in other models [58]. By incorporating intermediate representations through neurons that respond to curvatures and shapes with their associated mathematical formulation we expect to contribute on more extensive work for a representation that becomes more abstract and closer to how the primate visual system represents an object. When we achieve that goal, we think it would be the time to apply learning approaches.

References

1. Ramón y Cajal, S.: Sobre las fibras nerviosas de la capa molecular del cerebelo. Rev. Trim. Histol. Norm. Patol. **1**, 33–49 (1888)
2. Ramón y Cajal, S.: The croonian lecture: La fine structure des centres nerveux. Roy. Soc. Lond. Proc. Ser. I **55**, 444–468 (1894)
3. Ramón y Cajal, S.: Variaciones morfologicas, normales y patologicas del reticulo neurofibrilar. Trab. Lab. Investig. Biol. Madrid. **3**, 9–15 (1904)
4. Hubel, D., Wiesel, T.: Receptive fields of single neurones in the cat's striate cortex. J. Physiol. **148**, 574–591 (1959)
5. Hubel, D., Wiesel, T.: Receptive fields and functional architecture of monkey striate cortex. J. Physiol. **195**(1), 215–243 (1968)
6. Poggio, T., Serre, T.: Models of visual cortex. Scholarpedia **8**(4), 3516 (2013)
7. Tsotsos, J.K.: Behaviorist intelligence and the scaling problem. Artif. Intell. **75**(2), 135–160 (1995)
8. Fukushima, K.: A neural network model for selective attention in visual pattern recognition. Bio. Cybern. **55**(1), 5–16 (1986)
9. Barlow, H.: Visual experience and cortical development. Nature **258**(5532), 199–204 (1975)
10. Hubel, D., Wiesel, T.: Receptive fields, binocular interaction and functional architecture in the cat's visual cortex. J. Physiol. **160**, 106–154 (1962)
11. Hubel, D., Wiesel, T.: Receptive fields and functional architecture in two nonstriate visual areas (18 and 19) of the cat. J. Neurophysiol. **28**, 229–289 (1965)
12. Grossberg, S.: Some nonlinear networks capable of learning a spatial pattern of arbitrary complexity. PNAS **2**(59), 368–372 (1968)
13. Grossberg, S.: Neural pattern discrimination. J. Theor. Biol. **2**(27), 291–337 (1970)
14. Grossberg, S.: A neural model of attention, reinforcement and discrimination learning. Int. Rev. Neurobiol. **18**, 263–327 (1975)
15. Marr, D.: Vision: A computational investigation into the human representation and processing of visual information. W.H. Freeman, NY (1982)
16. Zucker, S.W.: Computer vision and human perception: an essay on the discovery of constraints. In: Proceedings of the International Conference on Artificial Intelligence, pp. 1102–1116 (1981)
17. Fukushima, K.: Neocognitron: a self organizing neural network model for a mechanism of pattern recognition unaffected by shift in position. Biol. Cybern. **36**(4), 193–202 (1980)
18. Fukushima, K., Miyake, S., Ito, T.: Neocognitron: a neural network model for a mechanism of visual patter recognition. IEEE Trans. Syst. Man Cybern. **13**, 826–834 (1983)
19. Fukushima, K.: Neocognitron: a hierarchical neural network capable of visual pattern recognition. Neural Netw. **1**, 119–130 (1988)
20. Crick, F.: Function of the thalamic reticular complex - the searchlight hypothesis. PNAS **81**(14), 4586–4590 (1984)
21. von der Malsburg, C.: Nervous structures with dynamical links. Ber. Bunsenges. Phys. Chem. **89**, 703–710 (1985)
22. Crick, F., Koch, C.: Towards a neurobiological theory of consciousness. **2**(263–275), 203 (1990)
23. Anderson, C., Van Essen, D.: Shifter circuits: a computational strategy for dynamic aspects of visual processing. PNAS **84**(17), 6297–6301 (1987)

24. Postma, E., van den Herik, H., Hudson, P.: Dynamic selection through gating lattices. In: IEEE International Joint Conference on Neural Networks, vol. 3, pp. 786–791 (1992)
25. Olshausen, B., Anderson, C., Van Essen, D.: A neurobiological model of visual attention and invariant pattern recognition based on dynamic routing of information. J. Neurosci. **13**(11), 4700–4719 (1993)
26. Heinke, D., Humphreys, G.: Attention, spatial representation, and visual neglect: simulating emergent attention and spatial memory in the selective attention for identification model (SAIM). Psychol. Rev. **110**(1), 29–87 (2003)
27. Orban, G.A.: Higher order visual processing in macaque extrastriate cortex. Psychol. Rev. **88**(1), 59–89 (2008)
28. Krüger, N., Janssen, P., Kalkan, S., Lappe, M., Leonardis, A., Piater, J., Rodríguez-Sánchez, A., Wiskott, L.: Deep hierarchies in the primate visual cortex: what can we learn for computer vision? IEEE Trans. Pattern Anal. Mach. Intell. **35**(8), 1847–1871 (2013)
29. Wallis, G., Rolls, E.: Invariant face and object recognition in the visual system. Prog. Neurobiol. **51**(2), 167–194 (1997)
30. von der Malsburg, C.: Self-organization of orientation sensitive cells in the striate cortex. Kybernetik **14**(2), 85–100 (1973)
31. Riesenhuber, M., Poggio, T.: Hierarchical models of object recognition in cortex. Nature Neurosci. **2**(11), 1019–1025 (1999)
32. Riesenhuber, M., Poggio, T.: Neural mechanisms of object recognition. Curr. Opin. Neurobiol. **12**(2), 162–168 (2002)
33. Serre, T.: Learning a Dictionary of Shape-Components in Visual Cortex: Comparison with Neurons, Humans and Machines. Ph.D. thesis, Massachusetts Institute of Technology (2006)
34. Serre, T., Wolf, L., Bileschi, S., Riesenhuber, M.: Robust object recognition with cortex-like mechanisms. IEEE Trans. Pattern Anal. Mach. Intell. **29**(3), 411–426 (2007)
35. Amit, Y.: A neural network architecture for visual selection. Neural Comput. **12**, 1141–1164 (2000)
36. Suzuki, N., Hashimoto, N., Kashimori, Y., Zheng, M., Kambara, T.: A neural model of predictive recognition in form pathway of visual cortex. BioSystems **76**, 33–42 (2004)
37. Rao, R., Ballard, D.: Dynamic model of visual recognition predicts neural response properties in the visual cortex. Neural Comput. **9**(4), 721–763 (1997)
38. Rao, R., Ballard, D.: Predictive coding in the visual cortex: a functional interpretation of some extra-classical receptive-field effects. Nature Neurosci. **2**(1), 79–87 (1999)
39. Fidler, S., Berginc, G., Leonardis, A.: Hierarchical statistical learning of generic parts of object structure. In: IEEE CVPR, pp. 182–189 (2006)
40. Weidenbacher, U., Neumann, H.: Extraction of surface-related features in a recurrent model of V1–V2 interactions. PLOS ONE **4**(6), e5909 (2009)
41. Heitger, F., Rosenthaler, L., von der Heydt, R., Peterhans, E., Kubler, O.: Simulation of neural contour mechanisms: from simple to end-stopped cells. Vis. Res. **32**(5), 963–981 (1992)
42. Murphy, T., Finkel, L.: Shape representation by a network of V4-like cells. Neural Netw. **20**, 851–867 (2007)
43. Azzopardi, G., Petkov, N.: Detection of retinal vascular bifurcations by trainable V4-Like filters. In: Real, P., Diaz-Pernil, D., Molina-Abril, H., Berciano, A.,

Kropatsch, W. (eds.) CAIP 2011, Part I. LNCS, vol. 6854, pp. 451–459. Springer, Heidelberg (2011)

44. Rodríguez-Sánchez, A., Tsotsos, J.: The importance of intermediate representations for the modeling of 2D shape detection: Endstopping and curvature tuned computations. In: IEEE CVPR, pp. 4321–4326 (2011)

45. Leventhal, A.G., Hirsch, H.V.: Cortical effect of early selective exposure to diagonal lines. Science **190**(4217), 902–904 (1975)

46. Rainer, G., Miller, E.K.: Effects of visual experience on the representation of objects in the prefrontal cortex. Neuron **27**(1), 179–189 (2000)

47. Tommasi, T., Quadrianto, N., Caputo, B., Lampert, C.H.: Beyond dataset bias: multi-task unaligned shared knowledge transfer. In: Lee, K.M., Matsushita, Y., Rehg, J.M., Hu, Z. (eds.) ACCV 2012, Part I. LNCS, vol. 7724, pp. 1–15. Springer, Heidelberg (2013)

48. Pinto, N., Cox, D., Dicarlo, J.: Why is real-world visual object recognition hard? PLOS Comput. Biol. **4**(1), 151–156 (2008)

49. Wang, G., Zhang, Y., Fei-Fei, L.: Using dependent regions for object categorization in a generative framework. In: IEEE CVPR, pp. 1597–1604 (2006)

50. Grauman, K., Darrell, T.: Pyramid match kernels: Discriminative classification with sets of image features. MIT Technical report CSAIL-TR-2006-20 (2006)

51. Mutch, J., Lowe, D.: Multiclass object recognition with sparse, localized features. IEEE CVPR, pp. 11–18 (2006)

52. Lazebnik, S., Schmid, C., Ponce, J.: Beyond bags of features: spatial pyramid matching for recognizing natural scenes categories. In: IEEE CVPR, pp. 2169–2178 (2006)

53. Zhang, H., Berg, A., Marie, M., Malik, J.: Svm-knn: Discriminative nearest neighbor classification for visual category recognition. In: IEEE CVPR, pp. 2126–2136 (2006)

54. Fei-Fei, L., Fergus, R., Perona, P.: Learning generative visual models from few training examples: an incremental bayesian approach tested on 101 object categories. In: IEEE CVPR, p. 178 (2004)

55. Olshausen, B.A., Field, D.J.: Emergence of simple-cell receptive field properties by learning a sparse code for natural images. Nature **381**(6583), 607–609 (1996)

56. Bell, A.J., Sejnowski, T.J.: The of natural scenes are edge filters. Vis. Res. **37**(23), 3327–3338 (1997)

57. Karklin, Y., Lewicki, M.S.: Emergence of complex cell properties by learning to generalize in natural scenes. Nature **457**(7225), 83–86 (2008)

58. Cadieu, C., Kouth, K., Pasupathy, A., Connor, C., Riesenhuber, M., Poggio, T.: A model of V4 shape selectivity and invariance. J. Neurophysiol. **98**, 1733–1750 (2007)

59. Pasupathy, A., Connor, C.: Responses to contour features in macaque area V4. J. Neurophysiol. **82**(5), 2490–2502 (1999)

60. Pasupathy, A., Connor, C.: Shape representation in area V4: Position-specific tuning for boundary conformation. J. Neurophysiol. **86**(5), 2505–2519 (2001)

61. Pasupathy, A., Connor, C.: Population coding of shape in area V4. Nature Neurosci. **5**(12), 1332–1338 (2002)

62. Rodríguez-Sánchez, A., Tsotsos, J.: The roles of endstopped and curvature tuned computations in a hierarchical representation of 2D shape. PLOS ONE **7**(8), 1–13 (2012)

63. Rodríguez-Sánchez, A.: Intermediate Visual Representations for Attentive Recognition Systems. Ph.D. thesis, York University, Dept. of Computer Science and Engineering (2010)

A Generic Model of Visual Selective Attention

Kleanthis C. Neokleous[1,2], Marios N. Avraamides[1],
and Christos N. Schizas[1(✉)]

[1] Department of Computer Science, University of Cyprus, Nicosia, Cyprus
{mariosav,schizas}@ucy.ac.cy
[2] Department of Psychology, University of Cyprus, Nicosia, Cyprus
kleneokl@cs.ucy.ac.cy

Abstract. We present a computational model for the understanding of the fundamental principles of visual selective attention. The model has important medical, social and engineering applications that could benefit the general public. The design of the model is guided by the state of the art in neurophysiological evidence and its performance has been evaluated by comparisons to behavioral data from psychological studies.

The model effectively links low level neural interactions with behavioral data, thus providing concrete explanations for psychological phenomena. The model was used to simulate finding from several behavioral experiments on visual selective attention, with emphasis on those eliciting controversies in the scientific literature.

Keywords: Visual selective attention · Computational modeling · Saliency map · Spiking neural network

1 Introduction

The purpose of the attentional mechanism can be realized by considering that for every instant of conscious life, a person receives millions of external stimulations from his/her sensory systems. In each eye there are about 125 million photoreceptors that are estimated to provide information down the optic nerve in the range of 108–109 bits per second. This amount of information exceeds by far of what the brain is capable to process and consciously experience. Visual selective attention mechanisms are responsible for maintaining the stability in the brain by biasing only the relevant and essential information for further processing in the visual cortex, while at the same time filtering out redundant stimulation.

Selective attention has important behavioral implications in our everyday life therefore a deeper understanding of its role could benefit the general public. For example, while driving, failure to sustain selective attention to the road when a distracting stimulus appears (e.g., an attractive advertisement board) may cause the driver to induce an accident. Also, deficits in the attentional system have been linked with clinical disorders and conditions such as the Attention-Deficit Hyperactivity Disorder (ADHD) and schizophrenia. For instance, failure to inhibit distracting information in order to remain focused on a task is considered by many psychologists as the underlying cause of ADHD, which is often associated with adverse life outcomes [1], while

© Springer International Publishing Switzerland 2014
L. Grandinetti et al. (Eds.): BrainComp 2013, LNCS 8603, pp. 63–75, 2014.
DOI: 10.1007/978-3-319-12084-3_6

abnormalities of attention have long been considered as core features of the cognitive dysfunction associated with schizophrenia. It has been shown by many studies that schizophrenics cannot modulate attention and they maintain consistently high levels of arousal during selective attentional tasks [2].

Finally, the field of "intelligent systems" can significantly profit from any newly acquired knowledge that cognitive modeling brings to surface, since combined with knowledge from computer science, it can provide a good basis for Computational Intelligence (CI) applications. Robots and other engineered systems that mimic biological capabilities as well as brain-computer interfaces are some of the potential areas of applications that can benefit.

Visual selective attention can operate either in a space/location-based or an object-based manner. In space-based attention, locations in the visual field are selected while in object-based attention, organized symbols of visual information are selected independently from their location in space [3].

A central distinction for both these types of attention however is made with regards to the endogenous and exogenous reallocation of the attentional focus.

Top-down or endogenous attention refers to the volitional modulation of neural activity that corresponds to an object or a location in space, and it functions in response to signals initiated by internal goals, that most likely originate in the parietal and frontal lobes of the brain. Bottom-up or exogenous attention is a faster and more automatic process that relies on the sensory saliency of stimuli registered by subcortical structures in the primary sensory cortices [4, 5].

2   The Model of Visual Selective Attention

2.1   Methodology

For the development of the model, scientific evidence and data from the fields of cognitive psychology and neurophysiology have been considered. The behavioral aspect of selective attention is mostly studied from the fields of cognitive/experimental psychology, in which the primary research methods involve experimentation with human participants, while information related to the low level mechanisms and the connectivity between different parts of the brain system is obtained from the fields of cognitive neuroscience [6].

The implementation and evaluation of the computational model was based on a recurrent process. Initially the model was designed based on scientific evidence about the low level neural interactions followed by an evaluation of its performance compared to several existing data from behavioral experiments. Simulation predictions were re-examined through the design and execution of new behavioral experiments, from which the obtained data were used for updating the parameters of the model. This procedure was repeated until the accuracy of the model's behavior was substantially confirmed.

Next, the model was used for simulating behavioral data from experimental studies that triggered some controversies and theoretical disagreements in an attempt to offer biologically-plausible explanations for these data. The tasks that have been simulated can be placed under two main categories of visual attention tasks. The first category refers to tasks in which the deployment of attention is focused on the temporal appearance of visual stimuli. The typical methodology used in these tasks is the rapid serial visual presentation (RSVP), which is a method of displaying a sequence of visual stimuli in rapid succession at the same location. One of the most famous attention related tasks using this paradigm is the attentional blink (AB) phenomenon, established by Raymond, Shapiro and Arnell [7]. The AB was simulated through the proposed computational model, and the findings have been presented in previous work [8, 9].

The second category refers to tasks in which the multiple stimuli are presented simultaneously in various spatial locations in the visual field. One such behavioral experiment that offered a new proposal for describing the attentional mechanisms at a theoretical framework but also triggered some disagreements is the perceptual load task, originally described by Lavie [10]. The findings of this task have been successfully reproduced and analyzed through computational simulations [11, 12].

What follows, is a general description of the model for both sub-model categories since the system has a coherent structure and its operational units follow the same principles.

2.2   Overview of the Computational Model

The model involves two stages of processing implemented through spiking neural networks (SNN). The first stage simulates the initial bottom-up competitive neural interactions among visual stimuli, while the second stage involves top-down semantic modulations of neural activity. During the progression of neural activity through the two stages of processing, the encoded stimuli compete for access to working memory (WM) through forward, backward, and lateral inhibitory interactions which modulate the strength of their neural response. This implementation is based on the biased competition framework [13] and on neurophysiologic findings showing that competition for neural representation in visual areas is initiated when two or more stimuli fall within the receptive fields of the same or nearby [14, 15] cells.

The model was implemented to operate in two stages for modeling purposes considering that the division relies only on the functions that each stage represents and not on the visual areas that are involved during attentional tasks. In fact, it is widely accepted that most of the early visual areas (e.g. V1, V2) are repeatedly active during the progression of neural activity in the visual cortex [16].

The first stage of the model corresponds to the initial representations of any incoming stimuli. These representations are created in the model according to the "saliency map" theory that explains how the overall saliency at each location in the visual field can be calculated by integrating information across individual feature maps. For example, in the visual cortex and in area V1 in particular, a neuron's response has been found to be significantly suppressed based on several properties of contextual inputs that lie outside but near its receptive field [17–19]. Luminance contrast appears to be the initial variable on which saliency computation is based, since it is the first type of information extracted by our visual system in the retina [20]. At higher levels of visual processing, other feature dimensions such as orientation, color and motion are encoded and contribute to the overall visual saliency of a stimulus. At even higher levels in the visual pathway, "features" with increased level of complexity (e.g., semantic contrast) may influence visual saliency. Each level in the hierarchy of visual processing builds its receptive field selectiveness based on the output of the preceding layers [21].

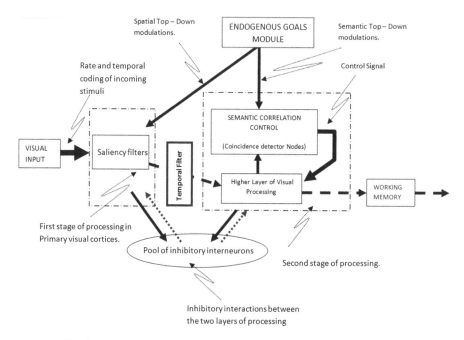

Fig. 1. The proposed computational model of visual selective attention.

The second stage of processing reflects the interaction between higher areas within the visual cortex and a top-down fronto-parietal network responsible for maintaining goal-directed activity (e.g. [3, 5]). More specifically, top-down signals in the second stage, correspond to the biasing of neural activity based on the semantic information that this neural activity conveys as it has been suggested by a number of studies with invasive recordings in the monkey visual area V4 [14, 22]. Top-down interactions during the computations performed in the second stage of processing can produce both neural amplification and neural synchronization in agreement with neurophysiological findings (e.g., [22, 23]). Attending a stimulus enhances the firing rate of the neurons that are linked to that specific stimulus and causes them to fire in a more synchronous rhythm. At the same time, the firing rates of neurons that correspond to unattended stimuli are suppressed. The evidence for synchronization in the human brain suggests that the temporal structure of neuronal spike trains is important for information processing. Nevertheless, this remains a controversial issue (see [24] for a review).

Finally, following the modulation of neural activity by top-down signals, the neural path leads to the working memory network. The working memory network will output a signal indicating perceptual awareness of an incoming stimulus if its neural activity is sufficient to activate the working memory nodes.

2.3   Generation of Input Stimuli

Each stimulus in the visual field is encoded with 12 input neurons whose receptive fields are associated with the spatial locations in which the stimuli appear. The stimuli are encoded through spike trains, i.e., series of discrete action potentials that are represented in the model as binary events (0's and 1's) denoting the absence or presence of a spike (action potential).

The firing rate of an input neuron can be seen as a Bernoulli process with probability P to have the value of 1 at any time bin of the spike train and 1 − PA, $(0 \leq PA \leq 1)$ to have the value of 0. The number of bins in a spike train is set in the model to equal the duration of each stimulus. For example, if a stimulus appears within the visual field for 100 ms then the neurons whose receptive fields correspond to that stimulus will generate spike trains that contain 100 time bins.

2.4   Saliency Map Model

For the saliency analysis in the first stage of processing we have adopted a saliency map model that was originally proposed by Koch and Ullman [25] as a neuromorphic vision algorithm. This algorithm, that has been implemented by Walther and Koch [26] into a Matlab toolbox (Saliency Toolbox - http://www.saliencytoolbox.net), can be used to produce saliency values for all spatial locations in the visual field. The overall saliency at each location in the visual field results from the integration of information across individual feature maps and is represented by a grayscale image indicating the calculated saliency for every pixel. The final saliency map is used in the model to generate the initial firing rates of the input neurons according to Eq. (1) (see also Fig. 2).

$$FR_{si} = \alpha(Max(Pj)) + \beta(\sum_{j=1}^{n} Pj) \tag{1}$$

In (Eq. 1), FRsi represents the firing rate of each of the 12 input neurons that correspond to the receptive field of stimulus Si. Max (Pj) is the maximum value of all the pixels that correspond to stimulus Si, and $\sum_{j=1}^{n} Pj$ is the total summation of the n pixel values (Pj) that correspond to stimulus Si. The terms α and β are weighting constants. The maximum pixel value for each stimulus reflects the general saliency of the stimulus while the summation value is used to incorporate the influence of the size of stimuli, as the model employs a fixed number of 12 neurons to encode incoming stimuli regardless of their size.

The values in the saliency map represent the extent to which locations in the visual field may attract attention in a solely bottom-up manner [27]. Although no semantic top-down modulation of neural activity takes place at early stages of processing, top-down spatial factors initiated by perceptual cues are allowed to influence the initial neural activity [28, 29] as discussed in the next subsection.

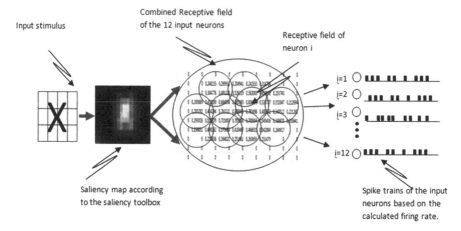

Fig. 2. Generation of initial firing rate according to the Saliency map algorithm.

2.5 Spatial Top Down Interactions

Spatial top down interactions are applied in the first stage of processing. More pre-cisely, in the case in which perceptual cues are used to prime the spatial location of an upcoming stimulus, top-down spatial factors in the model exert their influence on the initial firing rate of the input neurons. This interaction is compatible with findings from several studies documenting that cues may increase the neural activity of neurons that correspond to visual stimuli immediately after and even before the onset of the stimuli (e.g., [28, 29]). In the computational model, spatial top-down interactions are simulated by a sequence of spike trains originating from the endogenous goals module and are driven towards the input neurons whose receptive fields coincide with the primed spatial location.

2.6 Semantic Top-Down Interactions

To model the semantic interactions, templates that contain features of targets are stored and used for evaluating any visual input. These target representations are maintained in the endogenous goals module (Fig. 1) and recalled when tasks demand it. Following the neural interactions of the first stage of processing, the spike trains that correspond to any incoming stimuli will pass through a "temporal filter" that reorganizes their spikes appearance without altering their average firing rate. This mechanism is implemented in the model according to a pre-defined probability that reflects the degree of resem-blance between the features of any incoming stimulus and those of a target. Thus only the spike train patterns of a stimulus that shares similar features with the target will change significantly and become closer to the distinct spike train pattern that maintains the semantic representation of the target. The temporal filter mechanism in the model is inspired by a study of Crick and Koch [30] who suggested that the selection of stimuli could be made on the basis of synchrony across neurons. Crick and Koch [30] also claimed that visual selective attention could function in a way that it causes changes to the temporal structure of the neural spike trains that represent information to be selected and suggested that these temporal changes are a prerequisite for the presence of neural synchronization. This procedure modulates the timing of spikes within the spike train while the firing rate of the spike train remains unchanged.

Following the temporal filter operation, neural activity is conveyed to the correlation control module (CCM). The role of the CCM is to evaluate and compare the neural activity coming from the first stage of processing (that contains information about the nature of any incoming visual stimulus) and the activity that represents the top-down signals that maintain the properties of the target in a given behavioral context (i.e., endogenous goals possibly held in prefrontal cortical areas).The CCM is a neural network containing coincidence detector (CD) neurons inspired by what is currently known about the functional role of pyramidal cells, which are the main neurons found in the visual cortex. The pyramidal neurons have one large dendrite that branches upward into the higher layers of the cortex, as well as an axon which may be long enough to reach distant areas of the brain. Pyramidal neurons have been observed to respond best to the coincident activation of multiple dendritic compartments [31].

Coincidence detection neurons may function as a mechanism that controls the correlation between two streams of information that originate from different cortical areas. Therefore the CCM may represent anatomical locations where interaction between top-down signals and bottom up sensory information has been observed such as in visual area V4 (e.g., [14, 32, 33]).

Based on the degree of correlation, a control signal will be generated for the amplification of the incoming visual neural activity. The strength of the control signal depends on the total firing of the CD neurons of the CCM. For example, if two signals are correlated then the CD neurons will fire more frequently and will elicit a stronger control signal. As a result, the firing rate of the corresponding incoming stimulus is amplified. In addition, due to the impact of the coincidence detector neurons, in cases in which high correlation between an incoming stimulus and top-down signals occurs, a synchronous neural activity is observed between the neurons of the subsequent neural network layers of the model in agreement with the neurophysiological findings described in Sect. 2.2.

2.7 Competitive Inhibitory Interactions

To model the attentional process, competitive interactions that take place among stimuli that appear simultaneously at different spatial locations in the visual field are included. This competitive behavior is achieved using pools of inhibitory interneurons as shown in Fig. 3. The strength of the inhibition between the presented stimuli in the first stage of processing depends heavily on the levels of saliency. Thus, stimuli with high saliency values are able to exert stronger inhibition towards the representations of other stimuli that are present in the visual field.

In the second stage of processing, the level of inhibition that a stimulus exerts (indirectly through the pools of inhibitory neurons) depends on the strength of its semantic correlation with the endogenous signals. Higher correlation between stimuli results in increased firing rate and consequently in stronger inhibition towards other stimuli.

For spatial attention tasks lateral inhibition between neurons whose receptive field corresponds to separate spatial locations of the visual field are incorporated, while in RSVP tasks the competitive interactions between presented stimuli occur at different time windows. In the RSVP tasks, each incoming stimulus will receive inhibition from the stimuli that appeared before as well as by those that follow. This assumption is consistent with several studies of single cell recordings [34, 35] that show the effect of visual masking on the firing rate of neurons in the temporal cortex of monkeys. Thus, competition between the RSVP items, represented by backward and forward inhibition, will have the first impact on each of the neural responses in this model configuration. Even more, forward and backward masking in the proposed computational model, is intensified by reverberatory activity between the first and second stage of processing.

Within the working memory layer, separate working memory nodes are linked to different stimulus representations, therefore inhibitory interactions appear also in this phase of the modeling process. As previously explained, in the working memory network, an output signal indicating perceptual awareness of an incoming stimulus is initiated whenever a specific stimulus neural activity is sufficient to activate the working memory nodes. The same signal however, acts also in an inhibitory manner towards any newly generated signals from the CCM when the correlation control signal coincides with the perceptual awareness signal. This inhibitory process is necessary for preventing multiple stimuli entering working memory while it is occupied. Distinguishing brain signals from EEG and MEG studies support this notion [36, 37].

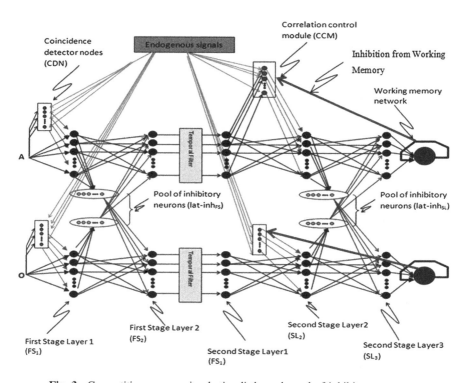

Fig. 3. Competition among visual stimuli through pool of inhibitory neurons.

3   Discussion

Several studies have been presented in the literature to propose candidate neural mechanisms for the attentional process. These results however, are usually compared with neurophysiologic studies that measure neural activity at the single neuron level. The proposed model is concentrated on the theoretical interpretations of behavioral experiments; therefore, a more abstract implementation was necessary. Still, the design of the model does not escape from the borderlines placed by neuroscience, and thus keeps its credibility and capability of predicting new findings. The combination of low level neural interactions and the more abstract psychological concepts as implemented in the model has provided the power to run simulations of behavioral phenomena, and at the same time to remain within the narrow limits of coupling interactions as these arise from the plethora of neurophysiologic evidence. Although the model does not follow an entirely biologically realistic implementation, the proposed approach offers the opportunity to contribute from a new perspective to the field of cognitive science.

The generic model of visual selective attention has been designed and used for simulating three debatable psychological experiments in the literature. These are the attentional blink phenomenon [7], the behavioral experiment that inspired the perceptual load theory [10], and the experiment that initiated a controversial debate on the relation between attention and consciousness [38]. The strategy we followed was to initially verify the model's achievement by comparing the simulation results with the experimental data, and afterwards to give some potential explanations for behavioral responses based on low level neural interactions, something that has not been clearly presented in the literature.

It is important to note that the model was indeed able to reproduce very closely the data derived from these three behavioral experiments [8, 9, 11, 12, 39] and it therefore represents a useful tool for evaluating the theories behind these results.

Appendix

The basic computational unit used in the model is the graded response neuron, defined by the membrane Eq. A1.

$$\tau_m \frac{dV}{dt} = E_L - V(t) + R_m I_s(t) \tag{A1}$$

V is the membrane potential of each neuron, τ_m is the membrane time constant, and E_L is the resting potential of the membrane. The membrane potential can be seen as a measure of the extent to which a node is excited. $I_s(t)$ represents the total synaptic current and is a simple combination of pre-synaptic excitation and bias currents that increase the membrane potential, with inhibition currents that reduce the membrane potential of the node. The total summation of the excitatory and inhibitory currents influences the actual membrane potential at each time instance. Finally, Rm is the membrane resistance of the neuron. In brief, Eq. 1 determines how the membrane potential V of each neuron develops over time after an input current Is is applied.

The value of the membrane potential increases until it reaches a specific threshold (V_{th}) at which a spike is emitted and V resets to its initial condition or resting potential V_{res}. Subsequently, a refractory period of 2 ms is applied before the neuron model is allowed to integrate again any pre-synaptic currents.

The term I_s in Eq. A1 quantifies the synaptic currents that are mediated by the excitatory receptors AMPA and NMDA (activated by glutamate, gAMPA and gNMDA) and the inhibitory receptor GABAA and GABAB, as shown in Eq. A2.

$$I_s(t) = (I_{AMPA}(t) + I_{NMDA}(t) + I_{GABA_A}(t) + I_{GABA_B}(t)) \tag{A2}$$

For the following analysis, the synaptic inputs will be considered as the total excitatory and inhibitory synaptic currents ($I_{exc}(t) + I_{inh}(t)$).

In the framework of the integrate-and-fire model, each pre-synaptic spike generates a post-synaptic current pulse that is driven towards the input of the following neuron as shown in (A3).

$$I_s(t) = (I_{exc}(t) + I_{inh}(t) = g_{exc}(t)(Es_{exc} - V) + g_{inh}(t)(Es_{inh} - V)) \tag{A3}$$

Where

$$g_{exc}(t) = \bar{g}_{exc}w_{exc}P_s(t), g_{inh}(t) = \bar{g}_{inh}w_{inh}P_s(t) \tag{A4}$$

is the maximal excitatory or inhibitory conductance and w_{exc}, w_{inh} refer to the excitatory and inhibitory synaptic weights.

$P_s(t)$ determines the synaptic conductivity and can be modeled by a simple exponential decay with time constant τs as shown in (A5).

$$P_s = \frac{1}{e^{\frac{t}{\tau s}}} + \frac{(\Theta(t - t_k)e^{\frac{t_k}{\tau s}})}{e^{\frac{t}{\tau s}}} \tag{A5}$$

In (A5), Θ represents the Heaviside step function (zero for negative arguments, unity for zero or positive arguments

$$\Theta(x) = \begin{cases} 0 & x < 0 \\ 1 & x > = 0 \end{cases} \tag{A6}$$

Coincidence Detector Nodes

Traditionally, coincidence detector neurons are modeled with a very short membrane time constant τ_m that can change rapidly. However, another way to model coincidence detection is based on a simple case in which separate inputs converge on a common target.

More precisely, if $\Psi(t)$ is a binary row vector denoting the states of neuron A and B at time t and $C(t + 1)$ the state of neuron C at t + 1.

$$C(t + 1) = \Theta(\Psi(t) - \theta) \tag{A7}$$

With Θ being the Heaviside step function, and θ the specific threshold for a number of pre-synaptic spikes that are needed to arrive synchronously in order for the output neuron C to induce a spike.

References

1. Barkley, R.A.: Behavioral inhibition, sustained attention, and executive functions constructing a unifying theory of ADHD. Psychol. Bull. **121**, 65–94 (1997)
2. Laurens, K.R., Kiehl, K.A., Ngan, E.T., Liddle, P.F.: Attention orienting dysfunction during salient novel stimulus processing in schizophrenia. Schizophrenia Res. **75**, 159–171 (2005)
3. Posner, M.I., Rothbart, M.K.: Research on attention networks as a model for the integration of psychological science. Ann. Rev. Psychol. **58**, 1–23 (2007)
4. Buschman, J., Miller, K.: Top-down versus bottom-up control of attention in the prefrontal and posterior parietal cortices. Science **315**(5820), 1860–1862 (2007)
5. Corbetta, M., Patel, G., Shulman, L.G.: The reorienting system of the human brain: from environment to theory of mind. Neuron **58**(3), 306–324 (2008)
6. Kastner, S., Ungerleider, L.G.: Mechanisms of visual attention in the human cortex. Ann. Rev. Neurosci. **23**, 315–341 (2000)
7. Raymond, J.E., Shapiro, K.L., Arnell, K.M.: Temporary suppression of visual processing in an RSVP task: An attentional blink? J. Exp. Psychol. Hum. Percept. Perform. **18**(3), 849–860 (1992)
8. Neokleous, Kleanthis C., Avraamides, Marios N., Neocleous, Costas K., Schizas, Christos N.: A neural network computational model of visual selective attention. In: Palmer-Brown, Dominic, Draganova, Chrisina, Pimenidis, Elias, Mouratidis, Haris (eds.) EANN 2009. CCIS, vol. 43, pp. 350–358. Springer, Heidelberg (2009)
9. Neokleous, C.K., Avraamides, N.M., Neocleous, K.C., Schizas, C.N.: A neural network model of the attentional blink phenomenon. Int. J. Eng. Intell. Syst. Electr. Eng. Commun. **17**, 115–126 (2009)
10. Lavie, N.: Perceptual load as a necessary condition for selective attention. J. Exp. Psychol. Hum. Percept. Perform. **21**(3), 451–468 (1995)
11. Neokleous, K.C., Avraamides, M.N., Schizas, C.N.: Computational modeling of visual selective attention based on correlation and synchronization of neural activity. In: Iliadis, L., Vlahavas, I., Bramer, M. (eds.) Artificial Intelligence Applications and Innovations III, pp. 215–223. Springer, Boston (2009)
12. Neokleous, K.C., Koushiou, M., Avraamides, M.N., Schizas, C.N.: A coincidence detector neural network model of selective attention. In: Proceedings of the 31st Annual Meeting of the Cognitive Science Society, Amsterdam, The Netherlands (2009)
13. Desimone, R., Duncan, J.: Neural mechanisms of selective visual-attention. Ann. Rev. Neurosci. **18**, 193–222 (1995)
14. Reynolds, J.H., Desimone, R.: Interacting roles of attention and visual salience in V4. Neuron **37**, 853–863 (2003)

15. Reynolds, J.H., Pasternak, T., Desimone, R.: Attention increases sensitivity of V4 neurons. Neuron **26**(3), 703–714 (2000)
16. Ioannides, A.A., Poghosyan, V.: Spatiotemporal dynamics of early spatial and category-specific attentional modulations. NeuroImage **60**, 1638–1651 (2012)
17. Nothdurft, H.C., Gallant, J.L., Van Essen, D.C.: Response modulation by texture surround in primate area V1: Correlates of popout under anesthesia. Vis. Neurosci. **1999**(16), 15–34 (1999)
18. Wachtler, T., Sejnowski, T.J., Albright, T.D.: Representation of color stimuli in awake macaque primary visual cortex. Neuron **37**(4), 681–691 (2003)
19. Shibata, K., Yamagishi, N., Goda, N., Yoshioka, T., Yamashita, O., Sato, M.A., Kawato, M.: The effects of feature attention on pre-stimulus cortical activity in the human visual system. Cereb. Cortex **18**, 1664–1675 (2008)
20. VanRullen, R.: Visual saliency and spike timing in the ventral visual pathway. J. Physiol. **97**, 365–377 (2003)
21. Chelazzi, L., Miller, E.K., Duncan, J., Desimone, R.: A neural basis for visual search in inferior temporal cortex. Nature **363**, 345–347 (1993)
22. Fries, P., Reynolds, J.H., Rori, A.E., Desimone, R.: Modulation of oscillatory neuronal synchronization by selective visual attention. Science **291**, 1560–1563 (2001)
23. Gregoriou, G.G., Stephen, J.G., Huihui, Z., Desimone, R.: High-frequency, long-range coupling between prefrontal and visual cortex during attention. Science **324**(5931), 1207–1210 (2009)
24. Rolls, E.T., Deco, G.: The Noisy Brain: Stochastic Dynamics as a Principle of Brain Function. Oxford University Press, Oxford (2010)
25. Koch, C., Ullman, S.: Shifts in selective visual attention: Towards the underlying neural circuitry. Hum. Neurobiol. **4**(4), 219–227 (1985)
26. Walther, D., Koch, C.: Modeling attention to salient proto-objects. Neural Netw. **19**, 1395–1407 (2006)
27. Zhaoping, L., Dayan, P.: Pre-attentive visual selection. Neural Netw. **19**, 1437–1439 (2006)
28. Silver, M.A., Ress, D., Heeger, D.J.: Neural correlates of sustained spatial attention in human early visual cortex. J. Neurophysiol. **97**, 229–237 (2007)
29. Shibata, K., Yamagishi, N., Goda, N., Yoshioka, T., Yamashita, O., Sato, M.A., Kawato, M.: The effects of feature attention on pre-stimulus cortical activity in the human visual system. Cereb. Cortex **18**, 1664–1675 (2008)
30. Crick, F., Koch, C.: Towards a neurobiological theory of consciousness. Semin. Neurosci. **2**, 263–275 (1990)
31. Spruston, N.: Pyramidal neurons: Dendritic structure and synaptic integration. Nat. Rev. Neurosci. **9**, 206–221 (2008)
32. Treue, S.: Visual attention: the where, what, how and why of saliency. Curr. Opin. Neurobiol. **13**, 428–432 (2003)
33. Ogawa, T., Komatsu, H.: Target selection in area V4 during a multidimensional visual search task. J. Neurosci. **24**, 6371–6382 (2004)
34. Rolls, E.T., Tovee, M.J., Panzeri, S.: The neurophysiology of backward visual masking: Information analysis. J. Cogn. Neurosci. **11**, 300–311 (1999)
35. Keysers, C., Perrett, D.I.: Visual masking and RSVP reveal neural competition. Trends Cogn. Sci. **6**, 120–125 (2002)
36. Ioannides, A.A., Taylor, J.G.: Testing models of attention with MEG. In: Proceedings of the IJCNN'03, pp. 287–297 (2003)

37. Luck, S.J.: The operation of attention—millisecond by millisecond—over the first half second. In: Ogmen, H., Breitmeyer, B.G. (eds.) The First Half Second: The Microgenesis and Temporal Dynamics of Unconscious and Conscious Visual Processes. MIT Press, Cambridge (2005)
38. Naccache, L., Blandin, E., Dehaene, S.: Unconscious masked priming depends on temporal attention. Psychol. Sci. **13**, 416–424 (2002)
39. Neokleous, K.C., Avraamides, M.N., Neokelous, C.K., Schizas, C.N.: Selective attention and consciousness: Investigating their relation through computational modeling. Cogn. Comput. **3**, 321–331 (2011)

COSFIRE: A Brain-Inspired Approach to Visual Pattern Recognition

George Azzopardi[(✉)] and Nicolai Petkov

Johann Bernoulli Institute for Mathematics and Computer Science,
University of Groningen, Groningen, The Netherlands
{g.azzopardi,n.petkov}@rug.nl

Abstract. The primate visual system has an impressive ability to generalize and to discriminate between numerous objects and it is robust to many geometrical transformations as well as lighting conditions. The study of the visual system has been an active reasearch field in neuropysiology for more than half a century. The construction of computational models of visual neurons can help us gain insight in the processing of information in visual cortex which we can use to provide more robust solutions to computer vision applications. Here, we demonstrate how inspiration from the functions of shape-selective V4 neurons can be used to design trainable filters for visual pattern recognition. We call this approach COSFIRE, which stands for Combination of Shifted Filter Responses. We illustrate how a COSFIRE filter can be configured to be selective for the spatial arrangement of lines and/or edges that form the shape of a given prototype pattern. Finally, we demonstrate the effectiveness of the COSFIRE approach in three applications: the detection of vascular bifurcations in retinal fundus images, the localization and recognition of traffic signs in complex scenes and the recognition of handwritten digits. This work is a further step in understanding how visual information is processed in the brain and how information on pixel intensities is converted into information about objects. We demonstrate how this understanding can be used for the design of effective computer vision algorithms.

Keywords: Computational models of vision · COSFIRE · Trainable filters · Feature detection · Shape · Handwritten digits · Retinal fundus images · Traffic signs

1 Introduction

"If our perception of a certain line or curve depends on simple or complex cells, it presumably depends on a whole set of them, and how the information from such sets of cells is assembled at subsequent stages in the path to build up what we call percept of lines or curves (if indeed anything like that happens at all) is still a complete mystery." writes D.H. Hubel in his Nobel Price lecture [26].

© Springer International Publishing Switzerland 2014
L. Grandinetti et al. (Eds.): BrainComp 2013, LNCS 8603, pp. 76–87, 2014.
DOI: 10.1007/978-3-319-12084-3_7

In the following, we propose a way how to assemble the information from Gabor filters, that are mathematical models of simple and complex cells, in order to construct detectors of more complex stimuli, such as lines, angles, curves, line bifurcations and, more generally, local combinations of line and curve segments. We also demonstrate the effectiveness of these detectors in practical applications.

The brain processes visual information in the so called visual pathway. It consists of two parts, namely the ventral and the dorsal streams, that are responsible for, roughly speaking, 'what' and 'where' aspects. We are concerned with how the ventral stream processes visual information, which takes an input signal from the retina and transforms it into meaningful object representation. This stream comprises cortical areas V1, V2, V4, TE and TEO [19,52].

Simple and complex cells referred to above are found in areas V1 and V2 [27,28]. The understanding of their properties have been the focus of numerous electrophysiological studies [2,14,15,35,51,53]. Later, computational models were developed aiming at computer simulations of the function of these neurons [1,3,33,47]. These computational models gave the basis for biologically motivated contour detection algorithms in digital image processing. In particular, two-dimensional Gabor functions were proposed for computational modelling of these cells [11,30]. Gabor functions were then widely applied in diverse computer vision tasks, including edge detection [32,37], texture analysis [9,17,23,29,49,50], image coding and compression [12], person identification based on iris pattern analysis [13], image enhancement [10], face recognition [36], motion analysis [42], and retrieval from image databases [54]. Further refinements of these models, include non-classical receptive field inhibition [43], also called surround suppression, and the filters that deploy this mechanism were shown to be effective detectors of object contours [21,22].

In contrast to areas V1/V2, there is still little knowledge on how visual information is processed further in subsequent areas of the ventral pathway. Area V4 receives input from V1/V2 and is known to comprise neurons selective for various aspects of visual information, such as shape [38], color [55] or texture [24]. In this paper we are concerned with shape and, therefore, we are mainly interested in the function of shape-selective V4 neurons. An account of the properties of this type of neuron was given by Pasupathy and Connor [38]. They investigated the activations of such neurons in macaque monkeys, using a systematically designed data set of relatively simple contour features similar to those illustrated by Fig. 1. They found that most (91 % of the 152) V4 neurons they studied were highly selective to curved contour features rather than to simple edges or bars. They also observed that V4 neurons are selective for the orientation of the contour feature, i.e. these neurons exhibited strong responses to angles and curves pointing in a specific direction. However, such a neuron may also be activated (with less than the maximum response) by stimuli differing slightly in orientation and/or curvature. Further analysis on V4 neurons was performed on a more complex data set including closed contour stimuli containing a combination of convex and concave contour elements [39]. The results of that study have shown that some V4 neurons are sensitive to a single convex or concave contour element,

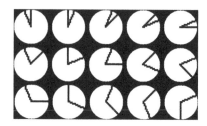

Fig. 1. Optimal stimuli for some V4 neurons that respond selectively to angles and curves, which can be characterized by two orientations such as two arms of an angle (redrawn from [38]).

while others are sensitive to a combination of adjacent contour elements. Moreover, the experiments of the referred authors reveal that on average V4 neurons have stronger responses to convex features rather than to concave ones which is consistent with the perceptual dominance of convexity found in psychophysics.

Similar to experimental neurophysiological studies, there is not much work on computational modelling of V4. A computational model of V4 neurons has been proposed in [44–46]. The response of a V4-like unit introduced in the referred papers depends on the Euclidean distance between a new input and a stored prototype where both input and prototype are local patterns of Gabor (energy) filter-like responses across different orientations and scales. Such a model will respond to an input pattern even if it contains only a part of the prototype. A missing part can, however, radically change a shape. For instance, a pattern that is formed by two line segments that make an angle is perceptually different from a pattern that consists of one of the constituent line segments. An Euclidean-distance model will, however, find these two patterns similar to a considerable extent. Furthermore, Euclidean-distance models are sensitive to the presence of noise or texture and to contrast variations. Those models are not invariant to any geometrical transformations.

There is psychophysical evidence [18] showing that curvatures are likely detected by an AND-type operation, which considers the responses of some afferent sub-units (sensitive for different parts of the curve pattern) and combines them by multiplication. This is in contrast to Euclidean-distance models that inherently involve addition. An AND-type model is activated only when it receives stimulation from all its afferent input, i.e. all contour parts that form a curve pattern are present. It will not respond when any of its inputs are not stimulated, i.e. any of the constituent parts of a curve pattern is absent. In the following, we propose and use such an AND-type model.

Fidler and Leonardis [16] propose to combine Gabor filter responses for vertex detection. They use local statistical analysis to identify two dominant orientations around a given point and use the corresponding channels in a bank of Gabor filters to detect vertices. This type of operator resembles the properties of shape-selective V4 neurons. At a next level they combine the responses of such operators in a similar way in order to define detectors of more complex

contour features that resemble the properties of some TEO neurons. Their approach is also vulnerable to contrast, noise and texture, and is also not robust to
geometrical transformations.

In the following, we propose nonlinear filters that can detect lines, vertices
and more complex contour features, similar to some V4 neurons. We call these
filters COSFIRE (Combination of Shifted Filter Responses). The response of
such a COSFIRE filter is assembled from selected responses of orientation-
selective filters. We configure such a filter by selecting given channels of a bank
of orientation-selective filters and combining their responses by a weighted geometric mean. The selection of channels is determined by the local pattern that
needs to be detected. This pattern is specified by the user as an area of interest
in a training image. The COSFIRE filters configured with given local patterns
can successfully detect the same and similar patterns in test images. The degree
of similarity/generalisation can be controlled by changing the values of certain
model parameters. We show how a COSFIRE filter achieves rotation-, scale- and
reflection-invariance.

The rest of this paper is organized as follows: In Sect. 2 we explain how a
COSFIRE filter can be configured by a specified prototype pattern of interest.
In Sect. 3, we demonstrate the effectiveness of the proposed COSFIRE filters by
applying them to three practical applications: the detection of vascular bifurcations in retinal fundus images, the detection and recognition of traffic signs
in complex scenes, and the recognition of handwritten digits. Section 4 contains
a discussion of some aspects of the proposed trainable approach and finally we
draw our conclusions in Sect. 5.

2   Computational Model and Its Implementation

A COSFIRE filter takes as input the responses of a collection of orientation-
selective filters that model V1/V2 cells. Here we use Gabor filters as they have
been widely used for more than two decades. Other orientation-selective filters,
such as CORF [4,5], may also be used. A COSFIRE filter response is then
computed as the weighted geometric mean of the responses of certain Gabor
filters at specific locations with respect to its receptive field center. The type
(orientation-selectivity and scale) of Gabor filters and the relative locations at
which we combine their responses are determined in an automatic configuration
process which we explain below.

2.1   Afferent Inputs: Gabor Filters

We denote by $|g_{\lambda,\theta}(x,y)|_{t_1}$ the thresholded response of a Gabor filter with orien-
tation preference of θ and a spatial wavelength preference of λ to an input image.
Such a filter is described by other parameters, namely bandwidth, spatial aspect
ratio, and phase offset, which we set as suggested in [41]. We normalize each
Gabor function that we use in such a way that the total sums of all the positive and negative values are 1 and -1, respectively. This normalization ensures

that the response to a line of width w will be largest for a symmetrical filter of preferred wavelength $\lambda = 2w$. It also ensures that the response to an image of constant intensity is 0. Without such normalization, this is true only for anti-symmetrical filters.

2.2 Configuration

A COSFIRE filter is configured by an automatic procedure that analyses the contour properties of a given local pattern, that we call a prototype. This is achieved in a single-step training phase where the user specifies a point of interest and a bounding box that surrounds a prototype of interest in a training image. Fig. 2a shows an input image with an enframed vertex that is considered as a prototype pattern.

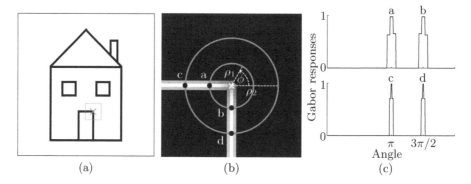

Fig. 2. (a) Training image of size 284×284 pixels. The cross marker and the gray bounding box around it indicate the specified local pattern of interest referred to as prototype. (b) The intensity pixels represent the superimposed thresholded responses ($t_1 = 0.4$) of a bank of Gabor filters with eight orientations ($\theta \in \{0, \frac{\pi}{8}, \ldots, \frac{7\pi}{8}\}$) and five wavelengths ($\lambda \in \{4, 4\sqrt{2}, \ldots, 16\}$) to the vertex prototype specified in (b). The top and bottom plots in (c) illustrate the Gabor responses along the inner and outer concentric circles in (b), respectively. The labels 'a','b','c', and 'd' indicate the local maxima points and are marked with black dots in (c). The location of each such point i is represented in polar coordinates (ρ_i, ϕ_i) relative to the specified point of interest.

The automatic analysis consists of three steps. *First*, we apply a bank of Gabor filters to the training image that contains the selected prototype, and threshold their responses using t_1, Fig. 2b. Here we use symmetric Gabor filters as the prototype is characterized by bar structures. *Second*, we consider the superimposed Gabor (thresholded) responses on the point of interest and along a number of k concentric circles (here $k = 2$) around that point. Then, we choose the locations along the concentric circles at which we achieve local maxima Gabor responses in an arc neighbourhood of $\pi/8$, Fig. 2c. These locations are converted to polar coordinates (ρ, ϕ) with respect to the given point of interest. They mark the positions of the dominant contours in the prototype. For each such a location we determine the channels (λ, θ) of the Gabor filters that exceed a fraction t_2 (here $t_2 = 0.5$) of the maximum response at that position. *Third*, we denote by S_f a set of 4-tuples that represents the channels and the respective locations of the Gabor filters that satisfy the above criteria for a prototype feature f:

$$S_f = \{(\lambda_i, \theta_i, \rho_i, \phi_i) \mid i = 1 \ldots n\} \tag{1}$$

where n is the number of involved Gabor filters. Each tuple $(\lambda_i, \theta_i, \rho_i, \phi_i)$ represents the characteristics of a contour part in the pattern of interest.

2.3 COSFIRE Filter Response

For each tuple $(\lambda_i, \theta_i, \rho_i, \phi_i)$ in set S_f we apply the Gabor filter with wavelength λ_i and orientation θ_i. Then we consider the Gabor responses in locations defined by the corresponding polar coordinates (ρ_i, ϕ_i). This is achieved by shifting the Gabor responses by ρ_i pixels in the direction opposite to ϕ_i. In this way the Gabor responses of interest meet at the same place, the one that we consider the support (or receptive field) center of the concerned COSFIRE filter.

Before shifting, however, we apply a blurring function to the Gabor responses in order to achieve some tolerance with respect to the preferred positions. For blurring we use a Gaussian function $G_\sigma(x, y)$ centered on the preferred position and compute the maximum of the weighted Gabor responses. The considered neighbours are determined by a standard deviation $\sigma = \sigma_0 + \alpha \rho_i$ that grows linearly with the distance ρ_i from the support center of the COSFIRE filter at hand. The positive values of parameters σ_0 and α are constants. The value of σ_0 is the standard deviation used at the support center of the concerned COSFIRE filter and the value α determines the extent of tolerance: tolerance increases with an increasing value of α. We denote by $s_{\lambda_i, \theta_i, \rho_i, \phi_i}(x, y)$ the blurred and shifted Gabor response for tuple $(\lambda_i, \theta_i, \rho_i, \phi_i)$ in set S_f, and denote by $r_{S_f}(x, y)$ the response of a COSFIRE filter:

$$r_{s_f}(x, y) = \left(\prod_{i=1}^{n} s_{\lambda_i, \theta_i, \rho_i, \phi_i}(x, y)^{\omega_i} \right)^{1/\sum_{i=1}^{n} \omega_i} \tag{2}$$

where $\omega_i = \exp^{-\frac{\rho_i^2}{2\sigma'^2}}$. Here we use $\sigma' = (-\rho_{\max}^2/2 \log 0.5)^{\frac{1}{2}}$ where $\rho_{\max} = \max_{i \in \{1 \ldots |S_f|\}} \rho_i$. With such a weighting scheme the weights in the center ($\rho = 0$) have a maximum value $\omega = 1$, and the farthest points ($\rho = \rho_{\max}$) have a minimum value $\omega = 0.5$.

Figure 3a illustrates the detected features in the input image shown in Fig. 2a. The circles surround the local maxima points in the COSFIRE response image that is obtained with Eq. 2.

2.4 Achieving Invariance to Geometric Transformations

We achieve invariance to rotation, scale and reflection by simply controlling some parameter values, instead of configuring COSFIRE filters by prototypes that are rotated, scaled or reflected versions of each other.

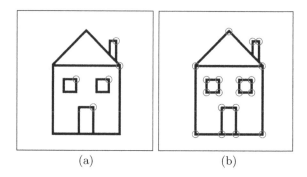

Fig. 3. Detection of features by a corner-selective COSFIRE filter which is applied in (a) a non-invariant mode and in (b) a rotation-invariant mode. The circles indicate the detected features.

We form a new set $\Re_\psi(S_f) = \{(\lambda_i, \theta_i + \psi, \rho_i, \phi_i + \psi) \mid \forall \ (\lambda_i, \theta_i, \rho_i, \phi_i) \in S_f\}$ by adding an offset ψ to the values of parameters θ_i and ϕ_i. The resulting set represents a COSFIRE filter that is selective for the same prototype f rotated by an angle ψ. Rotation invariance is then achieved by considering a set Ψ of equidistant ψ values and then taking the maximum response: $\hat{r}_{S_f} = \max_{\psi \in \Psi}\{r_{\Re_\psi}(x, y)\}$. Figure 3b illustrates the detection of all right-angled corners irrespective of their orientation ($\Psi = \{0, \pi/4, \ldots, 7\pi/8\}$).

Similarly, we form a new set $T_\upsilon(S_f) = \{(\upsilon\lambda_i, \theta_i, \upsilon\rho_i, \phi_i) \mid \forall \ (\lambda_i, \theta_i, \rho_i, \phi_i) \in S_f\}$ by multiplying with a factor υ the values of parameters λ_i and ρ_i. This results in a COSFIRE filter that responds to the prototype f scaled by a factor υ. A scale-invariant response is achieved by considering a set Υ of υ values equidistant on a logarithmic scale and then take the maximum response: $\tilde{r}_{S_f}(x, y) = \max_{\upsilon \in \Upsilon}\{r_{T_\upsilon(S_f)}(x, y)\}$.

A new set $\acute{S}_f = \{(\lambda_i, \pi - \theta_i, \rho_i, \pi - \phi_i) \mid \forall \ (\lambda_i, \theta_i, \rho_i, \phi_i) \in S_f\}$ results in a COSFIRE filter that is selective to the prototype f reflected about the y-axis. A reflection-invariant response is then computed as $\acute{r}_{S_f}(x, y) = \max\{r_{S_f}, r_{\acute{S}_f}\}$.

Finally, we denote by $\bar{r}_{S_f}$ the combined rotation-, scale- and reflection-invariant response by taking the maximum value of the rotation and scale-invariant responses of the filters S_f and $\acute{S}_f$: $\bar{r}_{S_f}(x, y) = \max\{\hat{r}_{\Re_\psi(T_\upsilon(S_f))}(x, y), \hat{r}_{\Re_\psi(T_\upsilon(\acute{S}_f))}(x, y)\}$.

3 Experiments

In [8] we demonstrated the effectiveness of the COSFIRE filters in three applications: the detection of vascular bifurcations in segmented retinal fundus images, detection and recognition of traffic signs embedded in images of complex scenes, as well as the recognition of handwritten digits, Fig. 4.

Retinal image analysis is gaining popularity as it gives the opportunity to take a non-invasive look at the cardiovascular system of human beings. One important step in this analysis is the detection of vascular bifurcations in the vessel tree. In [7] we evaluated our method, for the detection of vascular bifurcations in

(a)   (b)   (c)

Fig. 4. Trainable COSFIRE filters are effectively applied to three applications: (a) detection of vascular bifurcations in retinal fundus images, (b) detection and recognition of traffic signs in complex scenes and (c) recognition of (top) western Arabic and (bottom) Farsi handwritten digits.

retinal images, on two benchmark data sets and attained the following results: a precision of 96.94 % at a recall of 97.88 % on 40 images provided in the DRIVE data set [48] and a precision of 96.04 % at a recall of 97.32 % on 20 images taken from the STARE data set [25]. In these experiments, we first configured six COSFIRE filters in a training phase by using different prototypical bifurcations. Then we applied the configured filters to test retinal images in rotation-, scale- and reflection-invariant mode.

In order to show the versatility and robustness of the COSFIRE approach in [8] we performed experiments on a public data set[1] of outdoor scenes for the detection and recognition of three different traffic signs. This data set was originally published in [20]. We configured three COSFIRE filters to be selective for the three concerned prototypical traffic signs. For a data set of 48 images we were able to localize and recognize all the traffic signs in the data set.

We also demonstrated that the collective responses of a group of COSFIRE filters can also be used to form a shape descriptor. In [6] we applied this shape descriptor to the recognition of handwritten digits, an application that has been extensively used for the evaluation of shape descriptors. We achieved a recognition rate of 99.52 % on the MNIST data set [34] of 70,000 (60,000 training and 10,000 test) western Arabic digits. This result is comparable to the best results ever achieved by other state-of-the-art methods. Furthermore, we achieved a recognition rate of 99.33 % on a data set [31] of 80,000 (60,000 training and 20,000 test) Farsi digits, which is the highest recognition rate ever reported for this data set.

The shape descriptor that we propose is inspired by the neurophysiological concept of population coding. There is evidence [40] that the responses of multiple shape-selective neurons in area V4 of visual cortex can be effectively used as a signature to discriminate between complex shapes.

---

[1] Traffic sign data set is online: http://www.cs.rug.nl/imaging/databases/traffic_sign_database/traffic_sign_database.html.

4   Discussion

We propose a trainable COSFIRE approach to visual pattern recognition that is inspired by the shape selectivity of V4 neurons in visual cortex. In [8] we demonstrated that the response of COSFIRE filters to test stimuli used in electrophysiological measurements is similar to the response of some V4 neurons.

We demonstrated the effectiveness of the proposed filters in three practical applications: the detection of vascular bifurcations in retinal fundus images, the detection and recognition of traffic signs in outdoor scenes, and the recognition of handwritten digits.

The COSFIRE filters that we propose are trainable, in that the specific feature to which such a filter optimally responds is used to determine the structure of the filter. In a single-step training process, the user specifies a pattern of interest and that pattern is used to configure a corresponding COSFIRE filter. This selectivity is not achieved by template matching, but rather by the determination of the dominant orientations in the concerned pattern and their mutual geometrical arrangement. The proposed filters are highly nonlinear, in that such a filter will only respond when all parts of the concerned feature are present.

Although a COSFIRE filter has a preferred selectivity to the pattern that was used for its configuration, the filter also responds to similar patterns which differ - to a certain extent - in the orientations of the involved lines and edges. The degree of generalization is flexible and can be tuned to the specific needs of the user by proper selection of the filter parameters, We also demonstrate how these filters can be augmented with rotation, scale and refection invariance by simply manipulating some model parameters.

COSFIRE filters are conceptually simple and easy to implement: the filter output is computed as the (weighted) geometric mean of blurred and shifted responses of orientation-selective filters[2].

5   Conclusions

The trainable COSFIRE approach reviewed in this paper is a contribution to the understanding of the visual system of the brain. It shows how information from computational models of the responses of V1/V2 simple and complex cells, can be assembled at the next, V4 level, in order to construct detectors of more complex stimuli, such as angles, curves, line bifurcations and, more generally, local combinations of line and curve segments. We also demonstrated how this understanding of the visual system of the brain can be used to design effective computer vision algorithms.

References

1. Adelson, E.H., Bergen, J.R.: Spatiotemporal energy models for the perception of motion. J. Opt. Soc. Am. a-Optics Image Sci. Vis. **2**(2), 284–299 (1985)

---

[2] The Matlab and C++/OpenCV implementations of COSFIRE can be downloaded from http://matlabserver.cs.rug.nl.

2. Albrecht, D.G., De Valois, R.L., Thorell, L.G.: Visual cortical-neurons - are bars or gratings the optimal stimuli. Science **207**(4426), 88–90 (1980)

3. Andrews, B.W., Pollen, D.A.: Relationship between spatial-frequency selectivity and receptive-field profile of simple cells. J. Physiol. Lond. **287**, 163–176 (1979)

4. Azzopardi, G., Petkov, N.: A CORF computational model of a simple cell that relies on LGN input outperforms the Gabor function model. Biol. Cybern. **106**(3), 177–189 (2012)

5. Azzopardi, G., Petkov, N.: Contour detection by CORF operator. In: Villa, A.E.P., Duch, W., Érdi, P., Masulli, F., Palm, G. (eds.) ICANN 2012, Part I. LNCS, vol. 7552, pp. 395–402. Springer, Heidelberg (2012)

6. Azzopardi, G., Petkov, N.: A shape descriptor based on trainable COSFIRE filters for the recognition of handwritten digits. In: Wilson, R., Hancock, E., Bors, A., Smith, W. (eds.) CAIP 2013, Part II. LNCS, vol. 8048, pp. 9–16. Springer, Heidelberg (2013)

7. Azzopardi, G., Petkov, N.: Automatic detection of vascular bifurcations in segmented retinal images using trainable COSFIRE filters. Pattern Recogn. Lett. **34**(8), 922–933 (2013)

8. Azzopardi, G., Petkov, N.: Trainable COSFIRE filters for keypoint detection and pattern recognition. IEEE Trans. Pattern Anal. Mach. Intell. **35**(2), 490–503 (2013)

9. Bovik, A.C.: Analysis of multichannel narrow-band-filters for image texture segmentation. IEEE Trans. Signal Process. **39**(9), 2025–2043 (1991)

10. Cristobal, G., Navarro, R.: Space and frequency variant image-enhancement based on a gabor representation. Pattern Recogn. Lett. **15**(3), 273–277 (1994)

11. Daugman, J.G.: Uncertainty relation for resolution in space, spatial-frequency, and orientation optimized by two-dimensional visual cortical filters. J. Opt. Soc. Am. a-Optics Image Sci. Vis. **2**(7), 1160–1169 (1985)

12. Daugman, J.G.: Complete discrete 2-d gabor transforms by neural networks for image-analysis and compression. IEEE Trans. Acoust. Speech Signal Process. **36**(7), 1169–1179 (1988)

13. Daugman, J.G.: High confidence visual recognition of persons by a test of statistical independence. IEEE Trans. Pattern Anal. Mach. Intell. **15**(11), 1148–1161 (1993)

14. De Valois, K.K., De Valois, R.L., Yund, E.W.: Responses of striate cortex cells to grating and checkerboard patterns. J. Physiol. (Lond.) **291**, 483–505 (1979)

15. De Valois, R.L., Albrecht, D.G., Thorell, L.G.: Cortical cells: bar and edge detectors, or spatial frequency filters? In: S.J. Cool and III Smith, E. L. (eds.) Frontiers in Visual Science, pp. 544–56. Springer, Berlin (1978): Frontiers in Visual Science, Houston, TX, USA, March 1977

16. Fidler, S., Leonardis, A.: Towards scalable representations of object categories: Learning a hierarchy of parts. In: 2007 IEEE Conference on Computer Vision and Pattern Recognition, vol. 1–8, pp. 2295–2302 (2007)

17. Fogel, I., Sagi, D.: Gabor filters as texture discriminator. Biol. Cybern. **61**(2), 103–113 (1989)

18. Gheorghiu, E., Kingdom, F.A.A.: Multiplication in curvature processing. J. Vis. **9**(2), 1–7 (2009)

19. Goodale, M.A., Milner, A.D.: Separate visual pathways for perception and action. Trends Neurosci. **15**(1), 20–25 (1992)

20. Grigorescu, C., Petkov, N.: Distance sets for shape filters and shape recognition. IEEE Trans. Image Process. **12**(10), 1274–1286 (2003)

21. Grigorescu, C., Petkov, N., Westenberg, M.A.: Contour detection based on non-classical receptive field inhibition. IEEE Trans. Image Process. **12**(7), 729–739 (2003)

22. Grigorescu, C., Petkov, N., Westenberg, M.A.: Contour and boundary detection improved by surround suppression of texture edges. Image Vis. Comput. **22**(8), 609–622 (2004)

23. Grigorescu, S.E., Petkov, N., Kruizinga, P.: Comparison of texture features based on gabor filters. IEEE Trans. Image Process. **11**(10), 1160–1167 (2002)

24. Hanazawa, A., Komatsu, H.: Influence of the direction of elemental luminance gradients on the responses of v4 cells to textured surfaces. J. Neurosci. **21**(12), 4490–4497 (2001)

25. Hoover, A., Kouznetsova, V., Goldbaum, M.: Locating blood vessels in retinal images by piecewise threshold probing of a matched filter response. IEEE Trans. Med. Imaging **19**(3), 203–210 (2000)

26. Hubel, D.H.: Exploration of the primary visual-cortex, 1955–78. Nature **299**(5883), 515–524 (1982)

27. Hubel, D.H., Wiesel, T.N.: Receptive fields, binocular interaction and functional architecture in cats visual cortex. J. Physiol. (Lond.) **160**(1), 106–154 (1962)

28. Hubel, D.H., Wiesel, T.N.: Sequence regularity and geometry of orientation columns in monkey striate cortex. J. Comp. Neurol. **158**(3), 267–294 (1974)

29. Jain, A.K., Farrokhnia, F.: Unsupervised texture segmentation using gabor filters. Pattern Recogn. **24**(12), 1167–1186 (1991)

30. Jones, J.P., Palmer, L.A.: An evaluation of the two-dimensional gabor filter model of simple receptive-fields in cat striate cortex. J. Neurophysiol. **58**(6), 1233–1258 (1987)

31. Khosravi, H., Kabir, E.: Introducing a very large dataset of handwritten Farsi digits and a study on their varieties. Pattern Recogn. Lett. **28**(10), 1133–1141 (2007)

32. Kovesi, P.: Image features from phase congruency. Videre **1**(3), 1–27 (1999)

33. Kulikowski, J.J., Bishop, P.O.: Fourier-analysis and spatial representation in the visual-cortex. Experientia **37**(2), 160–163 (1981)

34. LeCun, Y., Huang, F.J., Bottou, L.: Learning methods for generic object recognition with invariance to pose and lighting. In: Proceedings of the 2004 IEEE Computer Society Conference on Computer Vision and Pattern Recognition, vol 2, pp. 97–104 (2004)

35. Macleod, I.D.G., Rosenfeld, A.: Visibility of gratings - spatial frequency channels or bar-detecting units. Vision. Res. **14**(10), 909–915 (1974)

36. Manjunath, B.S., Shekhar, C., Chellappa, R.: A new approach to image feature detection with applications. Pattern Recogn. **29**(4), 627–640 (1996)

37. Mehrotra, R., Namuduri, K.R., Ranganathan, N.: Gabor filter-based edge-detection. Pattern Recogn. **25**(12), 1479–1494 (1992)

38. Pasupathy, A., Connor, C.E.: Responses to contour features in macaque area v4. J. Neurophysiol. **82**(5), 2490–2502 (1999)

39. Pasupathy, A., Connor, C.E.: Shape representation in area v4: Position-specific tuning for boundary conformation. J. Neurophysiol. **86**(5), 2505–2519 (2001)

40. Pasupathy, A., Connor, C.E.: Population coding of shape in area v4. Nat. Neurosci. **5**(12), 1332–1338 (2002)

41. Petkov, N.: Biologically motivated computationally intensive approaches to image pattern-recognition. Future Gener. Comput. Syst. **11**(4–5), 451–465 (1995)

42. Petkov, N., Subramanian, E.: Motion detection, noise reduction, texture suppression, and contour enhancement by spatiotemporal gabor filters with surround inhibition. Biol. Cybern. **97**(5–6), 423–439 (2007)

43. Petkov, N., Westenberg, M.A.: Suppression of contour perception by band-limited noise and its relation to non-classical receptive field inhibition. Biol. Cybern. **88**(10), 236–246 (2003)

44. Riesenhuber, M., Poggio, T.: Hierarchical models of object recognition in cortex. Nat. Neurosci. **2**(11), 1019–1025 (1999)
45. Serre, T., Kouh, M., Cadieu, C., Knoblich, U., Kreiman, G., Poggio, T.: A theory of object recognition: computations and circuits in the feedforward path of the ventral stream in primate visual cortex. AI Memo 2005–036/CBCL Memo 259, Massachusetts Inst. of Technology, Cambridge (2005)
46. Serre, T., Wolf, L., Bileschi, S., Riesenhuber, M., Poggio, T.: Robust object recognition with cortex-like mechanisms. IEEE Trans. Pattern Anal. Mach. Intell. **29**(3), 411–426 (2007)
47. Shapley, R., Caelli, T., Morgan, M., Rentschler, I.: Computational theories of visual perception. In: Spillmann, L., Werner, J.S. (eds.) Visual Perception: The Neurophysiological Foundations, pp. 417–448. Academic, New York (1990)
48. Staal, J., Abramoff, M.D., Niemeijer, M., Viergever, M.A., van Ginneken, B.: Ridge-based vessel segmentation in color images of the retina. IEEE Trans. Med. Imaging **23**(4), 501–509 (2004)
49. Tan, T.N.: Texture edge-detection by modeling visual cortical channels. Pattern Recogn. **28**(9), 1283–1298 (1995)
50. Turner, M.R.: Texture-discrimination by gabor functions. Biol. Cybern. **55**(2–3), 71–82 (1986)
51. Tyler, C.W.: Selectivity for spatial-frequency and bar width in cat visual-cortex. Vis. Res. **18**(1), 121–122 (1978)
52. Ungerleider, L.G., Mishkin, M.: Two Cortical Visual Systems. MIT Press, Cambridge (1982)
53. Von Der Heydt, R.: Approaches to visual cortical function. Rev. Physiol. Biochem. Pharmacol. **108**, 69–150 (1987)
54. Wu, P., Manjunath, B.S., Newsam, S., Shin, H.D.: A texture descriptor for browsing and similarity retrieval. Signal Process.-Image Commun. **16**(1–2), 33–43 (2000)
55. Zeki, S.M.: Color coding in rhesus-monkey prestriate cortex. Brain Res. **53**(2), 422–427 (1973)

Toward the Development of Cognitive Robots

Antonio Bandera[1]([✉]) and Pablo Bustos[2]

[1] ISIS Group, Dpto. Tecnología Electrónica, University of Malaga, Málaga, Spain
ajbandera@uma.es
http://www.grupoisis.uma.es
[2] RoboLab, Escuela Politécnica, University of Extremadura, Cáceres, Spain
pbustos@unex.es
http://robolab.unex.es

Abstract. With the aim of endowing robots with the ability to engage people in real social interactions, it is currently typical that novel architectures for robot control take into account in its internal design concepts and schemes originated from cognitive theories. The objective is that robots will be able to emanate responses at human interaction rates and exhibit a pro-active behaviour. This pro-active behaviour implies that the internal architecture of these robots should not only be able to perceive and act. It should also be able to perform off-line reasoning. This paper introduces RoboCog, a new cognitive architecture whose four core elements are a deep -in the concrete-abstract dimension- and hybrid -in the symbolic-numeric dimension- representation of the current state, including the robot itself and the observed world; a set of agents that provide broad functionalities such as navigation, body movement control, dialog or object recognition, and as a result build and maintain this representation; an internal emulation and planning facility where foreseen courses of action can be inferred and tested; and an Executive module that coordinates the interactions among all others. Furthermore, agents themselves can reproduce internally this architecture, including their own replicas of the four elements. The typical scheme of 3-tier architectures is therefore replaced by a recursive estructure that provides a more flexible scenario, where the responses of all agents are tied together by the use of a common inner representation. Preliminar results of the proposed architecture in real scenarios show how RoboCog is able to enhance the effectiveness and time-of-response of complex multi-degree-of-freedom robots designed to collaborate with humans.

Keywords: Robotics · Cognitive architectures · Simulation theory of cognition

1 Introduction

Cognitive neuroscience robotics integrates studies on robotics, cognitive science and brain science. The long term aim is to translate models that explain the functionality of the human brain to the domain of socially interactive robots. These

© Springer International Publishing Switzerland 2014
L. Grandinetti et al. (Eds.): BrainComp 2013, LNCS 8603, pp. 88–99, 2014.
DOI: 10.1007/978-3-319-12084-3_8

robots should share the environment with humans, emanating and understanding a continuous and dense stream of social signals. This challenging scenario demands new strategies for robot control, which should intimately link the robot body with its dynamic surroundings. This can be only achieved if perception and action are closely tied, but this is not probably sufficient. The robot must be able to predict the result of an observed or executed action, as this could be the only way to quickly anticipate what the next action will be. The aim is to imitate the human capabilities for actively perceiving others' actions, predicting their intentions at different levels of abstraction and quickly learning from the observation of others' behaviours. If we have a look to recent theories on cognitive neuroscience, it appears to be clear that motor representations provide a functional connection between mind and body, but also that they provide the basis for processes such as action understanding, imitation and empathy [17]. Thus, on one hand, it can be stated that they play a critical role in social interaction, offering a means for people to take on the others' perspectives [17], but, on the other hand, the existence of these common representations, where states of mind and body are merged, could also explain how voluntary movements are performed, at sensorimotor level [12], where they enable determinations about the motor commands required to perform a task and predictions about the consequences of these commands, and at levels of increasing abstraction, corresponding to more global aspects (situational and rational) of action specification [13]. In order to extend this functionality to the ability of interacting with the environment, these motor representations should be complemented with information about other people or objects that populated the environment. Briefly, cognition is the ability that allows us to internally deal with the information about ourselves ant the external world and, hence, this ability is subject to the existence of an internal active representation handling all this information.

With the aim of replicating the aforementioned framework into artificial agents, classical cognitive systems posit an inner realm richly populated with internal tokens that stand for external objects and states of affair [4]. These internal representations, however, are not valid to generate predictions or reasoning. Recent works suggest that cognitive architectures cannot work on a passive, bottom-up fashion, simply waiting to be activated by external stimuli. Instead, these architectures must continuously use memory to interpret sensory information and predict the immediate future. These predictions about the outer world can be used to actively drive the resources to relevant data in top-down modes of behaviour, allowing an efficient and accurate interpretation of the environment [4,11]. The necessity of employing internal simulation for rapidly creating new concepts and react to unanticipated situations using previous experience is postulated in the EU FP7 project XPERIENCE (http://www.xperience.org). In this proposal, internal simulation is addressed by structural bootstrapping, an approach that leverages existing experience to predict unexplored action effects and to focus the hypothesis space for learning novel concepts. The generative modeling is employed at all levels of cognitive development, and linked to the outer reality through enacted grounding and categorisation. Planning, prediction and action selection are here considered at the internal simulation stage. In the

EU FP7 project NEURALDYNAMICS (http://www.neuraldynamics.eu/), it is postulated that the scene representation must actively drive the visual exploration, the pre-segmentation and the creation of instances in the working and long-term memories, updating them when information changes. Including an extended version of the outer world, the representation must address the predicted visibility of elements on the scene as gaze changes and respond to failures detecting predicted object by updating the scene representation.

Our proposed approach is closely related to these projects although it advocates different types of representations. We adopt the approach that an internal model should be hierarchically defined at several levels of abstraction, as a tool to simultaneously hold different interpretations of the world. In agreement with Deb Roy, we support the view that the task planner should not be included in the same loop that updates this structure, but be built over the mental model [16]. This deep hybrid representation is computationally defined as a top-level graph from which other more specific graphs can be derived online. Each one encodes reality at a different abstraction and functional level, adapting more and more to the details of the current situation. The most abstract level corresponds to a graph in which nodes are variables with attributes and edges are logical binary predicates. The graph is built as the robot tries to achieve its mission and, at any time instant, the graph holds the robot's immediate beliefs about itself and its surrounding world. Agents propose changes to the graph as a result of their interaction with it and with the world. Emulators and planners are an special type of agent that takes the model and a domain theory to anticipate probable curses of action or to search for specific curses of action that lead to the solution of a problem.

In the scenarios where our experiments are conducted, this model includes the robot (self-modelling), humans, objects and the room. This model is not available only as a passive representation of the outer world, it is intensively used as a form of virtual reality [18]. This idea emerges from our previous work. In the VISOR project (http://www.grupoisis.uma.es/visor), funded by the EU FP6 EURON, a simple example of this hypothesis was tested: in order to improve a marker-less, upper-body human motion capture system based on face and hands detection, the whole person is modelled as a virtual human. Only face and hands are roughly detected and tracked from the real scene, but the whole upper-body motion is extracted from the virtual world (the mental model). Furthermore, the virtual model is also able to inform us about the region on the image where an occluded or disappeared hand could probably appear, and to correct false perceptions. If we add the environment model to this example, we will have here an example of the situation postulated by Prof. Owen Holland [11]: *at the heart of the mechanism is not just the body in the environment, it is a model of the body in a model of the environment.* This situation allows emanating predictions from the model, which can be correlated with real perceived information to drive attention, increase efficiency and filter noisy perception, while the contents of the mental model are also updated through experience.

The rest of paper is organised as follows: after presenting our psychophysics and brain-inspired foundations, the RoboCog cognitive architecture for robot control is described at Sect. 2. Then, Sect. 3 presents the experimental scenarios where the architecture has currently been evaluated. Finally, Sect. 4 draws the main conclusions and future directions of research and development.

2 Making Robot to Imagine for Acting

2.1 Foundations

Electrophysiological studies demonstrate that there are sensorimotor neurons that selectively discharge both during the execution of an action and during the perception of the same action executed by others. These neurons were called *mirror neurons* [15] and subsequent work has also shown that they do not only respond to the dynamic of the action, but also on the basis of the goal of the action. Thus, recent progress in cognitive neuroscience suggests that, in the case of understanding a purposeful action, the human brain gives higher priority to the information about the consequences or effects that this action embodies than to the information about the motion properties of this action. For instance, this assertion is postulated by the *common coding hypothesis* [14]. According to this theory, actions are coded in terms of the perceivable effects they will generate. Associations between motor patterns and sensory effects can then be used backward to retrieve a movement by anticipating its effects. Perception-action codes are also accessible during action observation, and perception activates action representations to the degree that the perceived and the represented actions are similar. This hypothesis has been reinforced over the last decade by an impressive number of findings from both psychophysics and cognitive neuroscience approaches, strongly supporting that it exists a direct connection between the neural and cognitive mechanisms involved in generating one's own action and the ones implied in perceiving the actions of others [5]. Neurophysiological data, both from cell recording in monkeys and neuroimaging studies in humans, also suggests that the perception of an action automatically triggers the simulation of this action, a process that could be at the basis of action understanding [8]. The *simulation theory* proposes that, when we perceive an action, we covertly mimic this action. Considering the interrelationships between perception and action, this theory implies the simulation of action, but also the simulation of perception. That is, *imagining and recalling things seen, heard or felt is essentially the same kind of processes as actually seeing, hearing or feeling something* [10]. The simulation theory also assumes the anticipation concept that is inherent to the common coding hypothesis and that can be referred as the subjective experience of action (i.e., the experience of agency): *The experience of preparing an action already predicts the effect of the action; and sensory information that an intended effect has occurred is retrospectively matched with the prediction* [9]. As G. Hesslow pointed out these internal, simulated perceptions could also trigger new covert actions [10].

On the other hand, brain studies establish the existence of relative hierarchies of motor control. For instance, the brain imaging experiments of action observation based on the method of repetition suppression conducted by S. Grafton

and A. Hamilton identified a distributed set of regions that are differentially activated as a function of the complexity of motor behavior [7]. From a psychological
point-of-view, E. Pacherie suggests that the process of action specification implies
three main stages, corresponding to the formation of future-directed intentions
(F-intentions), present-directed intentions (P-intentions) and motor intentions
(M-intentions) [13]. According to this dissertation, the representations formed
at each stage are quite different, but all of them can be considered as internal models, zooming increasing spatio-temporal areas of the world and of the
self-model of the agent. The resulting hierarchical model of action specification
puts on the top the overarching goal(s) and a deliberative planner (practical
reasoning), in the middle the situated goals provided by the top-stage planner
and a situational planner (motor program), and on the bottom the instantaneous goals provided by the situational planner and a sensorimotor planner.
These three stages use forward models to predict the next state of the system at
deliberative, situational or instantaneous levels. The bottom stage provides the
motion specifications to an execution module.

2.2 RoboCog: A Cognitive Architecture Based on Internal Simulation

Section 2.1 states that action execution and simulation, and action perception
are intimately tied, sharing a common motor representation. This representation
will be organised in a hierarchical way, providing different, but synchronised,
interfaces at levels of abstraction that range from the fine-grained aspects of
motor control to the symbolic ones needed by the rational control. The existence
of a deep, hybrid representation for action, perception and emulation will be the
core of RoboCog, the novel architecture for robot control described in this paper.
Together with this central representation, the main elements of RoboCog will
be the existence of a hierarchy of task-oriented modules, which will work at
deliberative, situational or sensorimotor stages, connected to a given interface
of the internal representation through a common Executive module, and of a
hierarchy of emulators, providing the simulation facilities at each of these stages.
Figure 1 shows an overview of the RoboCog architecture.

The central part of the architecture is occupied by the inner representation
of the outer world, whose interfaces ranges from the geometric (sensorimotor)
level to the symbolic (deliberative) one. These interfaces deliver models of the
outer world at a given abstraction level or stage. The whole structure is always
synchronised and changes at any levels of the structure will provoke updates
at the rest of levels. The base level of the representation is updated from the
software components at the HAL (Hardware Abstraction Layer).

Executive modules constitute the only way to access to the inner representation. They provide the corresponding model of the inner representation to the
task-oriented modules (the so-called CompoNets, as they will be internally composed by a set of software components) and also receive, from these CompoNets,
proposals for changing this model. The Executive module is the responsible of
validating if these changes are valid or not. When a change is accepted, the model

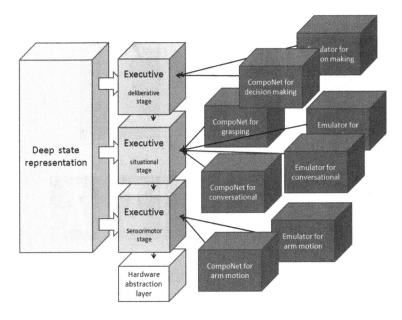

Fig. 1. Overview of the RoboCog architecture.

is updated inside the inner representation and this will imply the updating of the rest of layers (models) of the representation. For instance, if a person is detected at the situational stage, a symbolic node should be added at the rational stage, and a 3d model of the person will appear at the sensorimotor layer. Furthermore, at each stage, the corresponding Executive module manages the goal at a different abstraction level. For instance, at the deliberative stage, the Executive will try to execute a plan to reach a overarching goal. At situational stage, the Executive serves to implement plan actions inherited from the upper level. It will execute situated goals. The Executive module at the sensorimotor stage pursuits the correct achievement of an instantaneous goal. It is not the lowest level of the architecture, which will be occupied by the software components that implements the HAL, i.e. motor or sensor drivers.

In order to test if the received action is the best one to reach a goal, the Executive emulates its effects using a second set of compoNets, the so-called Emulators. The Emulator uses a copy of the model provided by the Executive at each stage of the hierarchy to generate a simulated perception of the outcome of the action. Figure 2 shows a simple example performed at the sensorimotor stage. The objective is that the robot touches a yellow box. The arm is moved using a forward model instead of an inverse one, and the simulation performed at the Emulator runs faster, providing the sequence of arm motions in advance. Alternatively, Emulators can provide intermediate perceptions that can allow the Executive to supervise the correct execution of the action (evaluating that the sequences of changes of the model are the same for the real and the simulated

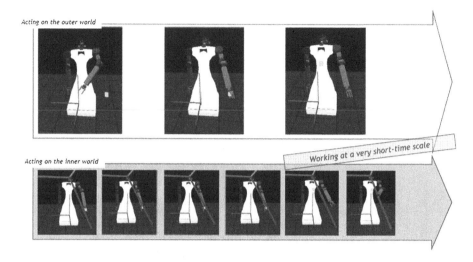

Fig. 2. Schematic representation of the simultaneous execution of a tracking action within a compoNet (top row) and an Emulator module (bottom row). The x-axis shows the temporal axis. The aim is that the robot touches the yellow box, and this is achieved by generating the correct motor commands for the arm. The Emulator allows to determine the sequence of commands in a faster way working over a inner model of the robot and environment. Hence, the real robot follows the sequence of arm motions in the real world (Color figure online).

execution of the action). Detected differences should launch warning commands to the Executive at the stage above and provoke a change on the course of action (goals) sent to the Executive at the stage below. Top-down processes of attention will be originated as a response to the warnings.

The architecture resembles the structure of the traditional 3-tier planning and execution architectures, but it can be noted that its spinal column (Inner models and Executive modules) is free of planning responsibilities. Delays and low responses can provoke that the changes to the model suggested by the compoNets will be rejected by the Executive, as the current reality reflected on the model does not allow them. However, the nature of the proposal also suggests the need of attentive components that, working on a top-down manner, drive the perceptual resources to the verification of the real appearance of any element 'artificially added' to the inner representation after an updating.

3   On-Going Experimental Scenarios

Reduced versions of this architecture have been tested in two use cases. In the first one, the architecture is endowed into a social assistant robot whose aim is to help clinic professionals to engage patients into a therapy for motor rehabilitation based on serious games. The architecture was mainly employed due to its ability to link a high-level planner with a set of situational behaviours. On the other hand, the second use case is a high demanding scenario of human-robot interaction, where the communication channels between the robot and the user is established through voice and gestures. Contrary to the first use case, the efforts here were focused on the situational stage and the synchronisation of all behaviours. Both versions run using an unique Executive module that manages the interfaces that the rest of compoNets need from the inner representation.

3.1 Hands-Off Assistant Robots for Motor Rehabilitation

Neuro-rehabilitation therapy pursuits the recovery of damaged neuronal areas and/or muscles from the repetitive practice of certain physical or mental activities. Obstetric brachial plexus palsy and cerebral palsy are among the most prevalent pathologies causing motor and cognitive deficits. The treatment of these lesions requires intensive and extended rehabilitation therapies in order to lessen their consequences on personal autonomy and working capacity. These therapies demand sustained dedication and effort by professionals, incurring in accretive costs for the institutions. Robotic Science has become in recent years a useful tool to address these issues related to the human rehabilitation domain. One of the most active research fields in this topic is the design of socially assistive robots. These robots are used in non-contact therapeutic interactions between the patient and the robot, exploiting embodiment, emotions, dialogs, personality, user models and socially situated-learning. They provide cost-effective solutions to the need of extended and dedicated one-on-one care, and also to monitor progress during physical therapy and daily life, providing tireless motivation, encouragement and guidance. Our initial hypothesis is that patients will get consistently engaged in a therapeutic non-physical interaction with a social robot, facilitating the design of new robot based therapies that will improve the patient recovery time and reduce the overall socio-economic costs.

Within this scenario, the project THERAPIST (http://www.therapist.uma.es) proposes the design and development of a socially interactive robot, which will be endowed with a specific instance of the RoboCog architecture. The design of this instance puts the emphasis on increasing the cognitive abilities at the decision-making stage of the architecture. For this end, the inner model at this stage provides a symbolic representation of the state encoding in a graph grammar. Using a set of grammar rules, the Executive is able to validate changes of the model, maintaining a inner representation that is coherent with the use case. The graph grammar is translated to PDDL (Planning Domain Definition Language) and then used by the Planning and Learning Architecture (PELEA [1]) to determine and monitor the course of action. PELEA combines two planners, one for high level actions and one for low level ones, with modules in charge of plan monitoring, goals generation and selection, re-planning triggering, etc. It also includes machine learning modules. In THERAPIST, the PELEA architecture will provide the plan actions, and there will not exist emulation functionalities at this stage of the architecture (Fig. 3).

Under the deliberative stage, the situational stage incorporates compoNets for verbal (dialogs) and non-verbal (emotions and gestures) interaction, person

Fig. 3. A snapshot of a rehabilitation session at the Hospital Universitario Virgen del Rocío (Seville). The robot Ursus is a robotic platform with moving head and arms, that makes intensive use of verbal and non-verbal tools to engage the patient in the therapeutic session.

detection, classification and tracking, and for navigation and homing. All these compoNets are not always activated, but they will be selectively turning on according to the task to achieve. This process is performed by the Executive module, that receives the situational goal from the deliberative stage. The hierarchy is completed with a sensorimotor stage, where the motor control and low-level perception are performed, and a HAL, mainly driven by the use of a RGBD camera for visual perception. A more extensive report of the use case has been recently published [3].

3.2 Control of Complex Humanoid Robots

Figure 4 shows the current aspect of Loki, an autonomous mobile robot built as a collaboration among the Universities of Castilla-La Mancha and Extremadura, Robotnik S.L.L and IADex S.L. Loki is composed of a mobile base, a rigid back spine, a torso with two arms and hands and an expressive head. The base of the robot has been designed to support a load of 200 Kg and can accommodate two 36 Ah/24 V batteries, power supplies, a battery charger, a DC/AC 2 KW inverter, two lasers or four Asus Xtion RGBD cameras attached to each side of the base, and a dual-socket, 12-cores, liquid-cooled Xeon board holding a NVIDA GTX650Ti GPU. This configuration provides enough autonomy and processing power to host our complete cognitive architecture on board. Each arm is composed of four Schunk servo-drives in a human-like upper arm configuration (3 degrees of freedom (dofs) for the shoulder and 1 for the elbow) and a forearm

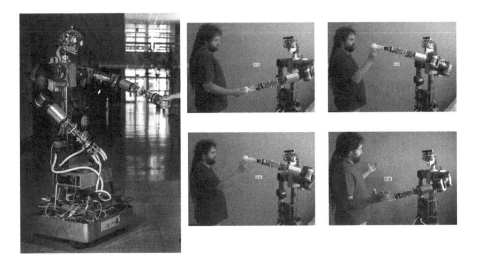

Fig. 4. (Left) The Loki robot; and (right) Loki playing with a human user.

with 3 additional dofs (a rotation along the forearm and two orthogonal rotations in the wrist). This two last dofs are built using a 3R Stewart platform that provides a great holding torque for the wrist. Attached to the top of the torso, Loki holds the expressive head Muecas. This head has a 4 dofs neck that uses the same kinematic construction as the forearms. The head holds a binocular visual system composed of two PointGrey Flea2 1 Mp cameras with 6 mm focal lenses and a RGBD sensor placed in the fronthead. The cameras are housed inside two hollow spheres made in Teflon. These eye-balls can pan independently and have a common tilt. The eyes are moved by means of three linear motors from Faulhaber that provide enough force to avoid the need of gear trains and to reach maximum angular speeds close to 600 deg/sec. Muecas also has an articulated yaw driven by a micro-servo and 2 dofs eyebrows, controlled by 4 servos as well.

The use case here is the modeling, building and understanding of a simple multimodal human-robot interaction task using the quasi-humanoid mobile manipulator Loki. The previous description of Loki illustrates the complexity of the robotic platform, but the scenario is also demanding due to the presence of a human user (see Fig. 4(Right)). Thus, the experiment consists on a simple game between the human and Loki. The human introduces herself and asks Loki to play the game. Upon acknowledge, she shows a yellow ball to the robot and it starts to track it, continuously fixating its gaze upon the ball with an RGBD sensor placed in the fronthead. After a human verbal indication, the robot reaches the ball with its hand and waits for a new interaction, or moves its arm back to a resting position after some courtesy delay. Loki tracks the object and accepts new speech commands during the whole span of the game. The development of this interaction game involves several problems such as generalized inverse kinematics, RGBD object detection and tracking, speech recognition and synthesis, and sequential task execution. All these problems present a significant degree of complexity, but the most challenging aspect is the integration and coordination of these capabilities in the control architecture that, further on, will facilitate the design of new and more complex tasks. The experiment is presented with details in a recently published paper [2].

In spite of fact that the game has been only evaluated in a research laboratory with domain expert players, some conclusions about the control architecture can be drawn. Thus, although a systematic evaluation of the robustness and accuracy of Loki's movements and perceptions remains to be done, the first set of experiments shows that the overall system is quite stable. From the point of view of the multimodal interaction through different situational compoNets, the architecture allows Loki to track in real time the ball position meanwhile it moves the arm to touch it. The inverse kinematics algorithm is also able to run in real time, even when positioning the head and the arm simultaneously.

4   Conclusions and Future Work

When making decisions that directly involve human users, the traditional 3-tier planning and plan execution scheme [6], which separates symbolic high-level planning from geometric plan execution, is not the best strategy. Because the generation of symbolic plans is relatively slow, the approach relies on a static (or almost static) world. Such an assumption is not only unrealistic, but also produces behaviors that does not react to changes and thus feels unnatural to humans. To solve this problem, this paper describes the current state of RoboCog, a cognitive architecture for robot control which is currently inside an active, iterative process of design, development and evaluation. RoboCog offers relevant differences with respect to similar approaches, being its main features the importance given to the motor representation and to the ability for simulating the action as a mechanism to achieve action understanding and robotic agency. The coupling of the deep state representations and the hierarchy of planners through the interfaces provided by the Executive buffers provide the necessary structure to implement this internal simulation.

The two use cases briefly presented here are an early test of the cognitive architecture. It is clear that a big challenge will be to handle the complexity of very large distributed computational systems when the whole architecture will be implemented. We also consider the need of integrating models of attention for action/perception focusing. Finally, it would be also an interesting research task to evaluate the extension of the temporal scale of emulation to the future but also to the past (learning).

Acknowledgments. This contribution has been partially granted by the Spanish Government and FEDER funds under coordinated project TIN2012-38079. RoboCog is a cognitive architecture being developed as a common effort among several research groups at different universities including the University of Extremadura (RoboLab), the University of Castilla-La Mancha (SIMD), the University of Málaga (ISIS and GISUM), the University Carlos III of Madrid (PLG) and the University of Jaén (M2P). The robotic therapy for motor rehabilitation is conducted with the group of Technological Innovation (GIT) and the Rehabilitation Department of the Hospital Universitario Virgen del Rocío (HUVR, Seville).

References

1. Alcázar, V., Guzmán, C., Milla, G., Prior, D., Borrajo, C., Castillo, L., Onaindia, E.: PELEA: planning, learning and execution architecture. In: Proceedings of the 28th Workshop of the UK Planning and Scheduling Special Interest Group, Brescia-Italy (2010)
2. Bustos, P., Martínez-Gómez, J., García-Varea, I., Rodríguez-Ruiz, L., Bachiller, P., Calderita, L., Manso, L.J., Sánchez, A., Bandera, A., Bandera, J.P.: Multimodal interaction with Loki. In: Workshop on Agentes Físicos, Madrid-Spain (2013)
3. Calderita, L.V., Bustos, P., Suárez-Mejías, C., Fernández, F., Bandera, A.: Therapist: towards an autonomous socially interactive robot for motor and neurorehabilitation therapies for children. In: Patients Rehabilitation Research Techniques Workshop (REHAB2013), Venice-Italy (2013)
4. Clark, A.: An embodied cognitive science? Trends Cogn. Sci. **3**(9), 345–351 (1999)
5. Decety, J., Grezes, J.: The power of simulation: imagining one's own and other's behavior. Brain Res. **1079**, 4–14 (2006)
6. Gat, E.: On three-layer architectures. In: Kortenkamp, D., Bonnasso, R.P., Murphy, R. (eds.) Artificial Intelligence and Mobile Robots, pp. 195–210. MIT Press, Cambridge (1998)
7. Grafton, S., Hamilton, A.: Evidence for a distributed hierarchy of action representation in the brain. Hum. Mov. Sci. **26**(4), 590–616 (2007)
8. Grezes, J., Frith, C.D., Passingham, R.E.: Inferring false beliefs from the actions of oneself and others: an fMRI study. NeuroImage **21**, 744–750 (2004)
9. Haggard, P., Tsakiris, M.: The experience of agency: feelings, judgments, and responsibility. Curr. Dir. Psychol. Sci. **18**, 242–246 (2009)
10. Hesslow, G.: The current status of the simulation theory of cognition. Brain Res. **1428**, 71–79 (2012)
11. Holland, O.: The future of embodied artificial intelligence: machine consciousness? In: Iida, F., Pfeifer, R., Steels, L., Kuniyoshi, Y. (eds.) Embodied Artificial Intelligence. LNCS (LNAI), vol. 3139, pp. 37–53. Springer, Heidelberg (2004)
12. Kawato, M., Wolpert, D.: Internal models for motor control. In: Bock, G.R., Goode, J.A. (eds.) Novartis Foundation Symposium 218: Sensory Guidance of Movement, pp. 291–307. Wiley, Chichester (1998)
13. Pacherie, E.: The sense of control and the sense of agency. Psyche **13**(1), 1–30 (2007)
14. Prinz, W.: Experimental approaches to action. In: Roessler, J., Eilan, N. (eds.) Agency and Self-Awareness, pp. 175–187. Oxford University Press, Oxford (2003)
15. Rizzolatti, G., Fadiga, L., Gallese, V., Fogassi, L.: Premotor cortex and the recognition of motor actions. Cogn. Brain Res. **3**, 131–141 (1996)
16. Roy, D., Hsiao, K., Mavridis, N.: Mental imagery for a conversational robot. IEEE Trans. Syst. Man Cybern. Part B **34**(3), 1374–1383 (2006)
17. Sommerville, J.A., Decety, J.: Weaving the fabric of social interaction: articulating developmental psychology and cognitive neuroscience in the domain of motor cognition. Psychon. Bull. Rev. **13**(2), 179–200 (2006)
18. Stein, L.A.: Imagination and Situated Cognition. AI Memo 1277, MIT AI Lab (1991)

Distance Measures for Prototype Based Classification

Michael Biehl[1]($\boxtimes$), Barbara Hammer[2], and Thomas Villmann[3]

[1] Johann Bernoulli Institute for Mathematics and Computer Science,
University of Groningen, P.O. Box 407, 9700 Groningen, The Netherlands
m.biehl@rug.nl
[2] CITEC Centre of Excellence, Bielefeld University, Universitätsstr. 21-33,
33594 Bielefeld, Germany
[3] Department of Mathematics, University of Applied Sciences Mittweida,
Technikumplatz 17, 09648 Mittweida, Germany

Abstract. The basic concepts of distance based classification are introduced in terms of clear-cut example systems. The classical k-Nearest-Neigbhor (kNN) classifier serves as the starting point of the discussion. Learning Vector Quantization (LVQ) is introduced, which represents the reference data by a few prototypes. This requires a data driven training process; examples of heuristic and cost function based prescriptions are presented. While the most popular measure of dissimilarity in this context is the Euclidean distance, this choice is frequently made without justification. Alternative distances can yield better performance in practical problems. Several examples are discussed, including more general Minkowski metrics and statistical divergences for the comparison of, e.g., histogram data. Furthermore, the framework of relevance learning in LVQ is presented. There, parameters of adaptive distance measures are optimized in the training phase. A practical application of Matrix Relevance LVQ in the context of tumor classification illustrates the approach.

1 Introduction

This contribution summarizes a tutorial talk which was meant as a first introduction to distance and prototype based machine learning techniques. Accordingly, our intention is not to give a complete overview of the field or to review all relevant literature. The paper may serve as a starting point for the interested reader to explore this practically relevant framework and active area of research.

The inference of classification schemes from previous observations, i.e. from labelled example data, is one of the core issues in machine learning [1–4]. A large variety of real world problems can be formulated as classification tasks. Examples include handwritten character recognition, medical diagnoses based on clinical data, pixel-wise segmentation and other image processing tasks, or fault detection in technical systems based on sensor data, to name only a few.

Throughout this contribution we assume that observations are given in terms of real-valued feature vectors in N dimensions. In general, the structure of the

L. Grandinetti et al. (Eds.): BrainComp 2013, LNCS 8603, pp. 100–116, 2014.
DOI: 10.1007/978-3-319-12084-3_9

data can be more complex and may require modified approaches, for instance the *pseudo-Euclidean* embedding of relational data. For this and other extensions of the concepts presented here, we refer the reader to [5,6] and references therein.

A variety of frameworks and training algorithms have been developed for the learning from examples, i.e. the data driven adaptation of parameters in the chosen classification model. They range from classical statistics based methods like Discriminant Analysis to the application of Multilayer Perceptrons or the prominent Support Vector Machine [1–4].

A particularly transparent approach is that of distance or similarity based classification [2,3,5]. Here, observations are directly compared with reference data or prototypes which have been determined in a training process from available examples. The similarity or, more correctly, *dis-similarity* is quantified in terms of a suitable distance measure.[1] The choice of appropriate measures is in the focus of this contribution. Most of the concepts discussed here can be applied in a much broader context, including supervised regression or the unsupervised clustering of data [5]. Here, however, we will limit the discussion to clear-cut classification problems and the use of prototype or reference data based classifiers.

In the next section we discuss two classical methods: the k-Nearest-Neighbor (kNN) approach [2,3,7] and Kohonen's Learning Vector Quantization (LVQ) [8,9] which – in their simplest versions – employ standard Euclidean distance. Mainly in terms of LVQ we discuss how to extend the framework to more general distance measures in Sect. 3.1. The use of divergences for the classification of histograms serves as one example. Section 4 presents the elegant framework of Relevance Learning Vector Quantization as an example for the use of adaptive distance measures. We conclude with a brief summary in Sect. 5.

2 Simple Classifiers Based on Euclidean Distances

When dealing with N-dimensional feature vectors, the use of Euclidean metrics for their pairwise comparison seems natural. In the following we discuss two classical methods which employ this measure in their simplest versions.

2.1 Nearest-Neighbor Classifiers

Arguably the simplest and by far most popular distance based scheme for vectorial data is the k-Nearest-Neighbor (kNN) classifier [2,3,7]. In this classical approach, a given set of P vectors in N-dim. feature space is stored together with labels which indicate their known assignment to one of the C classes:

$$\{\, \mathbf{x}^\mu, y(\mathbf{x}^\mu) = y^\mu \,\}_{\mu=1}^P \quad \text{where} \quad \mathbf{x}^\mu \in \mathbb{R}^N \quad \text{and} \quad y^\mu \in \{1, 2, \dots, C\}. \quad (1)$$

---

[1] In this article, we use the term *distance* in its general sense, not necessarily implying symmetry or other metric properties.

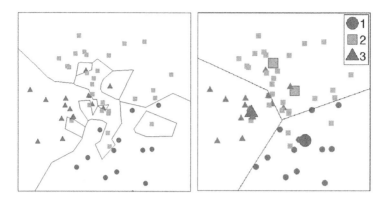

Fig. 1. Illustration of simple classification schemes based on Euclidean distance. Both panels display the same three class data set and decision boundaries represented by solid lines. **Left:** Nearest-Neighbor classifier. **Right:** Nearest Prototype classification, prototypes are marked by larger symbols as indicated by the legend.

An arbitrary feature vector $\mathbf{x}$ is classified according to the distances from the reference samples. In the most basic 1NN scheme, its (squared) Euclidean distance

$$d(\mathbf{x}, \mathbf{x}^\mu) = (\mathbf{x} - \mathbf{x}^\mu)^2 = \sum_{j=1}^{N} \left(x_j - x_j^\mu \right)^2 \tag{2}$$

from all reference samples $\mathbf{x}^\mu$ is computed and the data point is assigned to the class of the *Nearest Neighbor*:

$$y(\mathbf{x}) = y^* = y(\mathbf{x}^*) \quad \text{with} \quad \mathbf{x}^* = \operatorname*{argmin}_{\mathbf{x}^\mu} \{d(\mathbf{x}, \mathbf{x}^\mu)\}_{\mu=1}^{P} . \tag{3}$$

In the more general kNN classifier the assignment, Eq. (3), is replaced by a voting among the k closest reference vectors.

The kNN classifier is straightforward to implement and requires no further analysis of the example data in a training phase. Furthermore, theoretical considerations show that kNN schemes can achieve close to Bayes optimal classification if k is selected appropriately [2,3]. As a consequence, the kNN classifier continues to be applied in a variety of practical contexts and often serves as a baseline for comparison with other methods. Figure 1 (left panel) illustrates the 1NN classifier for an artificial three class data set in two dimensions. The prescription (3) results in a piece-wise linear tessellation of feature space.

Two major drawbacks of the approach are evident:

(I) For large data sets, the method involves considerable computational effort in the working phase. The naive implementation of (3) requires the evaluation of P distances and the identification of their minimum for each novel classification. Although clever search and sorting strategies can reduce the computational complexity [3], the basic problem persists for large data sets.

(II) More importantly, class boundaries can become very complex since every example is taken into account on an equal footing. The system is highly sensitive to single, potentially mislabelled examples or outliers. This bears the risk of over-fitting, i.e. the classifier can become too specific to the example set which may result in poor generalization performance with respect to novel data. The effect is clearly mildened when k neighbors are taken into account. However, too large k can yield overly smooth boundaries.

Both problems suggest to reduce the number of reference examples. The representation of the data set by a condensed set of examples was already considered in [10]. A variety of improved selection schemes have been proposed which aim at retaining relevant information contained in the data set, see e.g. [11] and references therein.

2.2   Learning Vector Quantization

Here we consider approaches which compute class representatives without restricting them to be elements of the training set. Each class is represented by at least one vector in a set of M labeled prototypes:

$$\left\{ \mathbf{w}^j, c^j \right\}_{j=1}^M \quad \text{where} \quad \mathbf{w}^j \in \mathbb{R}^N \quad \text{and} \quad c^j \in \{1, 2, \ldots C\}. \tag{4}$$

Together with the Euclidean measure, the prototypes parameterize piece-wise linear class boundaries. Similar to the 1NN classifier, a Nearest Prototype Scheme (NPC) assigns an arbitrary feature vector to class

$$y(\mathbf{x}) = c^* \quad \text{where } c^* \text{ is the label of } \mathbf{w}^* = \underset{\mathbf{w}^j}{\operatorname{argmin}} \left\{ d(\mathbf{x}, \mathbf{w}^j) \right\}_{j=1}^M. \tag{5}$$

The term *winner* is frequently used for the closest prototype $\mathbf{w}^*$ with respect to data point $\mathbf{x}$. More sophisticated voting rules, probabilistic or *soft* schemes can be devised, but here we limit the discussion to *crisp* classifiers.

The right panel of Fig. 1 illustrates the NPC scheme. The resulting decision boundaries are obviously much smoother than those of the corresponding 1NN classifier (left panel). The NPC scheme is less sensitive to details of the data set which is reflected by the fact that it misclassifies some of the training examples. In comparison to the 1NN scheme, this should result in superior generalization behavior in the presence of noisy examples and outliers.

Arguably the most attractive feature of prototype-based schemes is their interpretability [12]. Prototypes are defined in the feature space of observations and, hence, can be inspected by domain experts in the same way as the sample data. This is in contrast to Multilayer Perceptrons or other model parameterizations which are less transparent. Moreover, prototypes should be - in a sense - *typical* for their classes. Thus, the concept is complementary to, for instance, the Support Vector Machine approach [4] which puts emphasis on *atypical* samples close to the decision boundaries.

LVQ prototypes are determined from the example data by more or less sophisticated training procedures. A conceptually simple idea for their initialization is to compute the class-conditional means, which appears promising when classes are represented by single, more or less spherical clusters. In more realistic situations, LVQ prototypes could be initialized at random in feature space. More reasonably, their initial positions could be determined by means of class-wise unsupervised competitive learning [1–3] prior to the actual supervised training.

In the following we present two prominent prototype-based, iterative training schemes from the family of Learning Vector Quantization algorithms.

Kohonen's LVQ1. Kohonen's original Learning Vector Quantization algorithm [8,9,13], known as LVQ1, constitutes an intuitive, heuristic procedure for the computation of prototypes. It is reminiscent of competitive learning for the purpose of unsupervised Vector Quantization [2].

In LVQ1, single training examples are presented, for instance in randomized order. Upon presentation of example $\{\mathbf{x}, y\}$, the currently closest prototype $\mathbf{w}^*$ is determined in analogy to Eq. (5). Only the winner is updated according to

$$\mathbf{w}^* \leftarrow \mathbf{w}^* + \eta\ \Psi(c^*, y)\ (\mathbf{x} - \mathbf{w}^*) \quad \text{where} \quad \Psi(c, y) = \begin{cases} +1 \text{ if } c = y \\ -1 \text{ if } c \neq y. \end{cases} \quad (6)$$

Here, the learning rate $\eta > 0$ controls the step size. Note that Eq. (6) could be re-written as

$$\mathbf{w}^* \leftarrow \mathbf{w}^* - \eta\ \Psi(c^*, y)\ \frac{\partial}{\partial \mathbf{w}^*}\left[\frac{1}{2}(\mathbf{x} - \mathbf{w}^*)^2\right], \quad (7)$$

formally. The *Winner Takes All* (WTA) prescription moves the prototype $\mathbf{w}^*$ closer to or away from the feature vector if the class labels agree or disagree, respectively. As a consequence, the sample $\mathbf{x}$ – or other feature vectors in its vicinity – will be classified correctly with higher probability after the update. Intuitively, after repeated presentation of the data set, prototypes approach positions which should be typical for the corresponding classes.

A number of variations of the basic scheme have been suggested in the literature, aiming at better generalization ability or more stable convergence behavior, e.g. [9,14–17]. Several modifications update more than one prototype at a time, e.g. LVQ2.1 or LVQ3, or employ adaptive learning rates as for instance the so-called Optimized LVQ (OLVQ) [9]. However, the essential features of LVQ1 – competitive learning and label-dependent updates – are present in all versions of LVQ.

Generalized Learning Vector Quantization. Cost function based approaches [14–17] have attracted particular attention. First of all, convergence properties can be studied analytically in terms of their objective function. Moreover, cost functions allow for systematic extensions of the training schemes, for instance by including adaptive *hyperparameters* in the optimization [18,19].

Here we focus on the so–called Generalized Learning Vector Quantization (GLVQ) as introduced by Sato and Yamada [14, 15]. The suggested cost function is given by a sum over examples:

$$E = \sum_{\mu=1}^{P} e^{\mu} \quad \text{with} \ e^{\mu} = \Phi \left(\frac{d(\mathbf{w}^J, \mathbf{x}^\mu) - d(\mathbf{w}^K, \mathbf{x}^\mu)}{d(\mathbf{w}^J, \mathbf{x}^\mu) + d(\mathbf{w}^K, \mathbf{x}^\mu)} \right), \tag{8}$$

where $\mathbf{w}^J$ and $\mathbf{w}^K$ denote the *closest correct* and *closest incorrect* prototype, respectively, for a particular example $\{\mathbf{x}^\mu, y^\mu\}$. Formally,

$$\mathbf{w}^J = \underset{\mathbf{w}^j}{\operatorname{argmin}} \left\{ d(\mathbf{x}^\mu, \mathbf{w}^j) \mid c^j = y^\mu \right\}_{j=1}^{M}$$

$$\mathbf{w}^K = \underset{\mathbf{w}^j}{\operatorname{argmin}} \left\{ d(\mathbf{x}^\mu, \mathbf{w}^j) \mid c^j \neq y^\mu \right\}_{j=1}^{M}. \tag{9}$$

Popular choices for the monotonically increasing function $\Phi(z)$ in Eq. (8) are the identity $\Phi(z) = z$ or a sigmoidal like $\Phi(z) = 1/[1 + exp(-\gamma z)]$ where $\gamma > 0$ controls the *steepness* in the origin [14, 20]. Its argument obeys $-1 \leq z \leq 1$, negative values $z < 0$ indicate that the corresponding training example is correctly classified. Note that for large γ the cost function approximates the number of misclassified training data, while for small steepness the minimization of E corresponds to maximizing the margin-like quantities $[d(\mathbf{w}^K, \mathbf{x}^\mu) - d(\mathbf{w}^J, \mathbf{x}^\mu)]$.

One possible strategy to optimize E for a given data set is *stochastic gradient descent* based on single example presentation [1, 2, 21, 22]. The update step for the winning prototypes $\mathbf{w}^J, \mathbf{w}^K$, given a particular example $\{\mathbf{x}, y\}$, reads

$$\mathbf{w}^J \leftarrow \mathbf{w}^J - \eta \frac{\partial}{\partial \mathbf{w}^J} \Phi(e) = \mathbf{w}^J + \eta \, \Phi'(e) \frac{4 d_K}{(d_J + d_K)^2} \left(\mathbf{x} - \mathbf{w}^J \right)$$

$$\mathbf{w}^K \leftarrow \mathbf{w}^K - \eta \frac{\partial}{\partial \mathbf{w}^K} \Phi(e) = \mathbf{w}^K - \eta \, \Phi'(e) \frac{4 d_J}{(d_J + d_K)^2} \left(\mathbf{x} - \mathbf{w}^K \right) \tag{10}$$

where the abbreviation $d^L = d(\mathbf{w}^L, \mathbf{x})$ for the squared Euclidean distances has been introduced.

Note that in contrast to GLVQ, LVQ1 cannot be interpreted as a stochastic gradient descent, although Eq. (7) involves the gradient of $d(\mathbf{w}^*, \mathbf{x})$. Formal integration yields the function

$$\frac{1}{2} \sum_{\mu=1}^{P} \Psi(c^*, y^\mu) \left(\mathbf{x}^\mu - \mathbf{w}^* \right)^2$$

which is not differentiable at class borders. Crossing the decision boundary, a different prototype becomes the winner and the sign of Ψ changes discontinuously.

3 Extensions to General Distance Measures

Occasionally it is argued that all distance based methods are bound to fail in high-dimensional feature space due to the so-called *curse of dimensionality* and the related *concentration of norms*, see [23] for a general discussion thereof. The problem is evident in the context of, e.g., density estimation or histogram based techniques. However, we would like to emphasize that the argument does not necessarily carry over to the *comparison* of distances. Consider, for instance, the difference of two squared Euclidean distances

$$d(\mathbf{x}, \mathbf{x}^a) - d(\mathbf{x}, \mathbf{x}^b) = 2\,\mathbf{x} \cdot (\mathbf{x}^b - \mathbf{x}^a) + (\mathbf{x}^a)^2 - (\mathbf{x}^b)^2 \qquad (11)$$

which involves the projection of $\mathbf{x}$ into the low-dimensional subspace spanned by reference vectors $\mathbf{x}^a, \mathbf{x}^b$. The *concentration of norms* suggests, indeed, that the last two terms approximately cancel each other in high dimensions, while the first remains non-trivial. Moreover, in the context of LVQ, $\mathbf{x}^a, \mathbf{x}^b$ in (11) are replaced by prototypes which have been determined as *low noise* representatives of the data set.

Euclidean distance appears to be a natural measure and is by far the most popular choice in practice. However, one should be aware that other measures may be more suitable, depending on the nature of the data set at hand [24]. Both the kNN and the LVQ framework facilitate the use of alternative distance measures in a rather straightforward fashion as outlined in the following.

3.1 Example Metrics and More General Measures

Frequently, distances $d(\mathbf{x}, \mathbf{y})$ are required to satisfy the metric properties

$$d(\mathbf{x}, \mathbf{y}) = 0 \Leftrightarrow \mathbf{x} = \mathbf{y}, \quad d(\mathbf{x}, \mathbf{y}) = d(\mathbf{y}, \mathbf{x}), \quad d(\mathbf{x}, \mathbf{z}) \le d(\mathbf{x}, \mathbf{y}) + d(\mathbf{y}, \mathbf{z}). \quad (12)$$

However, in the prototype based or kNN classification of a query $\mathbf{x}$, these conditions can be relaxed. For example, the NPC with prototypes $\{\mathbf{w}^j\}$ is still well defined with a non-symmetric measure as long as only one of the two choices, $d(\mathbf{x}, \mathbf{w}^j)$ or $d(\mathbf{w}^j, \mathbf{x})$, is used consistently. Distances between different prototypes or between two data points are never considered explicitly in the scheme.

A large variety of distance measures can be employed for classification tasks. Discretized data, for instance, can be compared by means of the Hamming distance or more general string metrics. Specific measures have been devised for *functional data* where the order of the observed features is relevant, see [25,26] for examples.

In the following we outline how, quite generally, differentiable distance measures can be made use of in LVQ schemes. Then we briefly discuss three example families of measures which constitute important alternatives to the standard Euclidean choice.

Incorporation of Differentiable Distances in LVQ Schemes. In the working phase of kNN or prototype based classification, essentially any meaningful distance measure can be employed which is appropriate for the problem at hand. An important restriction applies, however, if gradient based training schemes like LVQ1 or GLVQ are used which require that the underlying distance is differentiable. Under this condition, a general LVQ1-like update can be written as

$$\mathbf{w}^* \leftarrow \mathbf{w}^* - \eta \ \Psi(c^*, y) \ \frac{\partial}{\partial \mathbf{w}^*} \ d(\mathbf{w}^*, \mathbf{x}) \tag{13}$$

in analogy with Eq. (7).

Similarly, the Euclidean distance in the GLVQ cost function (8) can be replaced by a more general, differentiable measure, yielding the update

$$\mathbf{w}^J \leftarrow \mathbf{w}^J + \eta \, \Phi'(e) \, \frac{2d_K}{(d_J + d_K)^2} \, \frac{\partial}{\partial \mathbf{w}^J} \, d(\mathbf{w}^J, \mathbf{x})$$

$$\mathbf{w}^K \leftarrow \mathbf{w}^K - \eta \ \Phi'(e) \, \frac{2d_J}{(d_J + d_K)^2} \, \frac{\partial}{\partial \mathbf{w}^K} \, d(\mathbf{w}^K, \mathbf{x}) \tag{14}$$

where the winners and all other quantities are defined as in (10). In the following we highlight a few families of differentiable distance measures which can be incorporated into LVQ in a straightforward way.

Minkowski Distances. A prominent class of distances corresponds to the so-called Minkowski measures

$$d_p(\mathbf{x}, \mathbf{y}) = \left(\sum_{j=1}^N |x_j - y_j|^p \right)^{1/p} \tag{15}$$

with $p > 0$ which includes the standard Euclidean distance for $p = 2$ or the so–called Manhattan metric for $p = 1$. Note that (15) is a metric only for $p \geq 1$, while it violates (12) for $p < 1$. However, in the latter case, $(d_p(\mathbf{x}, \mathbf{y}))^p$ becomes a metric [27]. Note that the Euclidean distance can be determined using the inner product

$$\langle \mathbf{x}, \mathbf{y} \rangle = \sum_{j=1}^N x_j \cdot y_j \tag{16}$$

by computing

$$d_2(\mathbf{x}, \mathbf{y}) = \sqrt{\langle \mathbf{x}, \mathbf{x} \rangle^2 - 2 \cdot \langle \mathbf{x}, \mathbf{y} \rangle + \langle \mathbf{y}, \mathbf{y} \rangle^2}. \tag{17}$$

For $p \neq 2$ and $p \geq 1$, an analogous calculation can be done using semi-inner products [28,29]. The use of Minkowski metrics with $p \neq 2$ has proven advantageous in several practical applications, e.g. [30,31], which can be accompanied by appropriate dimensionality reduction schemes, e.g. principal component analysis (PCA) [32,33]. Minkowski distances are either differentiable or can be replaced by differentiable approximations, see [27] and references therein. Figure 2 illustrates the influence of the parameter p in (15). It displays the unit circles in two dimensions corresponding to different Minkowski distances.

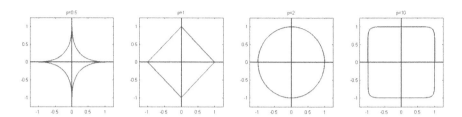

Fig. 2. *Unit circles* corresponding to Minkowski metrics, Eq. (15), in two dimensions with, from left to right, $p = 0.5$, $p = 1$ (Manhattan), $p = 2$ (Euclidean), and $p = 10$.

Divergences. In many practical problems, properties of the data are represented by histograms. Prominent examples are the characterization of images by color histograms or the *bag of words* representation for texts. In other domains, *intensity spectra* or other non-negative and normalizable functional data represent the objects of interest [34]. A large variety of statistical divergences are tailored for the comparison of positive measures or probability densities. Arguably, the non-symmetric Kullback-Leibler divergence is the most prominent example [35]. Here we exemplify the concept in terms of the symmetric Cauchy-Schwarz divergence

$$d_{CS}(\mathbf{x}, \mathbf{y}) = \frac{1}{2} \log\left[\langle \mathbf{x}, \mathbf{x} \rangle \cdot \langle \mathbf{y}, \mathbf{y} \rangle\right] - \log\left[\langle \mathbf{x}, \mathbf{y} \rangle\right] \tag{18}$$

which is obviously differentiable [36]. Figure 3 illustrates how d_{CS} differs from the standard Euclidean distance: Three normalized 50-bin histograms are displayed which satisfy $(\mathbf{x}^a - \mathbf{x}^b)^2 = (\mathbf{x}^c - \mathbf{x}^b)^2$. However, according to the Cauchy-Schwarz measure, $d_{CS}(\mathbf{x}^a, \mathbf{x}^b) \approx 1/2 \, d_{CS}(\mathbf{x}^c, \mathbf{x}^b)$, implying that the single peak $\mathbf{x}^a$ is considered to be closer to the broad unimodal $\mathbf{x}^b$ than the double peak histogram $\mathbf{x}^c$.

The incorporation of symmetric and non-symmetric, differentiable divergences into GLVQ training and classification is introduced in [37]. As an application example, the detection of Mosaic Disease in Cassava plants based on various image histograms is discussed there.

Kernel Distances. Kernel distances [38] can also be incorporated in prototype based learning and classification approaches, see e.g. [39, 40]. The so-called kernel trick consists of an implicit, in general non-linear, mapping to a potentially infinite dimensional space. This mapping space is equipped with an inner product which can be calculated from original data in terms of a so–called kernel $\kappa(\mathbf{x}, \mathbf{y})$ [41, 42]. The corresponding kernel distance is calculated as

$$d_{\kappa}(\mathbf{x}, \mathbf{y}) = \sqrt{\kappa(\mathbf{x}, \mathbf{x})^2 - 2 \cdot \kappa(\mathbf{x}, \mathbf{y}) + \kappa(\mathbf{y}, \mathbf{y})^2} \tag{19}$$

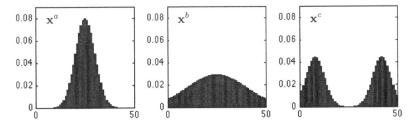

Fig. 3. Three normalized histograms $\mathbf{x}^a, \mathbf{x}^b, \mathbf{x}^c$ with 50 bins each. The pair-wise comparison in terms of Euclidean distance and Cauchy-Schwarz divergence, cf. Eq. (18), as discussed in Sect. 3.1

in complete analogy to the inner product based Euclidean distance calculation (17). A famous example is the Gaussian kernel

$$\kappa_G\left(\mathbf{x}, \mathbf{y}\right) = \exp\left(\frac{-\left(d_2\left(\mathbf{x}, \mathbf{y}\right)\right)^2}{2\sigma^2}\right) \tag{20}$$

with the kernel width σ.

The application of kernel distances frequently translates non-linear complex classification tasks into easier, linearly separable problems [41], as demonstrated for, e.g., image based face recognition in [43]. For LVQ schemes, the kernel distance is assumed to be differentiable, which implies that also the kernel $\kappa\left(\mathbf{x}, \mathbf{y}\right)$ has to be differentiable [44].

4 Adaptive Distances and Relevance LVQ

In an ideal situation, insight into the problem suggests the use of a specific, fixed distance measure. Very often, however, prior knowledge is limited and only a suitable parametric form of the distance can be specified. In Relevance Learning, a particularly elegant extension of LVQ, the corresponding parameters are adapted in the same data driven training process that identifies the prototypes.

4.1 Matrix Relevance LVQ

In the following we discuss Matrix Relevance LVQ as an extension of the basic Euclidean scheme [20]. An obvious problem of the standard measure is that all dimensions are taken into account on the same footing. First of all, some of the features may be very *noisy* and potentially corrupt the classifier. Furthermore, features can be correlated or scale very differently. Euclidean or other pre-defined measures are sensitive to rescaling and more general linear transformations of the features. Consequently, their naive use can be problematic in practice. Matrix Relevance LVQ in its simplest form addresses these problems by using a generalized quadratic distance of the form

$$d(\mathbf{x}, \mathbf{w}) = (\mathbf{x} - \mathbf{w})^\top \Lambda (\mathbf{x} - \mathbf{w}) \quad \text{with} \quad \Lambda = \Omega^\top \Omega \quad \text{where} \quad \Lambda, \Omega \in \mathbb{R}^{N \times N}. \tag{21}$$

Here the specific parameterization of Λ as a square guarantees that the distance is positive semi-definite: $d(\mathbf{x}, \mathbf{w}) \geq 0$.

The elements of the matrix Ω are considered adaptive quantities in the training process. The distance (21) is differentiable with respect to $\mathbf{w}$ and Ω:

$$\frac{\partial d(\mathbf{w}, \mathbf{x})}{\partial \mathbf{w}} = \Omega^{\top} \Omega \, (\mathbf{w} - \mathbf{x}), \qquad \frac{\partial d(\mathbf{w}, \mathbf{x})}{\partial \Omega} = \Omega \, (\mathbf{w} - \mathbf{x})(\mathbf{w} - \mathbf{x})^{\top} \qquad (22)$$

which facilitates gradient based updates of prototypes and distance measure. In the corresponding extension of LVQ1-like updates, the WTA prototype update (13) is combined with

$$\Omega \leftarrow \Omega - \eta_{\Omega} \; \Psi(c^*, y) \, \frac{\partial}{\partial \Omega} \, d(\mathbf{w}^*, \mathbf{x}). \qquad (23)$$

Generalized Matrix Relevance LVQ (GMLVQ) updates Ω according to

$$\Omega \leftarrow \Omega - \eta_{\Omega} \, \Phi'(e) \left(\frac{2 d_K}{(d_J + d_K)^2} \, \frac{\partial \, d(\mathbf{w}^J, \mathbf{x})}{\partial \Omega} - \frac{2 d_J}{(d_J + d_K)^2} \, \frac{\partial \, d(\mathbf{w}^K, \mathbf{x})}{\partial \Omega} \right) \qquad (24)$$

together with the prototype updates (14). Both, (23) and (24) can be followed by an explicit normalization to enforce $\sum_{ij} \Omega_{ij}^2 = 1$. The matrix learning rate η_{Ω} is frequently chosen smaller than that of the prototype updates. We refer the reader to [20, 45] for details and the full form of the updates and a discussion of their variants.

Note that the above correspond to only the simplest versions of matrix relevance learning. A number of non-trivial variations have been suggested, including the use of prototype- or class-specific localized matrices which yield piece-wise quadratic decision boundaries in feature space [20]. Rectangular matrices Ω can be employed in order to avoid the adaptation of $\mathcal{O}(N^2)$ degrees of freedom in high-dimensional data sets [45]. They facilitate also the discriminative low-dim. representation or visualization of labeled data sets [45, 46]. The restriction to diagonal matrices Ω and Λ reduces the scheme to a weighting of single features, which had been introduced earlier as RLVQ [47] and GRLVQ [48], respectively. Formally, Euclidean LVQ versions are recovered by setting Ω proportional to the N-dimensional identity matrix.

Similar parameterized distance measures have been used in the context of various classification frameworks. For instance, the cost function based optimization of a quadratic distance (21) can be integrated in an extended kNN approach as introduced in [49], see also references therein. As another example we would like to mention Radial Basis Function networks [1] which, in combination with relevance learning, have been applied in problems of vital importance recently [50].

A Matlab toolbox *Relevance and Matrix adaptation in Learning Vector Quantization*, including GMLVQ and a number of variants, is available at the website [51].

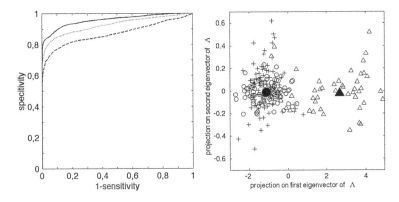

Fig. 4. Left: ROC curves as obtained by GLVQ (dashed), GRLVQ (dotted), GMLVQ (solid line) with respect to the detection of malignant ACC, see Sect. 4.3. **Right:** Visualization of the data set, displaying projections on the leading eigenvalues of Λ. In addition to malignant ACC (triangles) and benign ACA (circles), healthy control data (crosses) are displayed. Prototypes for ACA and ACC are marked by filled symbols.

4.2 Interpretation of the Relevance Matrix

It is instructive to note that the quadratic distance (21) can be rewritten as $d(\mathbf{w}, \mathbf{x}) = [\Omega(\mathbf{w} - \mathbf{x})]^2$, implying that plain Euclidean distance is applied after a linear transformation of feature vectors and prototypes. The transformation can account for the above mentioned problems of noisy or correlated features by assigning weights to single dimensions and pairs of features, respectively. Note that the diagonal element $\Lambda_{jj} = \sum_i \Omega_{ij}^2$ quantifies the total contribution of the original feature dimension j to the linear combinations $[\Omega(\mathbf{w} - \mathbf{x})]_i$.

The direct interpretation of Λ_{jj} as the *relevance* of feature j for the classification is only justified if different features are of the same magnitude, typically. This can be achieved by, for instance, a *z-score transformation* in a preprocessing step, such that $\sum_\mu x_j^\mu / P = 0$ and $\sum_\mu (x_j^\mu)^2 / P = 1$. Additional measures have to be taken in the presence of strongly correlated or linearly dependent features, see [12] for a detailed discussion of the interpretation of Λ and related regularization techniques.

It is instructive to note that, given Λ, a continuum of matrices Ω satisfies $\Omega^\top \Omega = \Lambda$. However, this does not pose a problem, since the ambiguity reflects invariances of the distance measure with respect to reflections or rotations of the data. For convenience, e.g. when comparing the results of different training processes, one can resort to a canonical representation of Ω in terms of the eigenvectors of Λ, see [12] for a more detailed discussion.

4.3 Example Application: Classification of Adrenal Tumors

We briefly illustrate the MRLVQ approach in terms of a recent medical application [52,53]. Tumors of the adrenal gland occur in an estimated 1–2 % of the population and are mostly found incidentally. The non-invasive differentiation between malignant Adrenocortical Carcinoma (ACC) and benign Adenomas (ACA) constitutes a diagnostic challenge of great significance. To this end, a panel of 32 steroid biomarkers – produced by the adrenal gland - has been suggested in [52] where details are given. The 24h excretion of these steroids has been analysed for a number of example patients with confirmed diagnosis, retrospectively. Preprocessing and normalization steps are also detailed in [52,53]. The available data set was analysed by means of GMLVQ in its simplest setting, employing one 32-dim. prototype per class and an adaptive $\Omega \in \mathbb{R}^{32 \times 32}$.

Standard validation procedures, for details see [52,53], were used to demonstrate that the resulting classifier achieves very good sensitivity (true positive rate) and specificity (1-false positive rate) with respect to the detection of malignancy. The obtained Receiver Operator Characteristics (ROC) [54] is shown in Fig. 4 (left panel). For comparison, the ROC is also displayed for simple GLVQ using the plain Euclidean distance in $\mathbb{R}^{32}$ and for a system restricted to an adaptive, diagonal Λ, which corresponds to GRLVQ [48]. Evidently, relevance learning and in particular the matrix scheme improves the performance significantly over the use of the naive Euclidean distance.

The resulting relevance matrix, see [53], shows that a few of the steroid markers play a dominant role in the classification as marked by large diagonal elements Λ_{jj}. Based on these results, a reduced panel of 9 markers was proposed in [52]. This reduction facilitates an efficient technical realization of the method, while the performance is essentially retained. The method constitutes a promising tool for the sensitive and specific differential diagnosis of ACC in clinical practice [52].

An additional feature of matrix relevance learning becomes apparent in this application example. Typically, relevance matrices become low rank in the course of training. Theoretical considerations which support this general, empirical finding are presented in [55]. As a consequence, the dominating eigenvectors of the relevance matrix can be used for the discriminative visualization of the labelled examples. Figure 4 (right panel) displays the projections of all ACA and ACC data and the obtained prototypes on the first two eigenvectors of Λ. In addition, healthy control data is displayed which was not explicitly used in the training process. The example demonstrates how the combination of prototype based and relevance learning can provide novel insight and facilitates fruitful discussions with the domain experts. For a similar application of GMLVQ in a different medical context, see [56].

5   Summary

This contribution provides only a first introduction to distance based classification schemes. To a large extent, the discussion is presented in terms of two classical approaches: the k-Nearest-Neighbor classifier and Kohonen's Learning Vector Quantization. The latter requires a training phase which tunes the classifier according to available training data. Examples for heuristic and cost function based training prescriptions are given. Mainly in the context of LVQ the use of generalized dissimilarity measures is discussed, which go beyond the standard choice of Euclidean distance. Relevance Learning is presented as an extension of LVQ, which makes use of adaptive distances. Their data driven optimization can be integrated naturally in the LVQ training process. As an example, matrix relevance learning is briefly presented and illustrated in terms of an application example in the medical domain.

This article and the suggested references can merely serve as a starting point for the interested reader. It is far from giving a complete overview of this fascinating area of ongoing fundamental and application oriented research.

References

1. Bishop, C.: Pattern Recognition and Machine Learning. Cambridge University Press, Cambridge (2007)
2. Hastie, T., Tibshirani, R., Friedman, J.: The Elements of Statistical Learning: Data Mining, Inference, and Prediction, 2nd edn. Springer, New York (2009)
3. Duda, R., Hart, P., Storck, D.: Pattern Classification, 2nd edn. Wiley, New York (2001)
4. Shawe-Taylor, J., Cristianini, N.: Kernel Methods for Pattern Analysis. Cambridge University Press, Cambridge (2004)
5. Biehl, M., Hammer, B., Verleysen, M., Villmann, T. (eds.): Similarity-Based Clustering. LNCS, vol. 5400. Springer, Heidelberg (2009)
6. Hammer, B., Schleif, F.-M., Zhu, X.: Relational extensions of learning vector quantization. In: Lu, B.-L., Zhang, L., Kwok, J. (eds.) ICONIP 2011, Part II. LNCS, vol. 7063, pp. 481–489. Springer, Heidelberg (2011)
7. Cover, T., Hart, P.: Nearest neighbor pattern classification. IEEE Trans. Inf. Theor. **13**, 21–27 (1967)
8. Kohonen, T.: Self-Organizing Maps, 2nd edn. Springer, Heidelberg (1997)
9. Kohonen, T.: Improved versions of learning vector quantization. In: International Joint Conference on Neural Networks, vol. 1, pp. 545–550 (1990)
10. Hart, P.: The condensed nearest neighbor rule. IEEE Trans. Inf. Theor. **14**, 515–516 (1968)
11. Wu, Y., Ianakiev, K., Govindaraju, V.: Improved k-nearest neighbor classification. Pattern Recogn. **35**, 2311–2318 (2002)
12. Strickert, M., Hammer, B., Villmann, T., Biehl, M.: Regularization and improved interpretation of linear data mappings and adaptive distance measures. In: Proceedings of the IEEE Symposium on Computational Intelligence (IEEE SSCI), IEEE, vol. 2013, p. 8 (2013)
13. Helsinki University of Technology: Bibliography on the Self-Organizing Map (SOM) and Learning Vector Quantization (LVQ). Neural Networks Research Centre, HUT (2002)
14. Sato, A., Yamada, K.: Generalized Learning vector quantization. In: Touretzky, D.S., Hasselmo, M.E. (eds.) Proceedings of the 1995 Conference, Cambridge, MA, USA, MIT Press. vol. 8, Advances in Neural Information Processing Systems, pp. 423–429 (1996)
15. Sato, A., Yamada, K.: An analysis of convergence in generalized LVQ. In: Niklasson, L., Bodn, M., Ziemke, T. (eds.) Proceedings of the International Conference on Artificial Neural Networks, Springer, pp. 170–176 (1998)

16. Seo, S., Obermayer, K.: Soft learning vector quantization. Neural Comput. **15**(7), 1589–1604 (2003)
17. Seo, S., Bode, M., Obermayer, K.: Soft nearest prototype classification. Trans. Neural Netw. **14**, 390–398 (2003)
18. Seo, S., Obermayer, K.: Dynamic hyperparameter scaling method for LVQ algorithms. In: IJCNN'06, International Joint Conference on Neural Networks, IEEE, pp. 3196–3203 (2006)
19. Schneider, P., Biehl, M., Hammer, B.: Hyperparameter learning in probabilistic prototype-based models. Neurocomputing **73**(7–9), 1117–1124 (2010)
20. Schneider, P., Biehl, M., Hammer, B.: Adaptive relevance matrices in learning vector quantization. Neural Comput. **21**(12), 3532–3561 (2009)
21. Robbins, H., Monro, S.: A stochastic approximation method. Ann. Math. Stat. **22**, 405 (1951)
22. Bottou, L.: Online algorithms and stochastic approximations. In: Saad, D. (ed.) Online Learning and Neural Networks. Cambridge University Press, Cambridge (1998)
23. Lee, J., Verleysen, M.: Nonlinear Dimension Reduction. Springer, New York (2007)
24. Hammer, B., Villmann, T.: Classification using non-standard metrics. In: Verleysen, M. (ed.) European Symposium on Artificial Neural Networks, ESANN 2005, pp. 303–316. d-side publishing (2005)
25. Lee, J., Verleysen, M.: Generalization of the Lp-norm for time series and its application to self-organizing maps. In: Cottrell, M. (ed.) Proceedings of the Workshop on Self-Organizing Maps (WSOM), Paris, Sorbonne, pp. 733–740 (2005)
26. Villmann, T., Hammer, B.: Functional principal component learning using Oja's method and Sobolev norms. In: Príncipe, J.C., Miikkulainen, R. (eds.) WSOM 2009. LNCS, vol. 5629, pp. 325–333. Springer, Heidelberg (2009)
27. Lange, M., Villmann, T.: Derivatives of Lp-norms and their approximations. Machine Learning Reports MLR-04-2013, pp. 43–59 (2013)
28. Giles, J.: Classes of semi-inner-product spaces. Trans. Am. Math. Soc. **129**, 436–446 (1967)
29. Lumer, G.: Semi-inner-product spaces. Trans. Am. Math. Soc. **100**, 29–43 (1961)
30. Golubitsky, O., Watt, S.: Distance-based classification of handwritten symbols. Int. J. Doc. Anal. Recogn. (IJDAR) **13**(2), 133–146 (2010)
31. Biehl, M., Breitling, R., Li, Y.: Analysis of tiling microarray data by learning vector quantization and relevance learning. In: Yin, H., Tino, P., Corchado, E., Byrne, W., Yao, X. (eds.) IDEAL 2007. LNCS, vol. 4881, pp. 880–889. Springer, Heidelberg (2007)
32. Joliffe, I.: Principal Component Analysis. Springer, New York (2002)
33. Biehl, M., Kästner, M., Lange, M., Villmann, T.: Non-euclidean principal component analysis and Oja's learning rule – theoretical aspects. In: Estevez, P.A., Principe, J.C., Zegers, P. (eds.) Advances in Self-Organizing Maps. AISC, vol. 198, pp. 23–34. Springer, Heidelberg (2013)
34. Villmann, T., Kästner, M., Backhaus, A., Seiffert, U.: Processing hyperspectral data in machine learning. In: Verleysen, M. (ed.) European Symposium on Artificial Neural Networks, ESANN 2013, p. 6. d-side publishing (2013)
35. Kullback, S., Leibler, R.: On information and sufficiency. Ann. Math. Stat. **22**, 79–86 (1951)
36. Villmann, T., Haase, S.: Divergence based vector quantization. Neural Comput. **23**(5), 1343–1392 (2011)

37. Mwebaze, E., Schneider, P., Schleif, F.M., Aduwo, J., Quinn, J., Haase, S., Villmann, T., Biehl, M.: Divergence based classification and learning vector quantization. Neurocomputing **74**, 1429–1435 (2011)
38. Schölkopf, B.: The kernel trick for distances. In: Tresp, V. (ed.) Advances in Neural Information Processing Systems, pp. 301–307. MIT Press, Cambridg (2001)
39. Inokuchi, R., Miyamoto, S.: LVQ clustering and SOM using a kernel function. In: Proceedings of the 2004 IEEE International Conference on Fuzzy Systems, vol. 3, pp. 1497–1500 (2004)
40. Schleif, F.-M., Villmann, T., Hammer, B., Schneider, P., Biehl, M.: Generalized derivative based kernelized learning vector quantization. In: Fyfe, C., Tino, P., Charles, D., Garcia-Osorio, C., Yin, H. (eds.) IDEAL 2010. LNCS, vol. 6283, pp. 21–28. Springer, Heidelberg (2010)
41. Schölkopf, B., Smola, A.: Learning with Kernels. MIT Press, Cambridge (2002)
42. Steinwart, I.: On the influence of the kernel on the consistency of support vector machines. J. Mach. Learn. Res. **2**, 67–93 (2001)
43. Villmann, T., Kästner, M., Nebel, D., Riedel, M.: ICMLA face recognition challenge - results of the team 'Computational Intelligence Mittweida'. In: Proceedings of the International Conference on Machine Learning Applications (ICMLA'12), pp. 7–10. IEEE Computer Society Press (2012)
44. Villmann, T., Haase, S., Kästner, M.: Gradient based learning in vector quantization using differentiable kernels. In: Estevez, P.A., Principe, J.C., Zegers, P. (eds.) Advances in Self-Organizing Maps. AISC, vol. 198, pp. 193–204. Springer, Heidelberg (2013)
45. Bunte, K., Schneider, P., Hammer, B., Schleif, F.M., Villmann, T., Biehl, M.: Limited rank matrix learning, discriminative dimension reduction, and visualization. Neural Netw. **26**, 159–173 (2012)
46. Biehl, M., Bunte, K., Schleif, F.M., Schneider, P., Villmann, T.: Large margin linear discriminative visualization by matrix relevance learning. In: Proceedings of the WCCI 2012 - IEEE World Congress on Computational Intelligence, IEEE Press (2012)
47. Bojer, T., Hammer, B., Schunk, D., von Toschanowitz, K.T.: Relevance determination in learning vector quantization. In: Verleysen, M. (ed.) European Symposium on Artificial Neural Networks, pp. 271–276 (2001)
48. Hammer, B., Villmann, T.: Generalized relevance learning vector quantization. Neural Netw. **15**(8–9), 1059–1068 (2002)
49. Weinberger, K., Blitzer, J., Saul, L.: Distance metric learning for large margin nearest neighbor classification. In: Weiss, Y., Schölkopf, B., Platt, J. (eds.) Advances in Neural Information Processing Systems, vol. 18, pp. 1473–1480. MIT Press, Cambridge (2006)
50. Backhaus, A., Ashok, P., Praveen, B., Dholakia, K., Seiffert, U.: Classifying Scotch Whisky from near-infrared Raman spectra with a radial basis function network with relevance learning. In: Verleysen, M. (ed.) European symposium on Artificial Neural Networks, vol. 2012, pp. 411–416 (2012)
51. Biehl, M., Bunte, K., Schneider, P.: Relevance and matrix adaptation in learning vector quantization (2013). http://matlabserver.cs.rug.nl/gmlvqweb/web
52. Arlt, W., Biehl, M., Taylor, A., Hahner, S., Libe, R., Hughes, B., Schneider, P., Smith, D., Stiekema, H., Krone, N., Porfiri, E., Opocher, G., Bertherat, J., Mantero, F., Allolio, B., Terzolo, M., Nightingale, P., Shackleton, C., Bertagna, X., Fassnacht, M., Stewart, P.: Urine steroid metabolomics as a biomarker tool for detecting malignancy in adrenal tumors. J. Clin. Endocrinol. Metab. **96**, 3775–3784 (2011)

53. Biehl, M., Schneider, P., Smith, D., Stiekema, H., Taylor, A., Hughes, B., Shackleton, C., Stewart, P., Arlt, W.: Matrix relevance LVQ in steroid metabolomics based classification of adrenal tumors. In: Verleysen, M. (ed.) 20th European Symposium on Artificial Neural Networks (ESANN 2012), pp. 423–428, d-side publishing (2012)
54. Fawcett, T.: An introduction to ROC analysis. Pattern Recogn. Lett. **27**, 861–874 (2006)
55. Biehl, M., Hammer, B., Schleif, F.M., Schneider, P., Villmann, T.: Stationarity of matrix relevance learning vector quantization. Technical report MLR-01-2009, Machine Learning Reports, University of Leipzig (2009)
56. Biehl, M., Bunte, K., Schneider, P.: Analysis of flow cytometry data by matrix relevance learning vector quantization. PLoS ONE **8**(3), e59401 (2013)

Bayes Optimality of Human Perception, Action and Learning: Behavioural and Neural Evidence

Ulrik R. Beierholm[(✉)]

University of Birmingham, B15 2TT Birmingham, UK
U.Beierholm@bham.ac.uk
http://beierholm.net/

Abstract. The primary role of any biological nervous system (including the human) is to process incoming information in a way that allows motor choices to be made that increases the subjective utility of the organism. Or put slightly differently, "to make sure good things happen". There are a number of ways that such a process can be done, but one possible hypothesis is that the human nervous system has been optimized to maximize the use of available resources, thus approximating optimal computations. In the following I will discuss the possibility of the nervous system performing such computations in perception, action and learning, and the behavioural and neural evidence supporting such ideas.

Keywords: Optimality · Bayesian inference · Reinforcement learning · Behaviour · fMRI · Neural recordings

1 Introduction

Evolution is a continuous process forcing biological organisms to constantly evolve or face extinction (red queen hypothesis [36]). Any biological function that requires metabolic energy expenditure has to provide an important role to be worthwhile. As such it is probably fair to assume that the nervous system of an animal plays an important role for its ecological fitness. If it is so important what is the role that it performs, or rather the roles as it is unlikely to simply perform a single task? While the nervous system undoubtedly plays a large part in regulating physiological factors such as hormones and metabolism, in the following I will primarily focus on the elements required for motor planning.

According to this argument (as well described by e.g. Daniel Wolpert [21,40])[1] the primary role of the brain is not to 'think', write poems or contemplate modern existence. Instead the goal is to make decisions about how to change the physical environment through motor control, the only means through which the brain can influence its environment. The brain thus needs to collect information about the environment, make a motor decision and await to see the outcome of its choice in order to learn to improve its choices for the future.

---

[1] http://www.ted.com/talks/daniel_wolpert_the_real_reason_for_brains.html

© Springer International Publishing Switzerland 2014
L. Grandinetti et al. (Eds.): BrainComp 2013, LNCS 8603, pp. 117–129, 2014.
DOI: 10.1007/978-3-319-12084-3_10

The process may be imagined more clearly if we contemplate a fictive organism, e.g. a hungry frog on a lily pad. (Fig. 1). The animal needs to consume calories (e.g. flies for the sake of this argument) and needs to make motor choices that maximize the number of flies caught while minimizing the effort exerted.

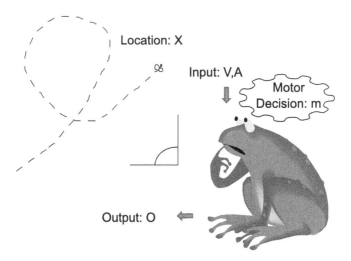

Fig. 1. Optimal behaviour: a frog on a lily pad has to infer the location of the flies, in order to perform a motor action to catch the fly. Based on the outcome of the action it can potentially learn about properties of its perceptual and motor system as well as the environment it is in (e.g. different lily pads might be preferable).

Given sensory input (e.g. visual and auditory stimuli) the animal first needs to infer the location of the insect (we are here disregarding whether or not frogs actually utilize sound for prey localization). Based on some estimate of this (see below) the animal can decide on a motor response that gives an optimal chance of catching the fly. Based on how well the motor response worked the animal learns about its perceptual system, motor control and the external environment.

In the follow the theoretical aspects of these processes, **inference**, **decision making** and **learning**, will be described in further details based on achieving the optimal behaviour for the animal.

2   Inference

Inference about states of the world becomes necessary due to stochastic properties and/or uncertainty about the states. If we have perfect knowledge about the state of the world in the past, present and future, no inference is necessary.

However the world does not present itself to us directly as von Helmholtz [18] and others have surmised. Instead we have to combine different sources of information in order to create a coherent interpretation of the world.

2.1   Bayesian Inference

Given such stochasticity and the need for inference, the most natural approach is to use Bayesian statistical inference which combines previous (prior) information with current estimates (based on a likelihood function) to provide an updated (posterior) distribution of possible states.

2.2   The Simple Case

Imagine for now that the frog has visual information, V about the location of the insect X. Given a visual cue V which is related to the true location X through a known stochastic process, $P(V|X)$, (see Fig. 2) and a prior distribution of possible estimates $P(X)$ the best way to combine these sources of information is through Bayes' theorem:

$$P(X|V) = \frac{P(V|X)P(X)}{P(V)} \tag{1}$$

where $P(V) = \sum P(V|X)P(X)$ functions as a normalizing term.

The new distribution of the state of the world is merely given as the normalised product of the prior knowledge $P(X)$ and the distribution for the new cue $P(V|X)$.

The location of the insect is now represented as a probability distribution based on the frogs visual estimate (and the uncertainty in that estimate), and its expectation about its location. This can be continuously updated (with a discounting over time if the insect is moving) and can for example also be used to estimate the velocity of the insect (and thus predict future locations).

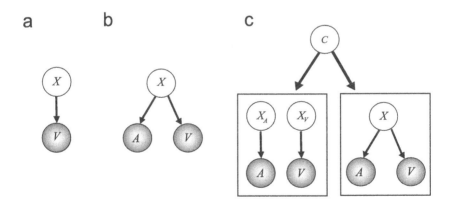

Fig. 2. Graphical models: (a) Simple model with one cause, S, and one cue, X. (b) Model with one source and two cues, X_V and X_A. (c) Causal inference model where the probability of either model is compared.

When the distributions are Normally distributed the calculations get further simplified since estimates based on the posterior distribution can easily be shown to be a linear combination of estimates of the prior and likelihood distributions with a weight specified by the covariances of the distributions.

2.3 Two Cues

A special case that has seen a lot of interest is the one of combining sources of information. Given two sources of information, e.g. audio A and visual V cues about a hidden property X, the information can again be combined in a similar fashion:

$$P(X|V, A) = \frac{P(V|X)P(A|X)P(X)}{P(V, A)} \tag{2}$$

Again, the new distribution of the estimate is given by the normalised product of the likelihood function for each of the two cues and the prior distribution.

From the viewpoint of our frog, if it has access to two sources of information about the location of the insect, it would be potentially beneficial to combine this information in a way that decreases the variance of the estimate of the location. This is exactly what the Bayesian cue integration does.

2.4 Causality

However, critically in order to perform such computations as described above, the causal structure underlying the cues needs to be known. E.g. it only makes sense to combine information from an audio and a visual cue if it is known that they refer to the same object. For large discrepancies in estimate (e.g. in space or time) from two cues automatic cue combination indeed becomes problematic. Hence it becomes necessary to estimate how likely it is that two cues are indeed from the same source, a process referred to as causal inference.

One of the simplest such cases (and yet most relevant) is the inference of whether two cues indeed were generated by one $(C = 1)$ or two sources $(C = 2)$.

$$P(C|V, A) = \frac{P(V, A|C)P(C)}{P(V, A)} \tag{3}$$

This allows inference about the probability of each of the causal structures given the cues, $P(C = 1|A, V)$ and $P(C = 2|A, V)$, allowing the estimation of a underlying source to be done through e.g. model averaging

$$\tilde{X} = P(C = 1|V, A)\tilde{X}_{C=1} + P(C = 2|V, A)\tilde{X}_{C=2} \tag{4}$$

where $\tilde{X}_{C=1}$ and $\tilde{X}_{C=2}$ are the estimates of X according to each of the two causal models.

This is equivalent to comparing the probability of competing hypotheses and doing averaging over them based on this value.

For the frog, if there are multiple insects nearby, it would be detrimental to combine cues from separate sources (e.g. audio from insect α and visual from insect β). Instead the causal relationship has to be estimated, i.e. the perceptual cues have to be attributed to the correct insects before any integration is performed.

2.5 Behavioural and Neural Evidence

While this may be optimal approach to combine information, does the human or animal brains actually use this? Behaviourally this has been studied in a large number of cases. For the single cue and its relationship with prior expectations e.g. in the way human subjects combine prior expectation of the speed of an object with the visually perceived speed [30,38].

For cue combination the Bayesian integration has been examined in a large number of human behavioural studies, showing optimal cue combination for e.g. audio-visual [1], visual-haptic [10] and slant and texture cues [20], i.e. for both within- and cross-modal stimuli.

For the estimation of causality it is perhaps somewhat surprising that the human brain seems to indeed be doing a calculation like this seemingly fast and effortless [21,29].

While there has been overwhelming support for such models in human behavioural experiments (see also [32]), the neural evidence is only now being uncovered.

A recent study [5] examined the neural recordings of awake ferret during development and found that spontaneous activity resembled what you would expect to record for a Bayesian system without visual input, e.g. just representing the prior expectations.

Intricate neural models of Bayesian inference have also been suggested using either neural networks [8], single neurons [3,24] as well as by single synapses [25]. While at least one study found neural activity in accordance with such models, [12], there is certainly potential for future experiment (see Fetsch et al. for a recent review [11]).

3   Choice and Movement

Statistical inference provides a probability distribution over the possible values of the unknown variable of interest. But critically it does not specify what you should do with that information. For that an optimal model requires you to take into account your subjective expected utility (SEU) of the options [4,27].

3.1 Utility Function

SEU describes the expectations that you have about possible outcomes and the subjective value that you assign to them. Obviously you will want make decisions that maximise the probability of a positive outcome for yourself:

$$\tilde{O} = \arg\max E < U(X,O) >= \arg\max \int U(X,O)P(X|A,V)dX \qquad (5)$$

The utility function can encapsulate phenomena such as rewards vs penalty trade off or risk aversion [27]. For perceptual problems it is often assumed that the utility of a choice decreases as the squared deviation from the true value $U(X, O) \sim (X - O)^2$. When the posterior probability of the unknown variable X is Normal distributed (as in several of the examples above) this leads to the optimal choice $O \sim \hat{x} \sim \int X P(X|A, V) dX$ although other utility functions will lead to other optimal responses [22].

For our pensive frog it has to decide not just which insect to try to catch, but calculate the best location to aim for given the movement of the insect. There may be biophysical costs involved making the motor response (muscle movement is not free) as well as opportunity costs if a better possibility of capture will be arriving soon. It is not easy being green.

3.2   Motor Control

The issue becomes a little more complicated when we take into account that not only do we not have perfect knowledge about the state of the world X (and thus have to infer a probability distribution over X, $P(X|A, V)$), we are also restricted in how we influence the world, not being able to directly do so in a way we wish. This is encapsulated by the problem of motor control; a specific motor signal ('point to the red dot on the screen') will lead to a distribution of outcome locations when repeated [33], $P(O|m)$. Furthermore the reaction time will not be perfect, hence variability in lag in response also has to be considered. An optimal decision thus also has to take such variability into account

$$m = \arg\max E < U > = \arg\max \int \int U(X, O) P(O|m) P(X|A, V) dX dO \quad (6)$$

where O refers to the eventual outcome, e.g. a location on a screen, while m is the motor command submitted. (The problem is actually more complex than this [31], but this will suffice for the current discussion).

The frog needs to have a representation of its own motor uncertainty, i.e. what is the locations that its tongue can reach, what is the variability etc. A fast moving insect may become less attractive if the speed is too large once the variability of the motor response is taken into account.

3.3   Behavioural and Neural Evidence

There is currently more behavioural than neurophysiological evidence for the brain utilizing optimal decision making and motor control, one exception being the study by Wunderlich et al. that showed activity in prefrontal cortex that was consistent with optimal use of reward cues.

Behaviourally there are however a large number of studies. Whiteley and Sahani [39] gave subjects a perceptual task where subjects had to integrate the potential payoffs when deciding on different options, showing that perceptual judgements can be influenced by the subjective utility.

In a series of experiments Trommershauser and colleagues studied the ability of human subjects to account for their own movement variability (motor noise), showing near optimal performance on simple tasks [33,34,42] but sub-optimal performance as the complexity increases.

4   Learning

Optimal behaviour also requires adapting to the environment through learning how the organism interacts with the environment as well as about the environment itself.

4.1   Bayesian Learning

Any parameters in the proposed mechanisms above have to be learnt and adapted to the statistics of the environment. Priors and likelihoods have to reflect respectively the statistics of the environment, and the variability in the perceptual system (e.g. visual).

In our frog example the animal has to learn e.g. how reliable its visual system is relative to the auditory system or the variability of its motor system. However it will also learn about the environment itself, e.g. which lily pad allows it to have a better chance of catching flies?

The obvious way to learn all of these variables is to utilize Bayesian inference for the parameters themselves. Bayesian models are excellent for this, due to the way new information is integrated, i.e. the posterior of a variable at time point t is

$$P(X|V_{1:t}) = \frac{P(V_t|X)P(X|V_{1:t-1})}{P(V_{1:t})} \tag{7}$$

where the posterior at time $t - 1$ becomes the prior for the update at time t. However very little is currently known about how the nervous system would achieve this, from a theoretical as well as experimental viewpoint. It would be advantageous if the updating of the parameters could happen 'online' i.e. while the animal is interacting with the environment, although 'off-line' updating, e.g. while sleeping, may also be possible for some variables [19].

4.2   Reward Learning - Model Based

A special case of learning that has gathered a lot of attention, partly due to its link with the literature on Pavlovian and Operant conditioning, is that of reward learning. Compared to the full sensory input available to an organism, only utilising a reward as a single signal for learning seems somewhat impoverished in the available information. However, the goal of the organism as argued above should be to optimise the potential future rewards from the environment, making it undoubtedly the most important single sensory signal to the organism.

In reward learning the total expected future rewards due to taking action a_t while in state s_t are calculated over a fixed time horizon or with a discount γ of future rewards

$$Q(s_t, a_t) = \sum_t^\infty \gamma^t E < r_t >= E < r_t > +\gamma E < r_{t+1} > +\ldots \qquad (8)$$

$$= E < r_t > +\gamma \sum_{s_{t+1}} P(s_{t+1}|s_t, a_t) \max_{a_{t+1}} Q(s_{t+1}, a_{t+1}) \qquad (9)$$

where $E < r_t >$ is the expected reward at time step t (substituting for the expected utility proposed above). Optimal behaviour (often referred to as a policy $\hat{\pi}$) is to choose the action that maximises future rewards, $\arg\max_{a_t} Q(s_t, a_t)$.

Optimal learning can still rely on Bayesian mechanisms, e.g. to try to estimate the probabilities for transitioning between states or receiving rewards. Such approaches are often referred to as model-based reinforcement learning due to their reliance on the establishment of a statistical model of the environment.

For our frog it now has to worry about not just the expected instantaneous outcome, but also what will happen at later times. It may for example be advantageous to move to a different lily pad to increase future expected rewards, despite the instantaneous cost in terms of movement and opportunity cost.

4.3 Reward Learning - Model Free

An alternative approach to the model-based RL does not rely on a model of the environment, instead approximating the expected reward $Q(s_t, a_t)$ by the learnt values from previous experiences. The goal is thus still to maximize the total expected future rewards (or utility) but this is achieved by approximating future rewards with past rewards. One approach updates $Q(s_t, a_t)$ after each trial according to:

$$Q(s_t, a_t) \rightarrow Q(s_t, a_t) + \alpha(r_t + \gamma \max_{a'} Q(s_{t+1}, a') - Q(s_t, a_t)) \qquad (10)$$

This method is referred to as Q-learning [37], and while it is an approximation to the optimal model it can be shown (given certain assumptions) to converge to the true values of $Q(s_t, a_t)$.

In the model-free reinforcement learning there is no explicit model of the environment, instead there is an assumption that the world is stationary and thus that past rewards are a predictor of future rewards. This will of course lead to deviations from optimal behaviour in situations where the environment does indeed vary [7].

For our frog, moving to the lily pad that has previously had most flies around it may be a generally good choice, but if things change in the lake (e.g. rise in water level) then this may no longer be a good choice, indicating how relying on past performance can be dangerous.

4.4 Behavioural and Neural Evidence

Behaviourally optimal updating of parameters has been studied in both perceptual [13] and motor control systems [14]. Furthermore a few imaging studies have examined Bayesian learning of parameters, e.g. Hampton et al. found that neural activity in prefrontal cortex during a reversal learning task corresponded more closely to a model-based or Bayesian learner than a model-free reinforcement learning model [17].

The relationship between model based and model-free learning and their relative behavioural and neural evidence has been reviewed in a few papers (e.g. [7,9]) but the largest amount of evidence of near-optimal learning probably relates to the study of model free learning.

The discovery that the phasic firing of dopaminergic mid-brain neurons are seemingly encoding the reward prediction error of the model-free system [28] has led to a large number of studies relating reinforcement learning to both behaviour and neural recordings (see [9] for a recent review). The idea that the brain is encoding aspects of subjective utility through mechanisms similar to reinforcement learning is today no longer a controversial claim [26].

5 Discussion

In the sections above I have presented the different elements that goes into a model of optimal behaviour, inference, decision making and learning, and presented some of the evidence that the human (or animal) nervous system performs each of these computations.

5.1 Optimal Behaviour

However in a realistic environment an organism is faced with performing all of these within a task. In our toy example our pondering frog needs to infer the location of multiple flies, decide on the most valuable target and plan for the motor command that takes into account both perceptual and motor variability. After the movement it has to assess if it needs to update parameters for its visual estimation model, its motor precision as well as whether it in fact needs to choose a different target or move to a different more lucrative location.

Obviously experimentally incorporating all of these elements into a single task becomes complex too study (although for an approximation see [43]). Optimisation of behaviour requires a number of computational steps as outlined above, computations that can only be performed by the nervous system and which constitute one of its primary functions. Each step of this process may be performed in a separate neural population, or the nervous system may have a different way of splitting the task that is more amenable to the type of computations in neural hardware.

5.2 Limitations

While I have debated the evidence for optimal processing in the nervous system, there is certainly also evidence against such an idea. Some of the most well known examples are from Kahneman & Tverskys studies [35] which highlighted the non-optimal heuristic methods and biases typically used by subjects when faced with written questions related to inference or decision making. Certain criticism has been levelled at this approach (e.g. [15]) while others have tried to bridge the gap between the performance on perceptual-motor tasks and these cognitive tasks (e.g. [41]).

The concept of integrating the subjective utility into the decision making process has also been questioned in human cognition, especially in behavioural economics where researchers such as Allais [2] have shown clear inconsistencies incompatible with the use of a single subjective utility function.

The complexity of the task faced by an organism should not be underestimated. In the real world that a frog is operating in multiple targets, distractors, irrelevant clutter etc. require the animal to perform much more intricate computations than the ones outlined above. Clearly approximations will have to be made. As researchers in this field we have multiple avenues to proceed. One approach is to continually rely on new developments in theoretical models and ideas, expanding the complexity of the tasks that can be processed. A different approach is to abandon the optimal (or near optimal) scheme and instead find a process that is 'good-enough'. According to this idea, the performance of a real organism can be just as good when using simplified models, similar to heuristics [16]. The debate amongst researcher on these issues is still ongoing, regarding the level of approximation needed or heuristics employed. However even less neurophysiological evidence currently exists for such models, than for the optimal models described above.

An obvious omission from the analysis of behaviour above is the issue of social decision making. In our example the frog is a solitary creature who does not have to worry about competitive or collaborative influences from e.g. members of the same species. For some animals this seems fair, but humans are extremely social creatures who are daily interacting with up to hundreds of other humans. Due to space constraint I have not debated this very complex issue, one which the economic field of behavioural game theory [6,23] is dedicated to.

5.3 Conclusion

Evolution on this planet (earth) has shaped the form and behaviour of every species for at least 2 billion years, forcing each species to adapt to the dynamic environment they are placed in. Given this process and the evolutionary pressure faced, it would be surprising if the organisms had not been trying to improve their fitness by approximating optimal processing in the neural systems, optimising inference about properties of the environment and the choices and motor commands that can improve the utility of the organism. In the previous sections I have attempted to draft a rough sketch of the processes involved in such an optimization, and what we currently know about how the nervous system might be approximating optimal behaviour. I have only scratched the surface of such a comprehensive topic, a topic which has generated large discussions of the feasibility of the process itself, but I hope that in describing the current state of knowledge I have at least convinced the reader of the importance of considering the task of the organism when trying to understand the nervous system.

References

1. Alais, D., Burr, D.: The ventriloquist effect results from near-optimal bimodal integration. Curr. Biol. **14**(3), 257–262 (2004)
2. Allais, M.: Le comportement de l'homme rationnel devant le risque: critique des postulats et axiomes de l'ecole americaine. Econometrica **21**(4), 503–546 (1953)
3. Beck, J.M., Ma, W.J., Kiani, R., Hanks, T., Churchland, A.K., Roitman, J., Shadlen, M.N., Latham, P.E., Pouget, A.: Probabilistic population codes for bayesian decision making. Neuron **60**(6), 1142–1152 (2008)
4. Berger, J.: Statistical Decision Theory and Bayesian Analysis. Springer, New York (1980)
5. Berkes, P., Orbán, G., Lengyel, M., Fiser, J.: Spontaneous cortical activity reveals hallmarks of an optimal internal model of the environment. Science **331**(6013), 83–87 (2011)
6. Camerer, C.F.: Behavioral Game Theory: Experiments in Strategic Interaction (The Roundtable Series in Behavioral Economics). Princeton University Press, Princeton (2003)
7. Daw, N., Niv, Y., Dayan, P.: Uncertainty-based competition between prefrontal and dorsolateral striatal systems for behavioral control. Nat. Neurosci. **8**, 1704–1711 (2005)
8. Deneve, S., Latham, P.E., Pouget, A.: Efficient computation and cue integration with noisy population codes. Nat. Neurosci. **4**(8), 826–831 (2001)
9. Doll, B.B., Simon, D.A., Daw, N.D.: The ubiquity of model-based reinforcement learning. Curr. Opin. Neurobiol. **22**(6), 1075–1081 (2012)
10. Ernst, M.O., Banks, M.S.: Humans integrate visual and haptic information in a statistically optimal fashion. Nature **415**, 429–433 (2002)
11. Fetsch, C.R., DeAngelis, G.C., Angelaki, D.E.: Bridging the gap between theories of sensory cue integration and the physiology of multisensory neurons. Nat. Rev. Neurosci. **14**(6), 429–442 (2013)
12. Fetsch, C.R., Pouget, A., DeAngelis, G.C., Angelaki, D.E.: Neural correlates of reliability-based cue weighting during multisensory integration. Nat. Neurosci. **15**(1), 146–154 (2012)
13. Fiser, J., Berkes, P., Orbán, G., Lengyel, M.: Statistically optimal perception and learning: from behavior to neural representations. Trends Cogn. Sci. **14**(3), 119–130 (2010)
14. Franklin, D.W., Wolpert, D.M.: Computational mechanisms of sensorimotor control. Neuron **72**(3), 425–442 (2011)
15. Gigerenzer, G.: On narrow norms and vague heuristics: a reply to Kahneman and Tversky. Psychol. Rev. **103**(3), 592–596 (1996)
16. Gigerenzer, G., Todd, P.: Simple Heuristics That Make Us Smart. Ocford University Press, New York (1999)

17. Hampton, A.N., Bossaerts, P., O'Doherty, J.P.: The role of the ventromedial pre-frontal cortex in abstract state-based inference during decision making in humans. J. Neurosci. Off. J. Soc. Neurosci. **26**(32), 8360–8367 (2006)
18. Hatfield, G.C.: The Natural and the Normative Theories of Spatial Perception from Kant to Helmholtz. MIT Press, Cambridge (1990)
19. Hinton, G.E., Dayan, P., Frey, B.J., Neal, R.M.: The "wake-sleep" algorithm for unsupervised neural networks. Science **268**(5214), 1158–1161 (1995)
20. Jacobs, R.A.: Optimal integration of texture and motion cues to depth. Vis. Res. **39**, 3621–3629 (1999)
21. Körding, K., Beierholm, U., Ma, W., Quartz, S., Tenenbaum, J., Shams, L.: Causal inference in multisensory perception. Plos One **2**(9), e943 (2007)
22. Kording, K.P., Wolpert, D.M.: The loss function of sensorimotor learning. Proc. Natl. Acad. Sci. U.S.A. **101**(26), 9839–9842 (2004)
23. Lee, D.: Game theory and neural basis of social decision making. Nat. Neurosci. **11**(4), 404–409 (2008)
24. Ma, W.J., Beck, J.M., Latham, P.E., Pouget, A.: Bayesian inference with proba-bilistic population codes. Nat. Neurosci. **9**, 1432–1438 (2006)
25. Pfister, J.-P., Dayan, P., Lengyel, M.: Synapses with short-term plasticity are opti-mal estimators of presynaptic membrane potentials. Nat. Neurosci. **13**(10), 1271–1275 (2010)
26. Rutledge, R.B., Dean, M., Caplin, A., Glimcher, P.W.: Testing the reward predic-tion error hypothesis with an axiomatic model. J. Neurosci. **30**(40), 13525–13536 (2010)
27. Savage, L.J.: The Foundations of Statistics. Wiley Publishing, New York, NY (1954)
28. Schultz, W., Dayan, P., Montague, P.: A neural substrate of prediction and reward. Sci. **275**(5306), 1593 (1997)
29. Shams, L., Beierholm, U.R.: Causal inference in perception. Trends Cogn. Sci. **14**(9), 1–8 (2010)
30. Stocker, A.A., Simoncelli, E.P.: Noise characteristics and prior expectations in human visual speed perception. Nat. Neurosci. **9**(4), 578–85 (2006)
31. Todorov, E.: Optimality principles in sensorimotor control. Nat. Neurosci. **7**(9), 907–915 (2004)
32. Trommershauser, J., Kording, K., Landy, M.S.: Sensory Cue Integration (Compu-tational Neuroscience Series). Oxford University Press, New York (2011)
33. Trommershauser, J., Maloney, L.T., Landy, M.S.: Statistical decision theory and the selection of rapid, goal-directed movements. J. Opt. Soc. Am. A. Opt. Image Sci. Vis. **20**, 1419–1433 (2003)
34. Trommershäuser, J., Maloney, L.T., Landy, M.S.: Decision making, movement planning and statistical decision theory. Trends Cogn. Sci. **12**(8), 291–297 (2008)
35. Tversky, A., Kahneman, D.: Judgment under uncertainty: heuristics and biases. Sci. **185**, 1124–1131 (1974)
36. Van Valen, L.: A new evolutionary law. Evol. Theor. **30**, 1–30 (1973)
37. Watkins, C., Dayan, P.: Technical note Q-learning. Mach. Learn. **8**, 279–292 (1992)
38. Weiss, Y., Simoncelli, E.P., Adelson, E.H.: Motion illusions as optimal percepts. Nat. Neurosci. **5**, 598–604 (2002)
39. Whiteley, L., Sahani, M.: Implicit knowledge of visual uncertainty guides decisions with asymmetric outcomes. J. Vis. **8**, 1–15 (2008)
40. Wolpert, D.M., Landy, M.S.: Motor control is decision-making. Curr. Opin. Neu-robiol. **22**(6), 996–1003 (2012)

41. Wu, S.-W., Delgado, M.R., Maloney, L.T.: Economic decision-making compared with an equivalent motor task. Proc. Natl. Acad. Sci. U.S.A. **106**(15), 6088–6093 (2009)
42. Wu, S.W., Trommershauser, J., Maloney, L.T., Landy, M.S.: Limits to human movement planning in tasks with asymmetric gain landscapes. J. Vis. **6**, 53–63 (2006)
43. Wunderlich, K., Beierholm, U.R., Bossaerts, P., O'Doherty, J.P.: The human prefrontal cortex mediates integration of potential causes behind observed outcomes. J. Neurophysiol. **106**(3), 1558–1569 (2011)

Merging Attention and Segmentation: Active Foveal Image Representation

Rebeca Marfil$^{(\boxtimes)}$, Esther Antúnez, Fabián Arrebola, and Antonio Bandera

ISIS Group, Departamento de Tecnología Electrónica,
University of Málaga, Málaga, Spain
{rebeca,eantunez,rfarrebola,ajbandera}@uma.es

Abstract. Research on the brain information processing has focused on the interrelationships among cognitive processes. Thus, it is currently well-established that the units of attention on human vision are not merely spatial but closely related to perceptual objects. This implies a strong relationship between segmentation and attention processes. This interaction is bi-directional: if the segmentation process constraints attention, the way an image is segmented may depend on the specific question asked to an observer, i.e. what she 'attend' in this sense. When the focus of attention is deployed from one visual unit to another, the rest of the scene is perceived but at a lower resolution that the focused object. The result is a multi-resolution visual perception in which the fovea, a dimple on the central retina, provides the highest resolution vision. While much work has recently been focused on computational models for object-based attention, the design and development of multi-resolution structures that can segment the input image according to the focused perceptual unit is largely unexplored. This paper proposes a novel structure for multi-resolution image segmentation that extends the encoding provided by the Bounded Irregular Pyramid. Bottom-up attention is enclosed in the same structure, allowing to set the fovea over the most salient image region. Preliminary results obtained from the segmentation of natural images show that the performance of the approach is good in terms of speed and accuracy.

Keywords: Foveal segmentation · Pyramids · Visual attention

1 Introduction

In computer vision literature, segmentation essentially refers to a process that divides up a scene into non-overlapping, compact regions. Each region encloses a set of pixels that are bound together on the basis of some similarity or dissimilarity measure. A large variety of approaches for image segmentation has been proposed by the computer vision community in these last decades. And simultaneously, this community has been asked for a definition of what is a correct segmentation. As several authors have argued, the conclusion about this

© Springer International Publishing Switzerland 2014
L. Grandinetti et al. (Eds.): BrainComp 2013, LNCS 8603, pp. 130–142, 2014.
DOI: 10.1007/978-3-319-12084-3_11

problem definition is that it is not well posed. Given an image where objects at different resolution appears, the segmentation algorithm should tune its internal parameters to fit correctly to the representation scale of the objects. In this framework, what is the correct set of parameters? As it is pointed out by Mishra et al. (2012), the answer to this question depends on another question: what is the object of interest on the scene? [13].

Attention mechanisms are responsible for pre-selecting relevant information from the sensed field of view in biological vision systems. The aim is that the complete scene will be analyzed using a sequence of rapid eye saccades. Efforts have been made to imitate such attention behavior in artificial vision systems, because it allows optimizing the computational resources as they can be focused on the processing of a set of selected regions (for an extensive survey, see [9]). Most of the models of visual attention build different scales of the input image and determine saliency by considering the vicinity of the individual pixels in these scales. As it has been pointed out by [6], the use of such coarse-to-fine scales during feature extraction provokes fuzziness in the final conspicuity map. This drawback can be avoided by adopting a region-based methodology for the model of attention [12]. Segmentation arises then as a way to constrain selective attention, being the responsible of providing the 'proto-objects', i.e. the image units where attention is deployed. The mutual interaction between segmentation and attention is discussed with details in the work by [8]. As aforementioned, the reverse influence is also possible and segmentation can be modulated by the responses of selective attention. The necessity of this mechanism for adaptively selecting the appropriate scale is also present in the work by [4]. As they pointed out, *dealing with the full variety one expects in high-resolution images of complex scenes requires more than a naive weighted average of signals across the scale range* [4]. Such an average would blur information, resulting in poor detection of both fine-scale and large-scale contours.

In this paper, we propose a hierarchical image encoding where segmentation and bottom-up attention processes could be simultaneously performed. As other approaches, this structure will resemble the one of the human retina: it will only capture a small region of the scene in high resolution (fovea), while the rest of the scene will be captured in lower resolution on the periphery. This foveal structure is encoded as an extension of the Bounded Irregular Pyramid (BIP) [11]. The remainder of the paper is organized as follows: Sect. 2 provides an overview of the proposed method, describing the data structure and decimation process of the foveal BIP. The segmentation and saliency estimation are described at Sect. 3. Section 4 presents preliminary results on using this structure. Conclusions and future works are drawn on Sect. 5.

2   Foveal Representation Using the Bounded Irregular Pyramid: The FovealBIP

2.1   Cartesian Foveal Geometries (CFG)

Although we could have the impression that our vision system is able to process the entire visual field of view in a single fixation, only part of the retina

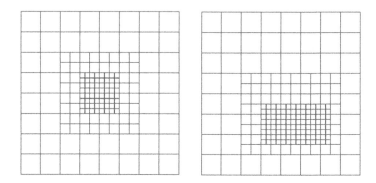

Fig. 1. (Left) fovea-centered CFG, and (right) adaptive fovea CFG.

(the fovea) permits high visual acuity. Surrounding this fovea, peripheral vision allows the recognition of well-known structures and the identification of similar shapes and movements, but it is not able to provide the visual acuity of the fovea. This multi-resolution encoding allows the human visual system to perceive a large field of view, bounding the data flow coming from the retina. Due to its inherent advantages, computational approaches have replied this non-uniform structure through methods such as the Reciprocal Wedge Transform (RWT), or the log-polar or Cartesian foveal geometries [15]. Specifically, Cartesian Foveal geometries (CFG) encode the field of view of the sensor as a fovea surrounded by a set of concentric rings with decreasing resolution [5]. In the majority of the Cartesian proposals, this fovea is centered on the geometry and the rings present the same parameters. Thus, the geometry is characterised by the number of rings surrounding the fovea (m) and the number of subrings of resolution cells -*rexels*- found in the directions of the Cartesian axes within any of the rings. Figure 1(left) shows an example of a fovea-centered CFG.

Among other advantages, there are CFGs that are able to provide a shiftable fovea of adaptive size [15]. Vision systems which use the fovea-centered CFG require to place the region of interest in the center of the image. That is usually achieved by moving the cameras. These movements need the selection of an endpoint and time for planning and execution. It is clear that a shiftable fovea can be very useful to avoid certain motor movements. Furthermore, the adaptation of the fovea to the size of the region of interest can help to optimise the consumption of computational resources. Figure 1(right) shows the rectangular structure of an adaptive fovea. The geometry is now characterised by the subdivision factors at each side of the fovea. It should be noted that the foveal geometry is not adequate for processing planar images. On the contrary, the aim is to use it for hierarchical processing. Thus, the whole structure (the *foveal polygon* [5]) can be drawn like Fig. 2 shows. There are a first set of levels of abstraction built from the fovea to the waist (the first level where the complete field of view is encoded). In the figure, levels 1 and 2 on this hierarchy are built by decimating the information from the level below and adding the data from the corresponding

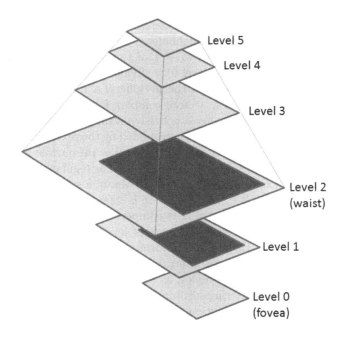

Fig. 2. Foveal structure for adaptive fovea lattices.

ring of the multi-resolution image. Over the waist, there are a second set of levels. All these levels encode the whole fiel of view and are built by decimating the level below. Typically, the decimation process inside the CFGs have been conducted using regular approximations [5]. Then, all levels of the foveal polygon can be encoded as images. The problems of regular decimation processes were early reported [1,7], but here, these processes were justified due to the simplicity for processing [15]. In this work, we propose to build the foveal polygon using the irregular decimation process provided by the Bounded Irregular Pyramid (BIP) [10].

2.2 Foveal Poligon

The data structure of the BIP is a mixture of regular and irregular data structures: a $2 \times 2/4$ regular structure and a simple graph. The mixture of both regular and irregular structures generates an irregular configuration which is described as a graph hierarchy. In this hierarchy, there are two types of nodes: nodes belonging to the $2 \times 2/4$ structure, named *regular nodes* and *irregular nodes* or nodes belonging to the irregular structure. Therefore, a level l of the hierarchy can be expressed as a graph $G_l = (N_l, E_l)$, where N_l stands for the set of regular and irregular nodes and E_l for the set of arcs between nodes (intra-level arcs). Each node $n_i \in N_l$ is linked with a set of nodes $\{n_k\}$ of N_{l-1} using inter-level arcs, being $\{n_k\}$ the reduction window of n_i. A node $n_i \in N_l$ is neighbor of other node $n_j \in N_l$ if their reduction windows w_{n_i} and w_{n_j} are connected.

Two reduction windows are connected if there are at least two nodes at level l-1, $n_p \in w_{n_i}$ and $n_q \in w_{n_j}$, which are neighbors.

Figure 3 shows an example with $m = 1$ of the proposed structure. In this simple example, the input image (level 0) is divided up into a central part, the fovea, at the highest resolution, and the periphery, a ring of lower resolution surrounding the fovea (in Sect. 4, a more complex foveal polygon with $m = 3$ (Fig. 6) has been employed). The fovea is firstly decimated to obtain the central part of the data at level 1, which is then surrounded by the rexels of the periphery. In the figure, regular nodes are represented by cubes meanwhile irregular ones are drawn as circles. All rexels at level 0 are encoded as regular nodes. The fovea (of 8×8 pixels in the example) is decimated to obtain a set of 12 regular nodes and 2 irregular nodes. The $2 \times 2/4$ tessellation is shown in the figure: the region surrounded by the white-coloured ring is composed by 2×2 regular nodes at level 0, that are not linked to a regular node at level 1, but to an irregular one because of its position on the fovea. This white-coloured ring is also linked to one irregular node at level 1. On the contrary, the two larger regions on the fovea are encoded at level 1 by regular nodes, as they shape well in the 2×2 regular geometry. As there is only one ring surrounding the fovea, the level 1 will encode the whole scene at uniform resolution (waist). The following levels (from waist to the uppest level) are building by decimating the level bellow.

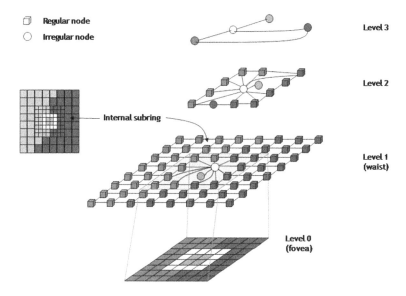

Fig. 3. Schematic representation of the decimation process inside the foveal bounded irregular pyramid (see text for details).

2.3   Decimation Scheme of the FovealBIP

According to the neighborhood definition explained in the previous subsection, two nodes x and y which are neighbors at level l are connected by an intra-level arc $(x, y) \in E_l$. Let ε_l^{xy} be equal to 1 if $(x, y) \in E_l$ and equal to 0 otherwise. Then, the neighborhood of the node x can be defined as $\{\mathbf{y} \in N_l : \varepsilon_l^{\mathbf{xy}}\}$. It can be noted that a given node $\mathbf{x}$ is not a member of its neighborhood, which can be composed by regular and irregular nodes. Each node $\mathbf{x}$ has associated a $v_{\mathbf{x}}$ value. Besides, each regular node has associated a boolean value $h_{\mathbf{x}}$: the homogeneity [11]. At the base level of the hierarchy G_0, the fovea, all nodes are regular, and they have $h_{\mathbf{x}}$ equal to 1. Only regular nodes which have $h_{\mathbf{x}}$ equal to 1 are considered to be part of the regular structure. Regular nodes with an homogeneity value equal to 0 are not considered for further processing. The proposed decimation process transforms the graph G_l in G_{l+1} using the pairwise comparison of neighbor nodes. Then, a pairwise comparison function, $g(v_{\mathbf{x_1}}, v_{\mathbf{x_2}})$ is defined. This function is true if the $v_{\mathbf{x_1}}$ and $v_{\mathbf{x_2}}$ values associated to the $\mathbf{x_1}$ and $\mathbf{x_2}$ nodes are similar according to some criteria and false otherwise. When G_{l+1} is obtained from G_l, being $l < waist$, this graph is completed with the regular nodes associated to the ring $l + 1$. This process will require to compute the neighborhood relationships among the regular nodes coming from the ring and the rest of nodes at G_{l+1}. Over the waist level, G_{l+1} is built by decimating the level below G_l.

The building process of the fovealBIP consists of the following steps:

1. Regular decimation process. The $h_{\mathbf{x}}$ value of a regular node $\mathbf{x}$ at level $l+1$ is set to 1 if the four regular nodes immediately underneath $\{\mathbf{y_i}\}$ are similar according to some criteria and their $h_{\{\mathbf{y_i}\}}$ values are equal to 1. That is, $h_{\mathbf{x}}$ is set to 1 if

$$\{ \bigcap_{\forall \mathbf{y}_j, \mathbf{y}_k \in \{\mathbf{y_i}\}} g(v_{\mathbf{y}_j}, v_{\mathbf{y}_k}) \} \cap \{ \bigcap_{\mathbf{y}_j \in \{\mathbf{y_i}\}} h_{\mathbf{y}_j} \} \qquad (1)$$

Besides, at this step, inter-level arcs among regular nodes at levels l and $l+1$ are established. If $\mathbf{x}$ is an homogeneous regular node at level $l+1$ ($h_{\mathbf{x}} == 1$), then the set of four nodes immediately underneath $\{\mathbf{y_i}\}$ are linked to $\mathbf{x}$ and the v_x value is computed.

2. Irregular decimation process. Each irregular or regular node $\mathbf{x} \in N_l$ without parent at level $l+1$ chooses the closest neighbor $\mathbf{y}$ according to the $v_{\mathbf{x}}$ value. Besides, this node $\mathbf{y}$ must be similar to $\mathbf{x}$. That is, the node $\mathbf{y}$ must satisfy

$$\{\|v_{\mathbf{x}} - v_{\mathbf{y}}\| = \min(\|v_{\mathbf{x}} - v_{\mathbf{z}}\| : \mathbf{z} \in \xi_{\mathbf{x}})\} \cap \{g(v_{\mathbf{x}}, v_{\mathbf{y}})\} \qquad (2)$$

If this condition is not satisfy by any node, then a new node $\mathbf{x'}$ is generated at level $l+1$. This node will be the parent node of $\mathbf{x}$ and it will constitute a root node. Its $v_{x'}$ value is computed. On the other hand, if $\mathbf{y}$ exists and it has a parent $\mathbf{z}$ at level $l+1$, then $\mathbf{x}$ is also linked to $\mathbf{z}$. If $\mathbf{y}$ exists but it does not have a parent at level $l+1$, a new irregular node $\mathbf{z'}$ is generated at level $l+1$ and $v_{z'}$ is computed. In this case, the nodes $\mathbf{x}$ and $\mathbf{y}$ are linked to $\mathbf{z'}$.

This process is sequentially performed and, when it finishes, each node of G_l is linked to its parent node in G_{l+1}. That is, a partition of N_l is defined. It must be noted that this process constitutes an implementation of the union-find strategy [10].

3. Definition of intra-level arcs. The set of edges E_{l+1} is obtained by defining the neighborhood relationships between the nodes N_{l+1}. As aforementioned, two nodes at level $l+1$ are neighbors if their reduction windows are connected at level l.

4. For $l < waist$
   - The set of nodes N_{l+1} is completed with the rexels of the ring $l+1$. These rexels are added as regular nodes, N_{l+1}^{ring}.
   - The intra-level arcs between nodes of N_{l+1}^{ring} and the rest of nodes of N_{l+1} are computed as in step 3. Nodes of N_{l+1}^{ring} do not have a real reduction window at level l, they present a *virtual reduction window*. The virtual reduction window of a node $\mathbf{x} \in N_{l+1}^{ring}$ is computed by quadrupling this node at level l as shown in Fig. 4. Therefore, the reduction window of $\mathbf{x}$ is formed by the four nodes immediately underneath at level l.

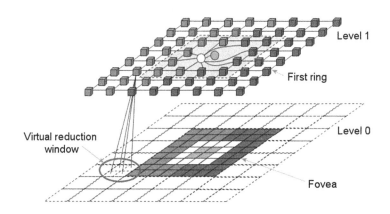

Fig. 4. Virtual reduction window of a node of a ring

3   Segmentation and Visual Attention

The fovealBIP has been employed for image segmentation and bottom-up visual attention. Following previous work [2], the image segmentation will be conducted in two consecutive stages. The pre-segmentation stage builds the lower set of levels of the foveal polygon (from l_0 to l_m with $l > waist$) according to the CIELab color features. On the top of this hierarchy, the perceptual grouping stage will employ edge and color information to obtain a second set of levels of abstraction. Within this hierarchy, the saliency values for bottom-up attention are estimated and the most relevant region is selected. Then, the fovea is moved to wrap this region and a new hierarchy of segmentation levels are computed. Next sections describe the pre-segmentation and perceptual grouping stages of the approach and the evaluation of features for bottom-up visual attention.

3.1   Pre-segmentation Stage

The pre-segmentation stage groups the image pixels and rexels into a set of photometric homogeneous regions (blobs) whose spatial distribution is physically representative of the image content. This stage is accomplished by means of the irregular foveal polygon described in Sect. 2, taking into account the CIELab color of the image pixels and the pairwise comparison of neighboring nodes: $g(v_{\mathbf{x}_i^{(l)}}, v_{\mathbf{x}_j^{(l)}})$ is true if the color difference between $\mathbf{x}_i^{(l)}$ and $\mathbf{x}_j^{(l)}$ is under a given threshold U_v, and false otherwise. In order to measure the color difference between two nodes, the $v_{\mathbf{x}}$ value of each node stores the mean color of its sons and the Euclidean distance is employed. That is, the distance between two nodes $\mathbf{x}_i^{(l)}$ and $\mathbf{x}_j^{(l)}$ at the pre-segmentation stage is defined as

$$\psi^\beta = \sqrt{(L_{\mathbf{x}_i^{(l)}} - L_{\mathbf{x}_j^{(l)}})^2 + \beta(a_{\mathbf{x}_i^{(l)}} - a_{\mathbf{x}_j^{(l)}})^2 + \beta(b_{\mathbf{x}_i^{(l)}} - b_{\mathbf{x}_j^{(l)}})^2} \tag{3}$$

where β is a parameter which allows to weight lightness and chrominance (grayscale images correspond to β equal to 0 and the usual CIELab space to β equal to 1).

3.2   Perceptual Grouping Stage

After the pre-segmentation stage, grouping regions aims at simplifying the content of the obtained partition. For managing this grouping, the irregular structure is used: the roots of the pre-segmented blobs at level l_m constitute the first level of the perceptual grouping multi-resolution output. Successive levels can be built using the decimation scheme described in Sect. 2 and a similarity criteria between nodes which has two main components: the color contrast between blobs and the edges of the image at the waist level computed using the Canny detector. This contrast measure is complemented with internal regions properties and with attributes of the boundary shared by both regions. To perform correctly, the nodes of the pyramid structure associated to the perceptual grouping stage store statistics about the CIELab color values of the nodes generated by the pre-segmentation stage which are linked to them. Then, the distance between two nodes $\mathbf{y}_i^{(l)}$ and $\mathbf{y}_j^{(l)}$, $\varphi^\alpha(\mathbf{y}_i^{(l)}, \mathbf{y}_j^{(l)})$, is defined as [2]

$$\varphi^\alpha(\mathbf{y}_i^{(l)}, \mathbf{y}_j^{(l)}) = \frac{d(\mathbf{y}_i^{(l)}, \mathbf{y}_j^{(l)}) \cdot min(b_{\mathbf{y}_i^{(l)}}, b_{\mathbf{y}_j^{(l)}})}{\alpha \cdot c_{\mathbf{y}_i^{(l)}\mathbf{y}_j^{(l)}} + (b_{\mathbf{y}_i^{(l)}\mathbf{y}_j^{(l)}} - c_{\mathbf{y}_i^{(l)}\mathbf{y}_j^{(l)}})} \tag{4}$$

where $d(\mathbf{y}_i^{(l)}, \mathbf{y}_j^{(l)})$ is the color distance between $\mathbf{y}_i^{(l)}$ and $\mathbf{y}_j^{(l)}$. $b_{\mathbf{y}_i^{(l)}}$ is the perimeter of $\mathbf{y}_i^{(l)}$, $b_{\mathbf{y}_i^{(l)}\mathbf{y}_j^{(l)}}$ is the number of rexels in the common boundary between $\mathbf{y}_i^{(l)}$ and

$\mathbf{y}_j^{(l)}$ and $c_{\mathbf{y}_i^{(l)}\mathbf{y}_j^{(l)}}$ is the set of rexels in the common boundary which corresponds to rexels of the edge detected by the Canny detector. α is a constant value used to control the influence of the Canny edges in the grouping process. Finally, it must be commented that the pairwise comparison function, $g(v_{\mathbf{y}_i^{(1)}}, v_{\mathbf{y}_j^{(1)}})$, is also implemented as a thresholding process. Then, $g(v_{\mathbf{y}_i^{(1)}}, v_{\mathbf{y}_j^{(1)}})$ is true if the distance measure between both nodes is under a given threshold U_p, and false otherwise. This threshold U_p will be typically different to U_v. The perceptual grouping process is iterated until the number of nodes remains constant between two successive levels.

3.3   Bottom-Up Visual Attention

Contrary to the typical strategy for bottom-up attention, in our framework feature maps are not computed in parallel across the visual field and combined into a salience map. The foveal polygon allows integrating image features into a single hierarchy. Each layer of the polygon is built considering color, brightness and edge strength using the decimation algorithm and segmentation stages described at Sects. 2 and 3. Thus, the foveal image is partitioned into regions by a perceptual grouping algorithm, optimizing the interaction with proto-objects and not just with disembodied spatial locations. Once the foveal polygon is built, the saliency value of each proto-object is obtained using color and brightness contrast measures [12]. Center-surround contrasts are estimated in our model using a region-based framework: a region of the partition at level l of the foveal polygon is linked with its corresponding region in the multi-resolution image through a set of inter-level arcs. In the upper level of the hierarchy each region corresponds with a 'proto-object' of the foveal image and its associated set of inter-level arcs allows to determine the shape of the 'proto-object' in the image (feedback connection) (see [10] for a detailed explanation of a segmentation process inside irregular pyramids). Figure 5c shows the bottom-up saliency values associated to the multi-resolution image of Fig. 5a. Figure 5b shows the segmentation result at the waist. It should be noted that the color or saliency values of Figs. 5b and 5c have been propagated from the waist to a virtual image, where the fovea and peripheral rings are included.

(a)   (b)   (c)

Fig. 5. (a) Original multi-resolution image; (b) segmentation result from the waist level; and (c) bottom-up saliency values from the waist level (see text for details).

4   Experimental Results

Figure 6 shows the segmentation results for several image of uniform and non-uniform resolution. In both cases, the BIP has been used to perform the segmentation process using the same segmentation parameters. It can be noted that the performance on the segmentation of the fovea is very similar in the uniform and non-uniform images. However, when the multi-resolution image is used, the segmentation speed is significantly greater. This is clearly due to the difference on size among the uniform and non-uniform images. Thus, the size of the uniform images in Fig. 6 is 320×480 (153,600 pixels) and the size of their non-uniform counterparts ranges from 9,780 to 18,930 rexels. The loss on visual acuity in the

Fig. 6. The first and second rows show several uniform images and the results from the perceptual grouping stage. The third and fourth rows show a foveated version of the same images at (a) and the results from the perceptual grouping stage. Contours have been drawn in white over the segmentation images

Fig. 7. The first column shows an uniform image and the segmentation result obtained using the BIP. The second and third columns show a foveated version of the same images at the first column and the segmentation results. After conducting a first fixation using a centered fovea, the fovea is then moved to the regions where human faces can be. The image features and inhibition of return (IoR) mechanism have been taken from previous work [14]. Contours have been drawn in white over the segmentation images

peripheral rings do not imply that they will not be interesting for the bottom-up component of attention. Figure 6 illustrates how the main regions on the scene are present on the segmentation images. In fact, the segmentation results at the peripheral part are smoother than in the fovea, providing larger regions. This issue benefits that they will be chosen as the new focus of attention.

The aim of the proposed framework is to enclose the bottom-up attention inside the structure for multi-resolution image segmentation. Once a saliency image is computed, the fovea is moved to the most salient image region. The fovea will be segmented at high resolution, providing details about the objects (e.g. the face details of the koala). These details could be necessary for object recognition and could also anchor the fovea over this part of the scene until this recognition is conducted (top-down attention) or other part of the scene is more relevant (bottom-up attention). Although this top-down behavior has not been currently implemented in our framework, it could resemble the role of fixational eye movements -the involuntary eye movements- during a fixation. Encoded as a graph, a previously learned model of the object (e.g. of a face, with eyes and mouth) can drive this behavior (see [3] for our work on this topic using uniform images). On the other hand, the peripheral field of view will be perceived at lower resolution. But this part of the scene, encoded as larger blobs, usually drives the bottom-up attention. Using a static image, this effect is illustrated at Fig. 7. The fovea explored the scene and is moved to the faces and hands of the people (blobs of skin color) on the scene. It can be noted that, when the fovea is over a face, the rest of blobs of skin color are clearly delimited in the segmentation image.

Finally, there is a major disadvantage on the method, associated to the quadtree effect on the segmentation results. In a first view, this can be interpreted as an inconvenience, but it must be noted that we are dealing with multi-resolution images. The association of a $2^n \times 2^n$ area to a rexel allows us to visualize our non-uniform images as planar images. But these rexels could come from a multi-resolution sensor, being not associated to a square-shaped region (although our approach will maintain the 2×2 virtual reduction windows for processing).

5   Conclusions and Future Work

The recent work on so-called *object-based* visual attention provides interesting new cross-talk between two traditionally separate research fields, one concerning visual segmentation and grouping processes, and the other concerning selective attention. Within this interesting ways crossing, this paper proposes to translate the interaction between both processes to a multi-resolution framework. With respect to the segmentation results, fixating the fovea over the most relevant region on the scene, our approach automatically segments the rest of the image with less acuity. With respect to the visual attention results, all image information (from the fovea and the peripheral rings) influences on the evaluation of the saliency values, and next fixations can be located on other parts of the scene. Combining hierarchical segmentation and saliency estimation, our approach is able to quickly determine what is the next region of interest on the scene, as this search is performed in the high levels of the hierarchy.

Current work focuses on testing the framework in real robots. For this end, there are several issues to solve. Firstly, we must consider that the proposed approach does not deal with different cameras to obtain the peripheral and foveal images, but obtains all the scene information from a single sensor. These multi-resolution images can be obtained from foveating cameras[1]. The system should also add a second sensor for providing disparity (depth) information. Furthermore, as it was pointed out by Mishra et al. (2012), future work should be focused on incorporating models of the objects in this framework. These models could be used to define a top-down component for attention and segmentation. Thus, the perceptual grouping of the segmentation process (Sect. 3.2) could include not only low-level cues, but also mid-level relationships (e.g. a human face includes eyes and mouth) to correctly define the contours of an object of interest on the image [13]. Considering these objects as a whole, the attention system could be tuned to search for specific kinds of objects on the scene. In order to correctly use these models, the irregular decimation process should preserve the topology of the perceived scene. Dual graphs or combinatorial maps could be employed for this purpose.

---

[1] http://www.novasensors.com/vsafc.htm

Acknowledgments. This work has been partially granted by the Spanish Government and FEDER funds project no. TIN2012-38079-C03-03. This article is the result of the work of the group of the Integrated Action AT2009-0026, constituted by Spanish and Austrian researchers.

References

1. Antonisse, H.J.: Image segmentation in pyramids. Comput. Graph. Image Process. **19**, 367–383 (1982)
2. Antúnez, E., Marfil, R., Bandera, A.: Combining boundary and region features inside the combinatorial pyramid for topology-preserving perceptual image segmentation. Pattern Recogn. Lett. **33**(16), 2245–2253 (2012)
3. Antúnez, E., Palomino, A., Marfil, R., Bandera, J.P.: Perceptual organization and artificial attention for visual landmarks detection. Cogn. Process. **14**(1), 13–18 (2013)
4. Arbeláez, P., Maire, M., Fowlkes, C., Malik, J.: Contour detection and hierarchical image segmentation. IEEE Trans. Pattern Anal. Mach. Intell. **33**, 898–916 (2011)
5. Arrebola, F., Camacho, P., Sandoval, F.: Generalization of shifted fovea multiresolution geometries applied to object detection. In: Del Bimbo, A. (ed.) ICIAP 1997. LNCS, vol. 1311, pp. 477–484. Springer, Heidelberg (1997)
6. Aziz, M.Z., Mertsching, B.: Color saliency and inhibition using static and dynamic scenes in region based visual attention. In: Paletta, L., Rome, E. (eds.) WAPCV 2007. LNCS (LNAI), vol. 4840, pp. 234–250. Springer, Heidelberg (2007)
7. Bister, M., Cornelis, J., Rosenfeld, A.: A critical view of pyramid segmentation algorithms. Pattern Recogn. Lett. **11**, 605–617 (1990)
8. Driver, J., Davis, G., Russell, C., Turatto, M., Freeman, E.: Segmentation, attention and phenomenal visual objects. Cogn. **80**, 61–95 (2001)
9. Frintrop, S., Rome, E., Christensen, H.: Computational visual attention systems and their cognitive foundations: a survey. ACM Trans. Appl. Percept. **7**(1), 1–39 (2010)
10. Marfil, R., Molina-Tanco, L., Bandera, A., Rodriguez, J.A., Sandoval, F.: Pyramid segmentation algorithms revisited. Pattern Recogn. **39**, 1430–1451 (2006)
11. Marfil, R., Molina-Tanco, L., Bandera, A., Sandoval, F.: The construction of bounded irregular pyramids with a union-find decimation process. In: Escolano, F., Vento, M. (eds.) GbRPR. LNCS, vol. 4538, pp. 307–318. Springer, Heidelberg (2007)
12. Marfil, R., Bandera, A., Rodríguez, J.A., Sandoval, F.: A novel hierarchical framework for object-based visual attention. In: Paletta, L., Tsotsos, J.K. (eds.) WAPCV 2008. LNCS (LNAI), vol. 5395, pp. 27–40. Springer, Heidelberg (2009)
13. Mishra, A., Aloimonos, Y., Cheong, L., Kassim, A.: Active visual segmentation. IEEE Trans. Pattern Anal. Mach. Intell. **34**(4), 639–653 (2012)
14. Palomino, A., Marfil, R., Bandera, J.P., Bandera, A.: A novel biologically inspired attention mechanism for a social robot. EURASIP J. Adv. Sig. Proc. (2011)
15. Traver, V.J., Bernardino, A.: A review of log-polar imaging for visual perception in robotics. Robot. Auton. Syst. **58**, 378–398 (2010)

Performance Analysis and Parallelization Strategies in Neuron Simulation Codes

Victor Lopez[(⊠)], Marçal Sola, and Jesus Labarta

Barcelona Supercomputing Center (BSC-CNS), Barcelona, Spain
{victor.lopez,marcal.sola,jesus.labarta}@bsc.es

Abstract. An important activity within the Human Brain Project (HBP) is to analyse and optimize the two main neuron simulation codes to improve their scalability and adapt them to efficiently work under an interactive supercomputing usage pattern. One application was already MPI + OpenMP while the other was pure MPI. We describe the analyses performed with the BSC tools and the initial efforts to hybridize the codes for better matching multicore architectures and to introduce the malleability that will be needed to operate under dynamic resource allocation environments of the future.

1 Introduction

When aiming at very large scale executions and operating in a very dynamic environment, malleability is an important property that applications should expose, to let schedulers and runtime systems to adapt the amount of resources allocated to a job or process as they run in order to react to changes in the environment. Examples of such variability in the amount of resources available may come from the application structure itself (i.e. migrating load imbalance) or from the system such as noise, heterogeneity in the devices, or activation/deactivation of mechanisms such as turbo-boost or node failures. A very important source of variability in future systems will derive from changes in the usage practices. We can envisage session based executions where a user launches a long running simulation on the available resources but periodically execute analytics jobs requiring a few processors/nodes to digest the intermediate results and based on them let the simulation continue, steer its future computation or launch further simulations or analyses. If no additional resources are available we would like to share the simulation resources with the analytics job such that both can proceed execution, getting interactive analytics response times while not significantly perturbing the simulation execution speed. We can also envisage that if one session finishes other session might like to use the available resources to accelerate the simulation or viceversa, that if an urgent session needs to be started, some of the resources of this one be shifted to the new one. All of these usage patterns require the applications to be able to dynamically adapt their parallelism structure dynamically, a property known as malleability.

Systems today are managed in pretty static ways, where a fixed number of cores are allocated to an application for its whole execution. The advantage is that the application programmer can partition the work among cores trying to match his conceptual model

L. Grandinetti et al. (Eds.): BrainComp 2013, LNCS 8603, pp. 143–156, 2014.
DOI: 10.1007/978-3-319-12084-3_12

of application computational complexity to his conceptual model of core and network performance. This is statically done when the application is started if not earlier as for example in many domain decomposition applications. The decisions taken often assume a perfectly homogeneous machine and knowledge of the computational structure. The disadvantage is that discordances between the conceptual models the programmer had and the actual application or system behaviour will result in inefficiency in the execution.

Tools that provide precise insight on the actual behaviour of applications and systems are thus becoming and ever growing need. Tools should allow developers to validate how their conceptual models hold true and adapt them based on the detailed observation of actual behaviour. Equally important for the efficient operation under the described dynamic environments is the ability of the runtime to adapt the parallelization structure of the application to the available resources. In order to enable such flexibility in mapping the application structure to the available resources a key issue is how the programmer describes the computations to be performed. Tasks based programming models provide a clean interface to describe the algorithmic structure and its potential concurrency in a portable way, decoupling programs from resources and increasing programmer productivity by letting their focus on the algorithms while the runtime handles architecture specificities and environment variability. It is actually a tight integration between tools, programming models and runtimes what is required to properly address the challenges of future interactive supercomputing systems.

The Human Brain Project (HBP) aims at integrating the community knowledge about the brain into computer models and simulations that could contribute to drastically increase our understanding of how it works and to improve our diagnosis and treating capabilities of its diseases. A key component of the project are the simulation engines to understand the dynamics of brain tissue consisting of millions of neurons and the impact of model parameters and characteristics in their electrical activity and its propagation. On one side, these applications pose huge computational requirements, on the other, the HBP envisaged usage modes match the described interactive supercomputing vision, where one or multiple coupled simulations, analytics applications and visualization will dynamically share the system resources.

The two main simulation codes in the HBP project are NEST and NEURON. NEST has been developed and used in different research projects at Juelich Supercomputing Center (JSC). NEURON was initially developed at Yale University and was tuned for highly parallel execution on the Blue Gene within the Blue Brain Project at EPFL where it is routinely used in production.

BSC is carrying out a long term effort to develop system software technologies considered as enables in the above vision. Trace based performance analysis tools such as Paraver and Dimemas, the OmpSs programming model, the NANOS++ runtime and the DLB dynamic load balancing library are components in such direction. The paper describes activity and initial results in applying those technologies within the HBO to the neuron simulation code. In the next sections we briefly describe the applications and BSC infrastructure. We then present performance analyses for the two applications and initial hybrid parallelization with MPI + OmpSs.

2   The Applications

NEST (NEural Simulation Tool) [1] is a simulator for spiking neural network models that focuses on the dynamics, size and structure of brain-scale neuronal network models rather than on the exact morphology of individual neurons. The neural system is defined at the level of neuron and synapses, where it considers an abstract assembly of nodes (neurons) which can have multiple connections with different properties (synapses). The interaction between nodes, or neuronal activity, is represented by spikes which are emitted by the nodes and propagated along the connections. Thus the connectivity can be described as a directed graph.

The application does not implement a specific network model but provides the user with a range of neuron and synapse models and efficient routines to connect them to complex networks. This way, the user can describe a network model and run the corresponding network simulation.

The simulation kernel is written in C++, using object oriented (OO) features and generic programming. Two parallel programming models can be used, MPI and OpenMP, which can be used together for a hybrid model parallel approach.

NEURON [2] is an open source simulation environment for empirically-based simulations of neurons and networks of neurons. It is particularly well-suited to problems that are closely linked to experimental data, especially those that involve cells with complex anatomical and biophysical properties. NEURON's computational engine employs special algorithms that achieve high efficiency by exploiting the structure of the equations that describe neuronal properties.

Beyond the analysis of the original NEURON code, we have been using the Bluron simulator, a modified version of NEURON developed by EPFL. The available version uses MPI without any support for multithreading.

3   BSC Infrastructure

3.1   BSC Tools

BSC Performance Tools team aims to provide a set of performance analysis tools for the user to solve any performance problem, or to simplify and facilitate the process of extracting information from the performance data. Some of the tools used in the analysis of NEST and Bluron are described here.

Paraver [3] is a very flexible performance tool developed at BSC that gives the user a global perception of the application behaviour by visual inspection to afterwards focus on the detailed quantitative analysis of the problems. The timeline display represents the behaviour of the application along time and processes, in a way that easily conveys to the user a general understanding of the application behaviour and simple identification of phases and patterns.

The ClusteringSuite [4], a set of programs based on cluster analysis that use data mining techniques for the classification of data, is applied to detect different trends in the application computation regions with minimum user intervention.

Finally the FoldingSuite [5] combines both instrumentation and sampling for trace-based performance analysis tools. The folding mechanism takes advantage of long execution runs and low frequency sampling to finely detail the evolution of the user code. These results are extremely useful to understand the behaviour of a region of code at a very low level.

3.2   OmpSs and DLB

The OmpSs Programming Model [6] designed by the Programming Models department at BSC is the effort to integrate different parallel features into a single programming model. In particular, the objective is to extend OpenMP with new directives to support heterogeneity by supporting other accelerator based APIs like CUDA or OpenCL, and asynchronous parallelism by the use data-dependencies between the different tasks of the program. The OmpSs environment is built on top of the Mercurium compiler and Nanos++ runtime system.

DLB (Dynamic Load Balancing) [7] is a dynamic library developed at BSC designed to speed up hybrid parallel applications by improving the load balance inside each computational node. It needs a malleable second level of parallelism (OmpSs in this case) so it can dynamically adapt the number of resources of this level at any time in which the unbalance is detected in the first level of parallelism (MPI).

4   Analysis of Applications

For each of the codes we performed different analyses running on MinoTauro, a cluster with 128 Bull B505 blades, each one of them composed by 2 Intel E5649 (6-Core) processor at 2.53 GHz, and 24 GB of main memory. In this section we describe the main results for each of the codes.

4.1   NEST

The first analyses aim at just reporting the execution times for different configurations (regarding computational resources, same problem size) to observe the overall application scalability and the performance of the hybrid parallel approach.

The public distribution of NEST includes some example scripts for the SLI interpreter describing a network of excitatory and inhibitory neurons and their connections for both, which will be randomly created. In particular we have used the Brunel Network model with a fixed problem size of 37500 neurons and 10 s of simulation time. The results have been obtained running the NEST simulator on MinoTauro using from 6 (half-node) to 120 MPI processes (10 nodes). For each core count fully populated nodes are used except for the initial 6 processes run. Figure 1 shows both pure MPI and Hybrid Scalability. In the first chart we can observe that with this given input the MPI simulator scales very well in all the scenarios. On the contrary, results obtained running the Hybrid versions show that none of distribution can increase the performance of the pure MPI version.

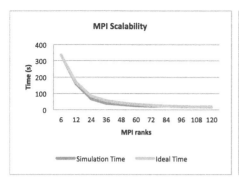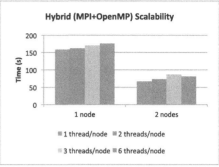

Fig. 1. MPI and hybrid scalability in NEST

To obtain a better understanding about the poor performance in hybrid parallel versions we analysed both simulations using Paraver. Figure 2 shows two screenshots of Paraver for two different simulations. Both traces inform about the IPC for a 12 ranks pure MPI version (a) and a hybrid 2 process per 6 thread version (b), so both executions are using the same number of resources. The information is represented in this case using a gradient which goes from light green, meaning low value, to dark blue, meaning the highest values. We can see four iterations of the pure MPI run while in the same time scale the hybrid version performs a few less than four iterations. The pure MPI version is averaging 0.9 Instructions per Cycle versus the 0.76 from the hybrid version.

We used the Clustering Suite to identify the application structure from the computation bursts of Paraver traces. The scatter plot at the top of Fig. 3 shows the number of instructions vs. IPC for each computation burst between MPI calls. The bottom

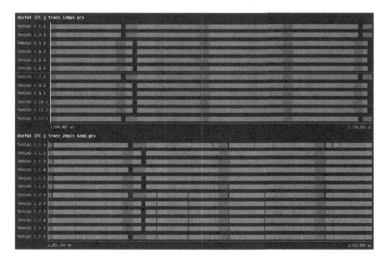

Fig. 2. IPC view comparison between a the pure MPI version (above) versus the hybrid version (below) (Color figure online)

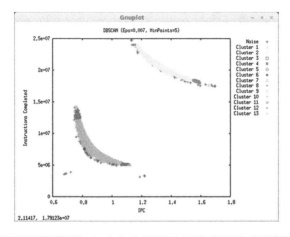

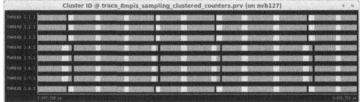

Fig. 3. Clustering scatterplot and time distribution (Color figure online)

timeline shows the actual time distribution of those clusters. The green cluster shows significant variability between instances in terms of both instructions and IPC, but still the dense structure of the cluster indicates that all those point correspond to the same computational structure. The analysis of the trace shows that although instances of the green cluster executing in parallel are actually very similar, there is variability along time, with the instances at some points in time have more instructions than those at other point in time.

The clustering analysis can be used as input to the folding process and obtain the analysis shown in Fig. 4, representing a synthetic average instance of the green cluster which shows a not very high overall IPC. Red points in Fig. 4 show the cumulative number of instructions from the beginning of the cluster for different measurements obtained by sampling. The green curve is a fit of the sampled points and its derivative in blue corresponds to the instantaneous Floating Point Instructions rate. We observe that it is actually not homogeneous during the cluster time lapse. We can clearly identify 3 different regions, and thanks to the instrumentation of the code and Paraver, we can locate them in the source code. Starting from the middle green highlighted section, where the Floating Point Instructions have the most significance, this behaviour belongs to the **update** function. This function is called every time step in the main loop and computes the spikes arriving from other neurons to the local neurons of the thread or process. After this one, we have the **gather_events** function, which happens to be represented by the rightmost yellow highlighted section corresponding to the

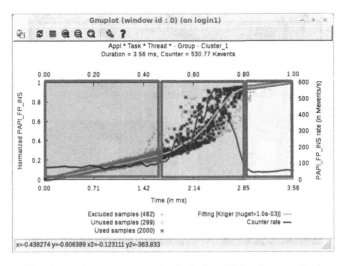

Fig. 4. Hardware counters detailed view (Color figure online)

packing of the data to be sent by the MPI calls that follow the cluster execution. This function is always ran by exclusively one thread per process and is the responsible to do the MPI communication to propagate the spikes of the local nodes and receive the foreign ones each iteration. Lastly, we have the **deliver_events** function, which is behaviour is highlighted red in the leftmost region of the plot. This function is called at the beginning of each iteration and is the responsible to deliver the spike events that were sent in the previous time step, either from MPI calls or from memory if the simulation is multi-threaded. As we can see, the FP rate in the gather and deliver phases is very low as they essentially correspond to data movement activities. The numerical computation of the neurons activity only constitutes around one third of the total iteration cost.

4.2   BLURON

The basic approach to parallelize a simulation with a large number of neurons is to assign a subset of them to then to each process. Simulating the propagation of potentials within a neuron is done iterating with a given time step. Every few such timesteps, a global communication takes place to propagate spikes to other neurons. Different types of neurons have different computational complexity associated and if the number of neurons assigned to each process is not large (as will occur if running on very large platforms), significant imbalance can result. This is shown in Fig. 5 for a case where 100 neurons are run on 128 cores. The view on top shows computation in black and MPI calls in red. The bottom view is the complementary one displaying in a gradient form light green to dark blue the duration of the computation phases. The last 28 processors have no neuron assigned to them. The inefficiency caused by the imbalance is very high.

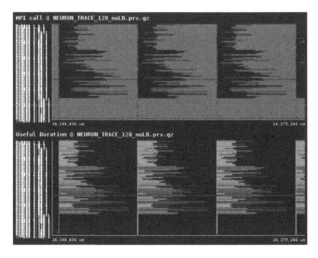

Fig. 5. Three iterations of the NEURON simulation for 100 neurons on 128 processes (Color figure online)

To address this imbalance the code can be configured to split some of the neurons on several processors based on an estimate of the computational cost of computing each neuron that is made at program initialization. This approach can improve load balance but now requires explicit communication every timestep between processors cooperating on one neuron. This behaviour is shown in Fig. 6 where 100 neurons are run on 64 processes. Inner step communications are seen in the top view, while the

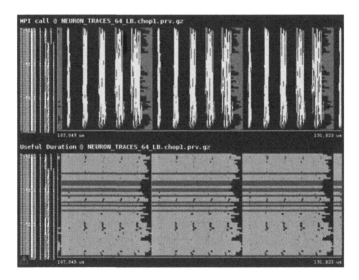

Fig. 6. Three iterations of the NEURON simulation for 100 neurons on 64 processes (Color figure online)

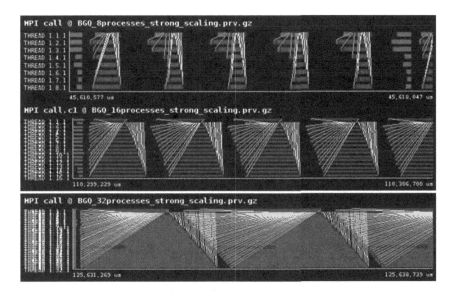

Fig. 7. Strong scaling one neuron onto 8, 16 or 32 processors (Color figure online)

lower timeline clearly identifies in dark blue the processors that get full neurons and light green the individual substeps for those that get parts of a neuron. The black region in the lower timeline shows that still the load balance achieved is not ideal.

When aiming at the extreme strong scale execution setups which are needed in some experiments, one neuron will be split into several processes. Figure 7 shows the behaviour when one single neuron is split into 8, 16 or 32 processes. We clearly see that there is a long (and growing with core count) time in MPI waits (brown) resulting in very poor performance. The figures also show a strong serialization behaviour, where all processes send data to the first one who performs a small computation and redistributes the generated value. The poor efficiency of this approach suggests that a shared memory parallelization to reduce overheads.

For our analysis we considered a use case based in a neuron distribution similar to the currently used in production, with about 10–15 neurons simulated per process. The scalability that we obtained with this configuration is shown in Fig. 8. Only the MPI scalability is considered, since the application has not been yet ported to use a shared memory based programming model.

Using Paraver, we can get detailed measurements of hardware counters in a very specific section. Figure 9 shows the Instructions Per Cycle ratio for some simulation timesteps. In particular the values go from 0.43 (light green) to 1.06 (dark blue).

In order to further analyse these low IPC regions, we used the Clustering suite to first clusterize and categorise the regions of code with similar behaviour and then the Folding suite to finely observe the hardware counters information for each cluster, and particularly the cluster that presented the lowest IPC. What we have found is shown in Fig. 10, where we can see the IPC and L3 miss ratios over time (blue line), and their cumulative value (green line). It is observed a drop in the IPC value induced by the increment of the cache misses. That is not strange at all and it suggests data intensive calculations.

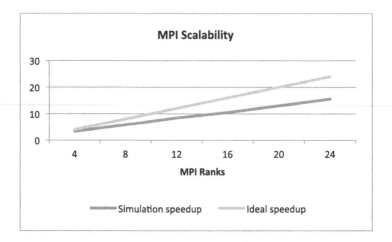

Fig. 8. MPI scalability in BLURON

Fig. 9. IPC of BLURON running on 4 MPI processes (Color figure online)

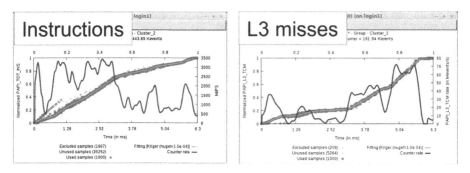

Fig. 10. Instantaneous MIPS and L3 miss rate for the more relevant cluster (Color figure online)

With all that, we decided to focus on the zones with high IPC, using OmpSs tasks to parallelize the work done by each of the MPI processes between the synchronization points.

As we said, this will imply that we will have some regions of the code that cannot be scheduled to be executed by multiple threads in parallel. To resolve this issue we would need to modify some algorithms of the application that are intended to work only with MPI.

5   Porting the Application to OmpSs

In this section we describe how the applications can be hybridized using OmpSs.

5.1   NEST

A very simple scheme of parallelization using OmpSs is shown in the Fig. 11. The left box has the original OpenMP code, with a big parallel section including the main simulator loop, being each parallel function called by all the threads, and a single directive protecting the MPI function. The right box shows a possible implementation of the same algorithm using OmpSs. The main loop is not affected by any directive and it is every function to be parallelized that has the *task* directive, in our case using *thread_nodes* as a dependency between both tasks. Then, we do not need to protect the MPI function with a single directive, since it is in the user code, only one thread will execute the function.

Figure 12 shows a zoomed trace of the OmpSs parallelization. The yellow events correspond to the deliver_events function, which, as it has been commented, is responsible to propagate the spikes from the previous MPI communication and suffers

```
#pragma omp parallel
{
    do {
        deliver_events(thread_nodes);
        update(thread_nodes);
        #pragma omp barrier
        #pragma omp single
        gather_events();      // MPI
    } while( ... )
}
```

```
do {
    #pragma omp task out(thread_nodes)
    deliver_events(thread_nodes);
    #pragma omp task in(thread_nodes)
    update(thread_nodes);
    #pragma omp taskwait
    gather_events();      // MPI
} while( ... )
```

Fig. 11. OpenMP vs OmpSs parallelization

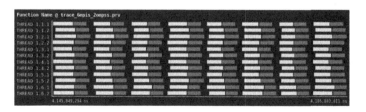

Fig. 12. Task view of some iterations of a hybrid version (6 MPI × 2 OmpSs threads) (Color figure online)

from poor performance. Being data movement dominated and thus memory bandwidth bound, this phase increases in duration as the number of threads increment, so it is one of the reasons that the hybrid versions do not perform as well as the pure MPI version. Possible parallelization strategies should look at ways to overlap the data movement phases in some cores with more computational intensive phases in others. The pink events correspond to the update function, which as it has been mentioned have a good overall performance and it scales well. Dark zones are non-taskified code, being the MPI communication in this case.

5.2 BLURON

We have parallelized the computation within an MPI process using OmpSs and tried to improve it using the Dynamic Load Balancing library, designed to speed up hybrid applications with nested parallelism by improving the load balance inside each computational node. It is important to note that, until now, we have been working with testing data and small scale executions. Therefore, results may vary in the future when we test with real data.

The cell membrane of the axon and soma of a neuron contain ion channels that allow it to propagate an electrical signal. These signals are generated and propagated by charge-carrying ions of different types, such as sodium (Na) or calcium (Ca2). To simulate the propagation of the spikes through the network of neurons, the application has to compute all those different mechanisms for each neuron. Something important to note is that the computation of the mechanisms for different neurons can be parallelized.

The region of the code that is more CPU intensive and has a higher IPC, as seen in Fig. 9, is composed by a *for* loop that just iterate over all those mechanisms in the way that Fig. 13 outlines. That is, each MPI process iterate over the different types of mechanisms defined in the simulation to perform the appropriate computations on the subset of neurons that have been assigned to this process. As a result, the mechanisms can be computed in parallel for different neurons. In order to parallelize these computations using threads in addition to the MPI processes, we had to decide the tasks granularity. We tried different approaches but the task schemes that performed better is the code described in the right box of Fig. 13. In this case we create a task for each type of mechanism which, as explained above, can be calculated in parallel. Another optimization that we introduced was the distinction of the mechanisms, considering only the most costly ones as tasks and serializing the ones that just were going to introduce overhead in the simulation.

Having done some executions with this configuration and tracing them, we obtained the result shown in Fig. 14. What can be seen in this Paraver trace, running a simulation with 4 MPI processes and 3 threads each, is the overlap of the execution of the tasks for one iteration of the main loop. More specifically, we can see for each MPI process the creation of the tasks by one thread (red) and the execution in parallel of the mechanisms in the form of tasks (pink).

We have been able to successfully parallelize with OmpSs this part of the code that computes the mechanisms associated to the neurons. However, as we have explained in

```
for (m : mechanisms) {
    for ( n : neurons) {
        calculate()
    }
}
```

```
for (m : mechanisms) {
    if (m.cost() > THRESHOLD) {
        #pragma omp task
        for ( n : neurons)
            calculate()
    } else {
        for ( n : neurons)
            calculate()
    }
}
#pragma omp taskwait
```

Fig. 13. OmpSs parallelization

Fig. 14. OmpSs tasks for BLURON (Color figure online)

the analysis section, there is another part of the code that may require a deeper analysis of the algorithms to figure out how to describe it efficiently with tasks. To mitigate the lack of parallelism for those cases we decided to use the DLB library.

At this point, the behaviour of the application resembles to what we can see in Fig. 14, which shows a trace including a few steps of a simulation. It is clear that the sequential segments will negatively affect the overall performance of the application. We thought that DLB, a library that can help to improve the load balance between MPI processes, could be a good option in this case. The strategy we followed was to shift a bit the computation of this two differenced segments of the code -the single and the parallel segments- for a few of the processes. That implies that at the same time we have some processes executing a sequential segment while others are in the parallel segment of the code. That allows DLB to take the unused cores of the MPI processes running sequential code and dedicate them to accelerate the computations on the other processes. This behaviour is shown in Fig. 15, running a simulation with 4 MPI processes and 3 threads each. In the figure we can see that while one process is on the sequential part, dark red segments in the picture, its cores are shared among other processes running the parallel segments, pink in the picture. That explains why some of the processes occasionally have more than three threads during the execution.

We are still actively working on this solution, looking for best configurations to see the performance we can achieve. However, we think that could be a good solution to consider alongside other proposed solutions, like the modification of the algorithms to allow a better parallelization.

Fig. 15. OmpSs tasks during a heterogeneous distribution of resources (Color figure online)

6 Conclusions

In this paper we have presented the analysis of the NEST and NEURON simulations codes constituting the main engines in the modelling capabilities within the HBP project. We have shown how the BSC tools can be useful to gain detailed insight in the behaviour of the applications both at the MPI level as well as at the sequential computation performance between MPI calls. This insight is extremely useful to identify how the OmpSs shared memory programming model can be used to address the specific performance issues. The experience is also proving very useful to co-design the tools and runtime implementations, ensuring that the OmpSs programming model an NANOS++ and DLB runtime libraries properly address the needs of a scientifically very relevant area such as neuroscience. Further experimentation especially at scale will be done to complete the initial results presented in this paper.

References

1. NEST Initiative, June 2014. http://www.nest-initiative.org/
2. NEURON|for empirically-based simulations of neurons and networks of neurons, June 2014. http://www.neuron.yale.edu/neuron/
3. Paraver|BSC-CNS, June 2014. http://www.bsc.es/computer-sciences/performance-tools/paraver
4. Cluster Analysis|BSC-CNS, June 2014. http://www.bsc.es/computer-sciences/performance-tools/clustering
5. Folding|BSC-CNS, June 2014. http://www.bsc.es/computer-sciences/performance-tools/folding
6. The OmpSs Programming Model|Programming Models@BSC, June 2014. http://pm.bsc.es/ompss/
7. Dynamic Load Balance|Programming Models@BSC, June 2014. http://pm.bsc.es/dlb

HPC and Visualization
for Human Brain Simulations

Towards Brain-Inspired System Architectures

Thomas Sterling, Maciej Brodowicz, and Timur Gilmanov[✉]

Center for Research in Extreme Scale Technologies,
School of Informatics and Computing, Indiana University, 420 N. Walnut St.,
Bloomington, IN 47404, USA
{tron,mbrodowi,timugilm}@indiana.edu

Abstract. Brain-inspired computing structures, technologies, and methods offer innovative approaches to the future of computing. From the lowest level of neuron devices to the highest abstraction of consciousness, the brain drives new ideas (literally and conceptually) in computer design and operation. This paper interrelates three levels of brain inspired abstractions including intelligence, abstract graph data structures, and neuron operation and interconnection. An abstract machine architecture is presented from which a lower bound on resource requirements for intelligence is to be derived. At the lowest level a new use of cellular automata architecture is discussed that mimics the fine-grain locality of action and high degree interconnectivity of neurons and their structures. Graph structures serve as a brain inspired intermediary abstraction between these two as the neocortex is organized as a directed graph. This paper shows how all of the pieces tie together and opens a new way of considering future computing structures through brain inspired concepts.

1 Introduction

Even as future directions of supercomputing are challenged by issues of scalability, power, reliability, and usability, the human brain demonstrates radical alternatives in technologies, structure, and operation that inspire revolutionary approaches to computing at unprecedented scales compared to contemporary computers. The brain comprises almost a hundred billion neurons; each with thousands of interconnects in less than 1500 cubic centimeters with a power budget of 20 Watts. Each neuron performs a complex algorithm a thousand times a second. Today, experts in the US, Europe, and Asia as well as other parts of the world are considering what can be derived from insights related to brain structure and operation in advancing technical approaches to goals in future Exascale computing for science, engineering, industry, commerce, the arts, and security. This paper examines three brain-inspired features of future generation computing: one abstract related to knowledge understanding and one physical to achieve effective degree and diversity of interconnectivity through semiconductor technology, both logically integrated by graph structures.

The phrase "brain-inspired" is as vague as it is provocative; both of real value. It suggests many potential opportunities and stretches the realm of possibilities well beyond conventional practices. As a result, it has motivated work

© Springer International Publishing Switzerland 2014
L. Grandinetti et al. (Eds.): BrainComp 2013, LNCS 8603, pp. 159–170, 2014.
DOI: 10.1007/978-3-319-12084-3_13

in a number of directions over many decades. Turing, after defining computability, prescribed a test for computer intelligence [1]. The vast networks of neurons have inspired the class of algorithms known as neural networks [2] that, among other areas, has demonstrated recent advances in natural language processing. Neural nets do not duplicate the brain but rather exhibit some properties reminiscent of and perhaps motivated by brain structures. Here, three properties of the human brain that inspire consideration of innovations in computing are identified: Consciousness, Intelligence, and Cellular Automata [3].

"Consciousness" is intuitive to everyone but lacks clarity of definition and is as much a part of philosophy as science. Therefore, it is deferred in this discussion, although tantalizing and important in the long term. Here, the latter two are examined in depth and tied to practical issues of future computing systems. "Intelligence" is addressed as a class of observable computing behavior. The project, Cognitive Real-time Interactive System (CRIS), is described to determine minimum bounds on resource requirements for intelligent systems. The generalized cellular automata hardware structure, inspired by neuron structures, is an innovative yet realistic concept to achieve advantages of low-level brain elements with future semiconductor device technologies. The Continuum Computer Architecture (CCA) project explores fine-grain hardware structures that take advantage of near nano-scale semiconductor technologies through brain-inspired physical characteristics including localized functionality and rapid result dissemination to wide array of distributed component destinations. These two brain-inspired computing forms are mutually supportive. Dynamic graph data structures are an intervening abstraction relating the two. Graphs may be considered brain-inspired as the complex topologies of the neurons of the brain are graphs. But many knowledge structures such as semantic nets and search space algorithms are manifest as graphs as well.

Intelligence is an attribute inspired by the human brain but neither defined nor limited by it. Further, not all mental attributes associated with the human brain need be ascribed to intelligence. A working definition of "intelligence" is required to guide the development and govern the operation of an intelligent system. Even if such a definition is not fully compliant with all possible interpretations, it must be viable, repeatable, testable, and realizable. Intelligence is the ability of an entity to understand its context including itself and react to it in real-time in response to intrinsic goals and derived objectives. This definition defers determination of the explicit class of entity or the nature of its context as well as the specification of its governing goals and objectives. It supports many possible manifestations of intelligent agents and their operational domain. It also implies a range of the property of intelligence, begging the question of a quantifiable metric by which to measure intelligence. Equally challenging is the pivotal verb: "to understand". The definition does establish the principal attributes of an intelligent system even if it alone fails to fully fix the meaning of key terms. Machine Intelligence is an algorithm representable in a mechanical system. Intelligence is an emergent behavior of a real-time system comprising the synergy of the distinct functional capabilities of learning, knowledge, planning, and understanding in a real-time context. The purpose of CRIS is to explore the resource requirements in time and space (memory capacity, execution elements, communication bandwidth, power) in order to realize the properties deemed essential to intelligence. The goal is to provide a quantifiable lower bound of such resources based on an abstract machine architecture comprising a synthesis of such functional elements. These are informed and inspired by understanding of the brain but not intended to duplicate brain functionality in all ways.

Conventional architectures, both individual processor cores and memory hierarchies, are becoming increasingly inadequate in terms of efficiency, scalability, power, generality, portability, and usability. But the brain inspires alternative structures; ones that exploit lightweight physical hardware structures while adapting to asynchronous operation. High connectivity over widely distributed destinations within the brain is a property rarely shared in conventional structures. The second extreme attribute is that of hyper-parallelism where each primitive element is capable of some independent and complex operation. Conventional systems do neither; the brain is exceptional at this at the level of neuron structures. Future nano-scale semiconductor technologies will favor tighter coupling for closer interaction while die-scale structures are loosely coupled and display asynchronous interaction. Cellular automata embodies many of the properties of neuron structures. However, conventional cellular automata are special purpose with interactions limited to nearest neighbor. CCA suggests an alternative version of cellular automata in which localized actions have global destinations through packet switching abstractions rather than line switched. Like neurons, many messages can be sent to different destinations. The unifying principle of graphs as the intermediate form representing both the abstraction of knowledge, planning, and searching for CRIS naturally lends itself to a new generation of implementation by CCA. This paper examines these levels of brain-inspired abstractions and their interrelationships for future computing systems.

2   Overview of Machine Intelligent System

Over the last six decades attempts to deliver a cognitive system that is capable of learning have been made. In spite of advances in natural language processing, planning, pattern matching, robotics, and other related disciplines, a truly cognitive system has not been delivered. With rapid technological advancements and digital information increase, new algorithms, utilizing both hardware and the available information, are being developed. Although seemingly capable of delivering certain elements of brain-inspired behavior, these algorithms lack in the critical component of being able to learn new concepts (self-adjust the algorithmic behavior of self) except in special cases.

2.1   Abstract Architecture for Machine Intelligence

An architecture that represents a Machine Intelligent (MI) system is comprised of a number of interrelated autonomous components, each of which serves key

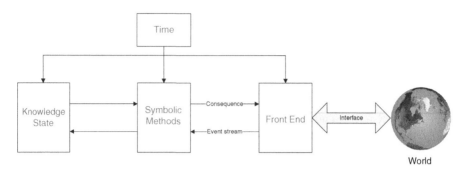

Fig. 1. Abstract architecture of a MI system.

functions in the entire system operation. These components can be divided into three groups at the top level, including the system's knowledge state, symbolic methods and front-end, see Fig. 1.

Knowledge state represents various types of knowledge that the system is continuously maintaining throughout its execution, while symbolic methods include a number of means for processing the accumulated knowledge as well as any other symbolic-based data. Finally, the front-end provides means for the system to exchange information with the outside world.

Such a system represents a closed execution loop by obtaining data stream at its front-end, which is then processed to obtain decisions about updating the knowledge state. This updated state is later used to provide an output stream to an external entity, which is referred to as the "World" in Fig. 1.

Knowledge is an essential part of any Machine Intelligence system that requires a well-defined representational hierarchy. Alternative knowledge representation techniques exist, including knowledge databases and ontology representation [4]. The proposed architecture differentiates knowledge into a number of classes beginning from relatively static foundational knowledge to most rapidly changing imperatives derived from input stream commands or otherwise implied by local context. Knowledge is further broken into universal knowledge, that any system might possess, such as fundamental facts about geography, history or physics, and unique knowledge that any system belonging to a particular environment needs to maintain, such as the machine's location, its internal system status, or what other agents it is currently interacting with in its surroundings.

One of the most important properties of the proposed MI system is that it has to be self-aware. A topic of self-awareness that goes back a few centuries has been a subject of discussion in the fields of psychology and philosophy. A definition of "self-aware" is proposed. Such systems need to identify themselves in the surrounding environment and recognizing what kind of entities (including other MI systems) it is presently interacting with. It is important for the system to model such aspects as identity (who am I?), physical location in space (where am I?), location in time (when am I?), and operation status (how am I?). Additionally, the system has to be aware of any entities in its neighborhood that can affect it, with whom/what it is presently maintaining a dialog, whether it is challenged by anything, and what are its current responsibilities alongside with how well it is advancing in achieving its goals. The system's objective function hierarchy models the latter, which is represented by a stack of goals to be satisfied. These goals are sorted by the complexity, with more coarse-grained declarative objectives located at the top of the hierarchy, and with fine-grained imperatives at the bottom.

The objective function module interacts closely with the active context stack that contains transient information about anything the system is interacting with, including knowledge, external agents, etc. Every new situation, event, objective or interaction requires a context, which is added to the active context hierarchy. Items in this hierarchy are linked to the corresponding objective function items. Due to the unstructured nature of processed information, it is possible that some of this relationships are "one:many", "many:one, or even "one:none" and "none:one". The active context stack is expected to become extremely dynamic at times when there is a need to process a large amount of fine-grained contextual information in the real-time regime. The stack, therefore, is growing and shrinking rapidly depending on the active contexts.

A mechanism that drives the knowledge query and update is referred to as Master Control Program (MCP). This mechanism is analogous to central nervous system for autonomic behavior. It ensures that a system is constantly going through an outer loop, executing required actions in bounded time. During the execution of a loop cycle, the MCP needs to perform a number of actions, such as (i) query the system's status by interacting with the self-awareness module; (ii) satisfy the objectives that are due this execution cycle; (iii) query all the I/O sensors to obtain updated information about the external environment; (iv) trigger the knowledge state update mechanisms, and (v) update current objective function and active context stack hierarchies. When satisfying the objectives, MCP needs to obey the axioms that are imposed by the developers and are hard-coded into the system's non-volatile read-only memory. This approach is necessary in order to guarantee that the system will not become dangerous to human beings under any circumstances. These rules can not be altered by the system itself and would require external interference (if need be). During the cycle of the execution loop, a number of symbolic methods are involved, which are described below.

The system's symbolic methods include learning, update mechanisms, planning, inference and conflict resolution. All of these methods are independent actors, that are operating on required tasks, taking current context information into consideration. Learning is one of the most essential methods allowing the system to modify its future actions based on the empirical information about its interaction with the environment. The update mechanisms ensure that the new information is processed and recorded in the machine's knowledge state base. Planning module supports for a plan derivation for various tasks. In case a machine does not know what type of metrics to use, or has to achieve a goal while generating a plan, it is attempting to utilize learning modules in order to express the goals through currently existing knowledge or obtain new knowledge about the problem. Finally, inference mechanisms allow to draw new conclusions about the facts available in the knowledge state, while conflict resolution ensures that all the constraints of present goals are satisfied.

The nature of brain-inspired computation and its processing similarities of those in human brain suggest the use of data structure that would resemble the brain's behavior. One such structure, that naturally represents neurons and their synapses, is graphs. Graph structures can be used for both knowledge storage, with facts of various types forming a tree-like conceptual hierarchy, and context and objective stack information. The information processed by the system varies greatly in terms of its life span, with some knowledge facts that are virtually never changed (such as axioms, or very slowly changing facts about the world) on one hand and pieces of knowledge that are extremely dynamic, such as active context stack frames, or objective functions, on the other. Graph data structures, that are capable of efficient representation and processing for both types of these knowledge types will be utilized. Algorithms that support extremely dynamic graph structures need to be considered.

2.2 Quantifying Metrics for Machine Intelligence

Taking the human brain as a reference Machine Intelligent system, a question about a rough estimate of required resources for an engineered MI system arises. How large of a system would be required in order to support Machine Intelligence? In fact, how should one measure such a system and what kind of units should be used? For that purpose, a set of metrics need to be considered. The introduced metrics need to be able to accurately measure some of the components of interest for a MI system, such as operation primitives. These primitives include I/O, knowledge state update, and query. Another set of important components include concurrency, storage, as well as energy and power.

A few examples of various metrics that will be used for the experiments include computational throughput, memory capacity, storage capacity, communication latencies, bi-section bandwidth interconnect, and energy consumption rate. The proposed metrics will be utilized to measure the performance of a simulation for the MI system.

3 Continuum Computer Architecture

The Continuum Computer Architecture is a 3-D computing medium intended to efficiently and scalably support the cognitive algorithms and data structures utilized by a machine intelligence system. This architecture is inspired by prominent brain properties that are immediately applicable to graph processing. In the sections below challenges of designing the knowledge processing hardware are described, the brain features that inspired particular facets of CCA are pointed out, trade-offs that define the design constraint space are analyzed, and the resultant system architecture is described.

3.1   Challenges of Knowledge Processing

Creation of an efficient graph processing component is associated with significant technological challenges. Current digital processors are designed for diametrically different purposes; they achieve high computational throughputs on numeric workloads in which data references exhibit high levels of locality. However, their performance drops off significantly when data access becomes unpredictable and sparse – such as graph operations. Graph processor implementation for machine intelligence that simultaneously satisfies the requirements of scale, response time, and energy using electronic processing technology available today is unfeasible. Superficial analysis of brain structure reveals that the count of synaptic connections is on the order of 10^4 for each neuron. This is more than an order of magnitude greater than the highest number of ports available in a low-level switch component of a state-of-the-art high-radix network. The neuron produces action potential (fires) at the rate of few hundred pulses per second. Its underlying electric activity consists of ionic current summation and integration on the capacitance of lipid bilayer coupled with the electrical properties of the axon [5]. With approximately a hundred billion neurons in a human brain, each with thousands of synaptic connections with complex chemistry, the aggregate operation rate necessary to effectively emulate brain activity may easily reach 10^{18} (1 Exa) per second. Since the brain operates on a power budget of roughly a fifth of that of a modern high-performance CPU dissipated in a volume of just over 1 l, the challenges of building an artificial knowledge processor capable of rivaling the human brain are nothing short of staggering.

3.2   Characteristic Features of the CCA

Brain-Inspired Properties. The brain exhibits a high degree of replication; even though there are various types of neurons, the overall brain structure is attained through extensive repetition of few similar "building blocks". CCA takes advantage of this by defining a minimal computing element, *fonton*, that connects with other elements in its immediate vicinity. The fonton is small enough to be implemented in a few thousand logic gates, reaching a diameter comparable to that of the average neuron (few tens of micrometers) in a modern CMOS process.

The neuron combines several functions: connectivity, analog signal processing, and even storage (accumulation of ionic charge). The fonton mirrors this by embedding processing logic, local registers, and a network router along with physical communication links. This approach avoids the pitfalls of discrete functional units connected by power-hungry buses with discrete memory modules and separate network hardware. The bandwidth available for each of the fonton components can be optimized to match the individual processing throughputs; their interactions may happen within a single clock cycle.

CCA inherits from the brain distributed control and quasi-independent operation. Due to limited amount of processing a single neuron can perform, every significant brain function requires formation and activation of ensembles of neurons. One of the side benefits of this is operational redundancy, in which functions affected by minor neural damage might be assumed by nearby healthy neurons. Due to inevitable production defects and component degradation affecting complex systems, this also introduces the necessary fault tolerance for contiguous operation of the CCA system. Even though some brain structures are developed for specific functionality (such as cerebellum with fast feed-forward neural paths optimized for motor control), many of them are largely interchangeable. CCA mimics it by providing uniform distribution of identical processing elements throughout the chip, forming a nearly isotropic computing medium throughout which higher level functions may be distributed arbitrarily.

Finally, the cerebral cortex, considered to be the locus of intelligence, is a stratified, but primarily 2-D structure. Its thickness is thought to be critically related to cognitive reasoning abilities. The CCA trivially replicates the 2-D layout with transistors instantiated on the surface of a flat piece of silicon. However, recently introduced die stacking [6] enables building in the third dimension.

Emergent Behavior. Unlike the brain, a CCA machine cannot redefine its physical connections over time. However, packet switching network permits logical organization of arbitrary aggregations of fontons, as long as routing is efficient. Packet switching is also a foundation of message-driven computing, in which parts of a program react to specific events rather than actively waiting or polling for them. This results in improved energy efficiency, as inactive software components may stay idle and minimize their resource footprint until a triggering event occurs. Since the speed of message packets in the medium is finite, locality and spatial distribution of the individual program components matter.

Even though the physical implementation of CCA hardware is envisioned as 3-D, this does not impose limits on logical dimensionality. Three dimensions provide natural simulation medium for many physical phenomena. However, logical organization of the interconnecting graph may be arbitrary. Moreover, since this connectivity is defined by routing tables modifiable by software, it can be shaped during the program execution.

The high degree of replication coupled with co-location of basic functions in all elementary components provides unprecedented aggregate processing bandwidth. Assuming a clock speed of 1 GHz and a conservative 10,000 fontons per die, the peak memory bandwidth achieves 240 TB/s using 8-byte wide register banks supporting two concurrent reads and one write access per cycle. For computations, a peak of 10 Tera-ops per die is possible.

Trade-Offs. Embedding the graph processor on a CCA platform offers a number of advantages with respect to in-brain processing. Unfortunately, nearly all of them are subject to trade-offs that reduce their effectiveness:

Speed: While the firing cycle of a neuron is measured in milliseconds, synchronous logic may be clocked at gigahertz frequencies, possibly higher if local clock domains are constrained to individual fontons or more exotic technologies are applied (Josephson junctions [7,8], quantum dots [9]). In CMOS process power dissipation increases with clock speed, often forcing the thermal constraints on practical designs even before technological clock limits are reached.

Scale: Unlike the brain, the volume of a CCA system is not restricted to that of the enclosing cranial cavity. However, crossing the die boundary may be associated with substantial performance sacrifice. Even 3-D stacking alone may reduce the number of closely interconnected fontons due to manufacturing rules. Increasing the overall processing power by connecting multiple 3-D stacks is possible, but results in a non-homogeneous structure. As the largest mass produced dies rarely exceed $500\,\mathrm{mm}^2$, manufacturing a homogeneous CCA system the size of human brain is difficult with available technology.

Connectivity: The ability to define and manipulate network properties in software is very appealing, but it still has to be mapped onto the 3-D physical mesh. This may result in increased diameter (counted in the number of interfonton links) of the implementation of a particular function. Fontons that act as routing intermediaries may have to be added to the resource pool. Increased diameter directly impacts the average number of communication hops a message must traverse on a path to destination, increasing latency, response time, and potentially energy consumed by the computation.

Energy: The power draw of a CCA implementation may be approximated through the analysis of current GPU designs, since they consist of highly replicated small processing cores operating at close to $1\,\mathrm{GHz}$. Thus, a 10,000-fonton die would use approximately $90\,\mathrm{W}$ to power 1.5 billion transistors on a $12 \times 12\,\mathrm{mm}$ chip manufactured in $28\,\mathrm{nm}$ process. This transistor count already provides for additional structures supporting off-die I/O and vertical interconnect. Stacking 10 dies brings the fonton count to 100,000 per structure in a volume just over $1\,\mathrm{cm}^3$, raising the power envelope to close to a kilowatt (!). Assuming $50\,\%$ loss of volume for power delivery, cooling, network, and structural enforcement, a brain-sized machine with peak performance of 65 Peta-ops would dissipate close to $0.6\,\mathrm{MW}$, demanding cooling water flow of about 15 liters per second ($10\,\mathrm{K}$ coolant temperature raise over ambient).

3.3   Architecture and Principles of Operation

Fonton. Figure 2 depicts the elementary building block of a CCA system. Its main components include minimal ALU, associative register file, and network interface. The processing within a fonton is controlled by a local state machine that coordinates the flow of requests that originate internally as well as those arriving from the network. There is no notion of explicit program counter; the operands necessary to execute a sequence of micro-operations are bundled with the relevant instructions to form a *token*, an atomic execution unit. Token execution modifies internal state of a fonton and potentially results in emission of tokens targeting the state of remote fontons.

The fonton is equipped with a minimal ALU that supports integer operations, along with pattern matching and bitwise permutations. Floating-point and extended integer arithmetic are higher-level functions that are synthesized

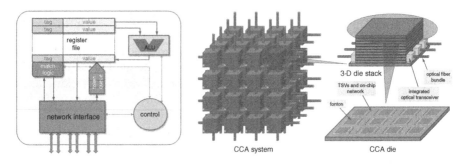

Fig. 2. *Fonton* element.   **Fig. 3.** Breakdown of CCA system components.

using fonton groups in adjacent locations. Although potentially slower, this provides unparalleled flexibility of matching the precision, resource footprint, and energy requirements to specific application.

Since physical memory is distributed across the system, traditional addressing schemes don't apply. Instead, fontons explicitly store associative tags along with the memory contents. The tags are unique for each entry, but also implement a form of wildcard addressing. As the location of fonton containing specific tag is not known a priori, part of the system manages a distributed address resolution service for non-local memory accesses by storing routing information in register files of predetermined fontons.

The network interface consists of six bidirectional links (two per dimension), connecting the neighboring fontons. A token packet, if traffic conditions permit, is sent over a link in a single cycle. The network interface can perform associative lookup on register tags to identify whether a token's target is local (the token is absorbed) or whether fonton contains related routing information (token's movement is modified).

Scaled Structures. Designing systems with large fonton counts requires special consideration (Fig. 3). Die stacking is a viable way to improve the resource count while preserving the homogeneous makeup of the device. While the inter-die interconnect has a different characteristics from that of the on-chip network, it uses matching technology – electrical signaling (for example, using Through-Silicon Vias [10]). Noting that the peak aggregate bandwidth of 2 PB/s is necessary to accommodate the maximum token flux through the stack boundary (256-byte packets assumed), a radically different approach is needed, such as on-die photonics with fiber optic links. Recent bandwidth record of just over 1 Pbit/s achieved in a 12-mode fiber [11] confirms the necessity of further development.

Operation. The remarkable similarity between the heavily cross-linked CCA hardware and vertex sets connected by edges of a graph helps efficiently map graph data structures onto execution resources. For small vertices, fontons provide sufficient storage to encode their local state and neighbor information;

otherwise, fontons are clustered to store complex node state. Token based operation is vital in implementation of graph algorithms. For example, searching a graph for vertices with certain properties would be inefficient if only one token is emitted per cycle for each link in a high-degree node. Instead, a parallel traversal may be initiated, in which tokens propagate as a 3-D "wavefront" with sufficient number of packets instantiated within few cycles after the launch of operation. This is typical of the brain as well.

4   Conclusions

Brain-inspired computing informs innovations in form and function for future generations of computing systems. Brains represent among the most complex systems known. They are exemplars of density, energy efficiency, performance, interconnectivity, 3-D structures, heterogeneity, hierarchical structures, real-time operation, intelligence, and self-aware behavior, as well as consciousness. Each of these conveys possible new concepts that may influence aspects of future computer system design and methods of operation. Brain-inspired computing is not the duplication of the brain but rather the borrowing of concepts derived from nature that suggest alternative approaches from those conventionally applied to computing. This paper has examined three general facets of brain-inspired computing structure and operation at three corresponding layers of abstraction. These are the high-level of the emergent behavior referred to as "intelligence", the low-level physical element and structure inspired by neurons, and the intermediate abstraction of the dynamic graph data structure, which is how the neurons of the brain are organized.

The CRIS project is exploring the high level abstraction of intelligence to provide a lower bound of the total resources required to achieve the functionality of one possible definition of "intelligence". The CRIS abstract architecture is defined to reflect functionality associated with and inspired by the behavior of the human brain rather than the emerging understanding of the physical distribution within the brain of distinguishable behavioral properties. While the CRIS architecture may not fully achieve intelligence, all functional components understood to contribute to intelligence is incorporated and therefore needs to be supported in real time. Therefore, analysis of means of implementing the functions and their respective duty cycles will yield the lower bound resource (time and space) assessment. The target abstract architecture, to which such high-level functionality is assumed to be implemented, is a graph-processing engine, the intermediate level brain-inspired concept.

The CCA project is exploring low-level implementation details of an innovative application of cellular automata to reflect brain-inspired neuronal properties and architecture. The key attributes to be considered are the localization of primitive operations within the separate basic components, the high degree connectivity of each component for input and output, event-driven operation, and graph topologies of structures. Conventional components do not work well in this class of high-density structures. Classical cellular automata are high density but physically of very limited interconnectivity physically and logically constrained to nearest neighbor. CCA extends the logical connectivity potentially to many orders of magnitude through packet switching treating the cellular fabric both as local operational units and global interconnectivity. CCA demonstrates that abstract graph structures can be implemented with neuronal-like packet switched components. This can provide a brain-inspired hardware implementation of the graph abstraction needed for the high-level also brain-inspired abstraction of intelligence. The implication of this work is that there are many and interrelated ways in which our emerging understanding of the brain is yielding new practical concepts for innovations in high performance computing.

References

1. Turing, A.M.: Computing Machinery and Intelligence. Mind **59**(236), 433–460 (1950)
2. Haykin, S.: Neural Networks: A Comprehensive Foundation, 1st edn. Prentice Hall PTR, Upper Saddle River (1994)
3. Toffoli, T., Margolus, N.: Cellular Automata Machines: A New Environment for Modeling. Scientific Computation. MIT Press, Cambridge (1987). http://books.google.com/books?id=HBlJzrBKUTEC
4. Doherty, P., Lukaszewicz, W., Skowron, A., Szalas, A.: Knowledge Representation Techniques - A Rough Set Approach. Studies in Fuzziness and Soft Computing, vol. 202. Springer, Heidelberg (2006)
5. Hodgkin, A.L., Huxley, A.F.: A quantitative description of membrane current and its application to conduction and excitation in nerve. J. Physiol. **117**(4), 500–544 (1952)
6. Topol, A.W.: Three-dimensional integrated circuits. IBM J. Res. Dev. **50**(4), 491–506 (2006)
7. Josephson, B.D.: Possible new effects in superconductive tunnelling. Phys. Lett. **1**, 251 (1962)
8. Likhariev, K.K., Semenov, V.K.: RSFQ logic/memory family: a new Josephson-junction digital technology for sub-terahertz-clock-frequency digital system. IEEE Trans. Appl. Supercond. **1**, 3–28 (1991)
9. Lent, C.S., Tougaw, P.D.: A device architecture for computing with quantum dots. Proc. IEEE **85**, 541–557 (1997)
10. Black, B., Annavaram, M., Brekelbaum, N., DeVale, J., Jiang, L., Loh, G.H., McCauley, D., Morrow, P., Nelson, D.W., Pantuso, D., Reed, P., Rupley, J., Sadasivan, S., Shen, J., Webb, C.: Die stacking (3D) microarchitecture. In: Proceedings of the 39th Annual IEEE/ACM International Symposium on Microarchitecture, MICRO-39, pp. 469–479, December 2006
11. NTT Corp.: World record one petabit per second fiber transmission over 50 km: equivalent to sending 5,000 HDTV videos per second over a single fiber. Press release, September 2012

Towards an Explorative Visual Analysis
of Cortical Neuronal Network Simulations

Torsten Wolfgang Kuhlen[1,3(✉)] and Bernd Hentschel[2,3]

[1] Forschungszentrum Jülich, Jülich Supercomputing Centre,
52425 Jülich, Germany
kuhlen@vr.rwth-aachen.de
[2] Virtual Reality Group, Department of Computer Science,
RWTH Aachen University, Seffenter Weg 23, 52074 Aachen, Germany
hentschel@vr.rwth-aachen.de
[3] JARA – High-Performance Computing, RWTH Aachen University,
Schinkelstraße 2, 52062 Aachen, Germany

Abstract. In neuroscientific analysis, visualization researchers have traditionally concentrated on medical imaging and microscopy data. While the visualization of experimental neuroscientific data is consequently on its way turning out increasingly mature tools, solutions for a visual analysis of neuroscientific simulation data are still in their infancy. For the assessment of large-scale neuronal network simulations, correlations between the brain's structure, function, and connectivity at the different temporal as well as spatial scales will have to be identified. The analysis of such ˋin silico experiments' requires immediate access to a number of heterogeneous data sources, e.g. connectivity information, spiking behavior of individual neurons, populations of neurons or entire brain regions. To address these requirements, we introduce a prototype of an interactive tool for the visual analysis of neuronal network models simulated via NEST. The tool strictly follows a multi-view approach, combining geometrical as well as abstract views to the data at multiple scales. Furthermore, we will discuss design parameters for adequate high-fidelity analysis workplaces, focusing on high-resolution or even immersive displays.

Keywords: Scientific visualization · In silico experiments · Multi-view analysis · Interactive Supercomputing

1 Introduction

Since Cajal's famous drawings of neuronal cell structures in the early 20th century, the discipline of scientific visualization has ever been playing a crucial role as a tool in Neuroscience. For the last two decades, visualization researchers mostly concentrated on medical imaging and microscopy data. Actually, the event of technologies like computer tomography or magnet resonance imaging has significantly pushed the field of volume visualization. A recent example which focuses on rendering massive volume data from electron microscopy can be found in Hadwiger et al. (2012). When we look at neuroscience-related papers published in the visualization community, we find that by far the largest share of publications is dealing with brain imaging data. A specific field that has

© Springer International Publishing Switzerland 2014
L. Grandinetti et al. (Eds.): BrainComp 2013, LNCS 8603, pp. 171–183, 2014.
DOI: 10.1007/978-3-319-12084-3_14

drawn significant attention in this regard is the computation and subsequent visualization of tractography data based on diffusion tensor magnetic resonance imaging (DT-MRI). DT-MRI provides a method for the assessment of white matter fiber tracts in the living human brain. The course of the fibers is estimated by measuring water diffusion in the brain. It should come at no surprise that DTI is so popular in the visualization community, since the images coming out of such visualizations are rather aesthetic and fascinating, and since visualization methods already developed in the field of Computational Fluid Dynamics, like particle tracing, could be adequately adopted and further advanced (see, among others (Weinstein et al. 1999; daSilva et al. 2001)). Recently, probabilistic tractography has attracted the attention of neuroscientists as well as visualization researchers (see Fig. 1). In contrast to the traditional deterministic approach, probabilistic tractography explicitly accounts for the uncertainty of the actual fiber tracts.

Fig. 1. Three-dimensional visualization of brain areas (gold, pink, brown) with fiber probabilistic bundle depicted by means of direct volume rendering (semi-transparent green). Imaging data provides additional anatomical context (Rick et al. 2011) (Color figure online).

When we look at the cellular level, scientific visualization has so far mostly concentrated on microscopy data that can also be captured conveniently on regular 3D volumes. The challenge here is to extract anatomical structures, like neurons and synapses, out of 2D image stacks (see Fig. 2). Examples of excellent work in this field can be found, e.g., in Roberts et al. (2011), Jeong et al. (2009), Dercksen et al. (2012), LaTorre et al. (2013).

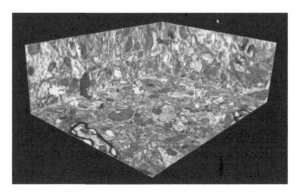

Fig. 2. Segmentation of neuronal structures out of a stack of electro-microscopy images (Morales et al. 2011)

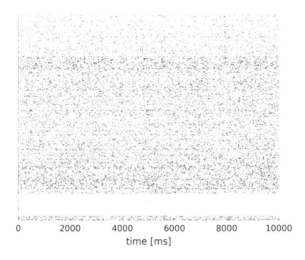

Fig. 3. Spikes dotted over time as a result from simulations of neuronal networks via NEST.

While the visualization of experimental neuroscientific data - be it on the macroscopic or the microscopic level - is on its way turning out increasingly mature tools, solutions for a visual analysis of neuroscientific simulation data are still in their infancy. Simulation in neuroscience ("in silico experiments") itself is still a rather new approach, so one might argue that the visualization community has simply not discovered this emerging field yet. This is particularly true for the simulation of large, biologically realistic neuronal networks, as they results from tools like NEURON (Carnevale and Hines 2006) or NEST (Gewaltig and Diesmann 2007). So far, neuroscientists working with these tools analyze simulation data mostly by looking at rather simplistic raster plots where neural activity is plotted over time, or at best at diagrams of derived parameters (see Fig. 3).

On these grounds, we argue that a more advanced visual analysis has the potential to further support neuroscientists to answer their research questions. Here, a close collaboration between neuroscientists and visualization scientists across their disciplines is absolutely mandatory in order to identify requirements and successfully develop valuable visualization tools for the analysis of in silico experiments. From discussions with neuroscientists at the Institute for Neuroscience and Medicine INM-6 at the Forschungszentrum Jülich, Germany, we learned that important research questions are to discover correlations of spiking activities between brain structures, function, and connectivity at the different temporal as well as spatial scales. As a consequence, highly complex and flexible data access patterns are required during an analysis of such neuroscientific data. As such, we set out to develop an interactive analysis tool that strictly follows a multi-view approach, combining geometrical as well as abstract views to the data at multiple scales. Moreover, since the neuroscientists' analysis workflow has an inherently explorative character, a useful tool should allow for an *explorative analysis*, making interactivity of the visualization a primary requirement.

After a very brief introduction to interactive visualization in the next section, the article will explain the multi-view paradigm in more detail in Sect. 3. We will demonstrate how we implemented this paradigm in a first prototype of an interactive tool for the visual analysis of NEST simulations. In Sect. 4, we will discuss some design parameters for a high-fidelity analysis workplace, focusing on high-resolution or even immersive displays. The article concludes with a summary and future work.

2 Interactive Visualization of Neuronal Network Simulation Data

In a nutshell, the discipline of scientific visualization has the goal to graphically illustrate scientific data in a way that researchers can gain insight into the phenomena they have measured in an experiment or simulated via a (high performance) computer. It was the famous computer scientist Richard Hamming, who already in the 1960's claimed that "The purpose of computing is insight, not numbers".

From an algorithmic point of view, visualization is typically described as a pipeline (Haber and McNabb 1990), starting with the simulation or experiment, and resulting in the images on some kind of display (see Fig. 4). While the end of the pipeline (rendering) refers to the discipline of computer graphics, the two arguably most interesting parts are located in the middle: filtering and mapping. Filtering describes any form of data transformation, e.g. the selection of a subset of the data, or the projection of data into a lower-dimensional space. Mapping is concerned with the actual conversion of data into graphical primitives from which scientists can eventually – i.e. after rendering – draw meaningful insight. In our mind, it is essential that domain scientists and visualization experts collaborate very closely in the design of these steps in order to come up with adequate solutions. Questions have to be answered like which data access patterns, which data processing methods, and which visualization metaphors have to be realized. Obviously, the answers to these questions heavily depend on the characteristics of the data like e.g., its size, dynamics, or dimensionality, but also on what research questions domain experts have with regard to their data.

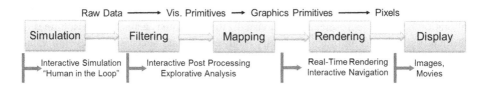

Fig. 4. The visualization pipeline with different interactivity levels

There are multiple levels of interactivity, depending on which parts of the visualization pipeline are made interactive. If no step in the pipeline at all is interactive, movies or just static images are produced in an off-line visualization process, mostly for publication or marketing purposes. Moreover, in a purely confirmative analysis, such a non-interactive approach can be appropriate for validating or discarding a hypothesis about a phenomenon in the data. This confirmative usage scenario is also targeted by solutions that offer real-time rendering and interactive navigation. This allows users to intuitively look at the data from multiple perspectives.

For the interactive rendering of large neuronal networks simulated via NEURON, good progress has been made recently in the Blue Brain Project (see http://bluebrain. epfl.ch/). Massively parallel rendering in distributed GPU clusters and advanced view-frustrum culling have been applied here to achieve real-time navigation through large populations of neurons with realistically shaped soma-branch-connections (Lasserre et al. 2012; Hernando et al. 2012). Furthermore, level-of-detail techniques have been leveraged, meaning that the data is available at multiple resolutions, and the details are only rendered when the experts decide to zoom into the data (see Fig. 5).

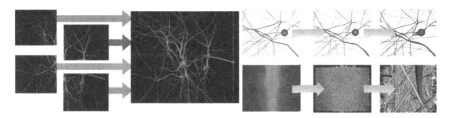

Fig. 5. Real-time navigation through large populations of simulated neurons via massively parallel rendering (left) and level-of-detail techniques (right).

Although these kinds of interactive geometrical rendering provide a significant contribution, they will not be able to answer important research questions on their own. Only if the preceding steps in the visualization pipeline provide interactive response times as well, the analysis process becomes truly explorative. Here, the scientist can directly operate on the simulation raw data and interactively define new visualizations in a trial-and-error process to find new hypotheses and assess the characteristics of a simulated phenomenon. In visualization science, providing tools that enable such an explorative analysis poses a great challenge in terms of performance. For quite some years now, the size of computed simulation results has increased faster than the possibilities of data processing and data analysis.

In the specific case of computational neuroscience, it turns out that a level of interactivity is needed that goes even beyond a sheer explorative post hoc analysis of computed simulation results. In fact, the notion of in silico experiments with large-scale, simulated neuronal networks would require a *computational steering* approach, where it is possible to directly influence the running simulation in an interactive and explorative manner. Only by such a "human-in-the-loop" philosophy, it will become possible to effectively gain insight into the structure and function of biologically realistic neuronal networks.

When neuroscientists strive to simulate neuronal networks up to the full brain scale, like in the European Flagship "The Human Brain Project", there will not even be the choice of traditional post processing. Here, a suitable visualization software framework must provide a tight coupling between visualization and simulation itself, which eventually leads to the concept of *interactive supercomputing*. Data size will become so huge here in both, spatial as well as temporal resolution, that it will be difficult to move or even store the data produced in such simulations. In the mid-term, *in situ visualization* as a special variation of interactive supercomputing is a promising option, if not the only possible strategy. In situ techniques produce the visualization on-the-fly, i.e. at simulation runtime, whereas the raw data is discarded once the visualization processing is done. Unfortunately, the explorative character of the visual analysis gets lost in the process, since the in situ approach obviously requires the visualization parameters to be fixed in advance.

If the simulation data is extremely huge or complex, like in the neuroscience domain, and if interactive response times are required over parts or even the complete visualization pipeline, a rather complex infrastructure is necessary. To achieve interactivity, there is no other option than to use High Performance Compute (HPC) resources not only for the simulation itself, but to leverage them for the visualization and analysis process as well. Unfortunately, how a powerful and flexible software framework should look like is still an open question in the visualization community. Although there are first software tools that combine massively parallel visualization computations and in situ capabilities, they are still in their infancy. Moreover, they are mostly tailored to simulation data from the field of Computational Engineering Science; hence it is not straightforward to adapt them to neuroscientific data. Consequently, it is a declared goal of the Human Brain Project to develop such an advanced interactive supercomputing framework. This, however, poses a formidable challenge.

3   A Multi-view Visualization of Brain Simulations

Apart from sheer interactivity and performance, user interface and workflow aspects represent further key challenges. In order to become a widely accepted part of a neuroscientist's daily work, an analysis tool has to feature an intuitive user interface and concise visualization metaphors; in addition it has – most importantly – to integrate seamlessly with existing workflows.

The identification of correlations between the brain's structure, function, and connectivity at the different temporal as well as spatial scales is essential for the assessment of large-scale neuronal network simulations. An understanding of these processes across scales requires immediate access to a number of heterogeneous data sources, e.g. connectivity information, spiking behavior of individual neurons, populations of neurons or entire brain regions, etc. To this end, multi-view visualizations promise to be a useful visualization design. The idea of multi-view visualization is to combine a number of specialized information displays and semantically link their content in order to interactively explore possible relationships in the data. In this context linking means that changes in either view are automatically transferred to all other views. Linking may relate to both, spatial as well as temporal aspects of the data.

In a close collaboration with domain scientists from the INM-6, we are currently developing an analysis framework that consistently builds on this multi-view paradigm. It combines structural and dynamic information via geometrical and more abstract views in order to effectively and efficiently support neuroscientists in the exploration phase of a neuronal network model analysis.

The central view in this framework consists of a geometrical representation of brain areas (see Fig. 6). In this central "control view", the aggregate neural activity per brain region is indicated via color-coding. Individual areas can arbitrarily be selected; each

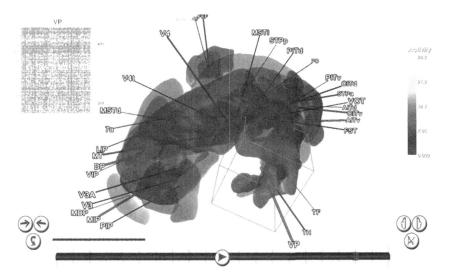

Fig. 6. Macroscopic "brain view" of a Macaque visual cortex model simulated with NEST. Upon selection of individual areas (green box), more detailed information is provided about the respective area, e.g. the spiking activity of neurons (top left) (Color figure online).

selection brings up the corresponding raster plot (see also Fig. 3). These plots, well-known from standard neuroscientific toolkits, allow for an analysis of the spiking activity in a population-resolved manner. They are synchronized in time with the macroscopic geometrical view, allowing users to quickly assess the interaction between microscopic and macroscopic scales.

Beyond these basic views, our tool offers dynamic bar plots of mean spike rates in each area, which in turn is semantically linked to the other views. This provides a quick overview of the model's activity, for instance to check whether the activity is too high or too low, or if there exist any specific oscillations. Additional plot views show time-varying mean activities for specific areas, revealing the mean rate at a more detailed level (see Fig. 7).

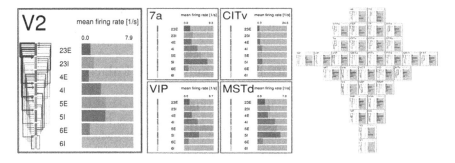

Fig. 7. Dynamic bar plots on mean spike rates – Overview of all areas (left), detailed views on populations for specific areas (middle), small multiples of all areas sorted by area hierarchy (right).

Beyond these geometrical and abstract, diagram-style views, we are currently developing and adding dynamic graph visualization views which will depict connectivity information in the form of either node-link diagrams or matrix views. This step has been motivated by related neuroscience work on connectivity (see, e.g. (Nordlie and Plesser 2010; Gerhard et al. 2011)). So far, two different graph-style views have been implemented (see Fig. 8): a connection graph where the diameter of the arrows indicates the connection strength between any two brain areas, and a highly dynamic "flux graph", which depicts the instantaneous activity flux between areas. Once more, all these views are semantically linked, helping the neuroscientists to reveal characteristic behaviors of network simulations. The overall tool and its functionality are described in more detail in Nowke et al. (2013).

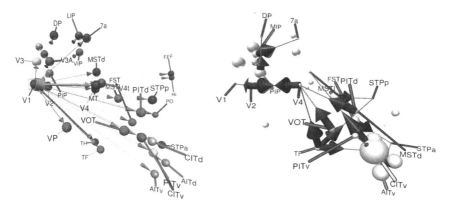

Fig. 8. Connection graph – arrow diameters represent the connection strength between a specific area and all other areas (left), and "activity flux" graph- arrow diameters represent instantaneous flux between areas (right)

We carried out initial expert reviews with neuroscientists based on a model simulating 32 areas of the visual cortex of a macaque brain which has been simulated using the NEST code. These studies indicate that a multi-view design, as developed in Aachen and Jülich, does not only significantly support the explorative analysis of simulated neuronal network models, but also serves as an important communication tool to explain models to stakeholders and a broader public across disciplines.

4   Towards a High-Fidelity Brain Analysis Workplace

While the prototype tool introduced in the previous section exclusively focuses on an explorative analysis of a single neuronal network simulation run, in the medium term, we strive to provide a much more comprehensive framework, which will not only support users to conduct a comparative analysis between multiple simulations with varying network parameters or even different simulation algorithms, but will also integrate experimental data for direct comparison. To achieve such an integrative analysis, the approach outlined above has to be extended in several ways. First, the framework has to provide defined extension points at which specialized views for a wide range of heterogeneous data items can be added. This should cater for data from multiple sources, multiple data modalities, and data at different spatio-temporal scales (from the molecular up to the macroscopic level). Second, the semantic linking across these views has to be described in a more abstract fashion, such that views that have been contrived at different points in time – i.e. that cannot possibly account for each other's existence – can seamlessly work together, nonetheless. Finally, the multi-view paradigm must work across multiple datasets, quite possibly from different applications and from different compute/storage sites.

Although web-based analysis tools are required, because they promise a convenient remote access to simulations and data from the scientist's desk, from a performance and infrastructural perspective, they obviously will not be able to adequately support a comprehensive, explorative multi-view approach. For a high-fidelity brain analysis workplace, a large, ultrahigh-resolution display might be essential, providing enough screen real estate to carry multiple views simultaneously, allowing users to switch between them at the blink of an eye. To this end, tiled display walls have become rather popular for the analysis of scientific data. These systems no longer rely on projection technology, but instead consist of multiple LCD monitors arranged in a matrix layout. In fact, such walls are envisaged in the Human Brain Project to serve as "cockpits" to steer and analyze neuronal network simulations and other neuroscientific data (see Fig. 9).

Fig. 9. Visual analysis of a NEURON simulation at a high resolution tiled display wall (Courtesy of the KAUST Visualization Laboratory at the King Abdullah University for Science and Technology and the Blue Brain Project, École Polytechnique Fédérale de Lausanne)

Since a simulation of biologically realistic networks, but also high-resolution experimental data like, for instance, polarized light imaging microscopy reveal highly complex three-dimensional structures, a stereoscopic display will help to assess complex spatial relationships in the data. A viewer-centered projection (VCP), where the user's head is tracked in order to provide a "quasi-holographic" view, will even further enhance the intuitiveness of a visual data inspection. A combination of stereoscopy and VCP eventually leads to *Immersive Virtual Reality* techniques (IVR). The probably most renowned immersive display is the so-called CAVE, where multiple rear-projected walls are arranged to form a room where the user is then fully surrounded by a virtual environment (Cruz-Neira et al. 1992). Figure 10 shows a concrete technical realization of such a CAVE at RWTH Aachen University. IVR does not only make it possible to visually perceive and explore three-dimensional geometrical object as if they really existed in physical space, but additionally allows for a direct interaction with objects in 3D space.

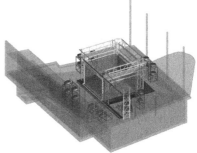

Fig. 10. The "aixCAVE" at RWTH Aachen University. By a combination of multiple rear-projection walls, stereoscopy and motion tracking, the user gets an immersive experience. In modern CAVEs like the one shown here, multiple projectors are used per projection wall in order to provide the high resolutions required in scientific data analysis.

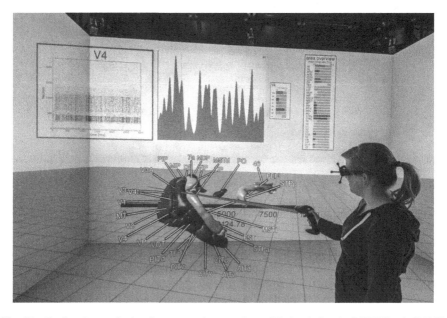

Fig. 11. Explorative analysis of a neuronal network model simulation in RWTH's aixCAVE. Like in the desktop version, multiple geometrical and diagram-style views are semantically linked to reveal correlations between structure, function and connectivity.

It is still an open question whether or not IVR techniques make sense in the context of neuroscientific visualization. In other domains of Computational Engineering Science, like Computational Fluid Dynamics, numerous success stories of fully-fledged solutions (Hentschel et al. 2008) as well as systematic studies (Laha et al. 2012; Laha et al. 2014) have already proven potential of IVR to significantly enhance explorative analysis processes. A first promising expert study with neuroscientists, who worked with a preliminary IVR version of the analysis tool introduced in the previous section (see Fig. 11), indicates that Virtual Reality techniques in fact support the visual analysis of large neuronal network models.

Making use of IVR is not a black-or-white decision. Fully immersive displays like a CAVE are only the top of a display pyramid. For neuroscientific analysis purposes single stereoscopic projection walls equipped with tracking for VCP and direct interaction might be appropriate already. Moreover, small semi-immersive VR systems that fit into office environments have recently become more and more popular. All in all, further research is necessary to find out what the "ultimate" display and interaction techniques are to support the Neuroscience community in an optimal way.

5 Summary

While the visual analysis of experimental neuroscientific data is an active and advanced field of research, analysis tools for an explorative analysis of simulation data related to large, biologically realistic neuronal network models are still in their infancy. So far, neuroscientists analyze the results of such "in silico experiments" mostly by looking at rather simplistic plots or conduct statistical analyses. In this article, we described an interactive tool for a visual analysis of such in silico experiments that follows a multiview strategy, semantically linking geometrical as well as abstract views to the data at the multiple scales in order to effectively and efficiently support neuroscientists in the exploration of neuronal network models. In the longer term, we strive at a much more comprehensive framework, where it will not only be possible to conduct a comparative analysis across multiple simulation runs with varying network parameters or even different simulation algorithms, but also a comparison of simulation and experimental data. To achieve such an integrative analysis, a semantic linking must be extended towards data from multiple modalities and sources. We suggest large, ultrahigh-resolution displays or even Immersive Virtual Reality displays to become the platform of a high-fidelity brain analysis workplace, because they provide enough display real estate to simultaneously depict multiple views.

In the EU-Flagship "The Human Brain Project" it is a designated goal to simulate neuronal network models up to the size of the whole human brain with its 10^{11} neurons and 10^{15} synapses. While the neuroscientists' research questions require complex and highly flexible access patterns to the simulation data, it is extremely expensive or even infeasible to store or move data at such a scale. It is still a long way to realize a visualization software framework that is able to cope with such huge and highly dynamic neuroscientific data. Such a framework must necessarily provide a tight coupling between visualization and simulation itself, eventually leading to the notion of interactive supercomputing.

References

Carnevale, N.T., Hines, M.L.: The NEURON Book. Cambridge University Press, Cambridge (2006)

Cruz-Neira, C., Sandin, D.J., DeFanti, T.A., Kenyon, R.V., Hart, J.C.: The CAVE: Audio visual experience automatic virtual environment. Commun. ACM **35**(6), 64–72 (1992)

Dercksen, V., Oberlaender, M., Sakmann, B., Hege, H.-C.: Interactive visualization – a key prerequisite for reconstruction of anatomically realistic neural networks. In: Linsen, L., Hagen, H., Hamann, B., Hege, H.-C. (eds.) Visualization in Medicine and Life Sciences II, pp. 27–44. Springer, Berlin (2012)

Gewaltig, M.-O., Diesmann, M.: NEST (NEural Simulation Tool). Scholarpedia **2**(4), 1430 (2007)

Gerhard, S., Daducci, A., Lemkaddem, A., Meuli, R., Thiran, J.P., Hagmann, P.: The connectome viewer toolkit: an open source framework to manage, analyze, and visualize connectomes. Front. Neuroinform. **5**, 3 (2011)

Haber, R.B., McNabb, D.A.: Visualization idioms: A conceptual model for scientific visualization systems. In: Shriver, B., Neilson, G.M., Rosenblum, L.J. (eds.) Visualization in Scientific Computing, pp. 74–93. IEEE Computer Society Press, Los Alamitos (1990)

Hadwiger, M., Beyer, J., Jeong, W.-K., Pfister, H.: Interactive volume exploration of petascale microscopy data streams using a visualization-driven virtual memory approach. IEEE Trans. Vis. Comput. Graph. **18**(12), 2285–2294 (2012)

Hentschel, B., Tedjo, I., Probst, M., Wolter, M., Behr, M., Bischof, C., Kuhlen, T.: interactive blood damage analysis for ventricular assist devices. IEEE Trans. Vis. Comput. Graph. **14**(6), 1515–1522 (2008)

Hernando, J., Schürmann, F., Pastor, L.: Towards real-time visualization of detailed neural tissue models: view frustum culling for parallel rendering. In: IEEE Symposium on Biological Data Visualization (BioVis), pp. 25–32 (2012)

Jeong, W., Beyer, J., Hadwiger, M., Vazquez, A., Pfister, H., Whitaker, R.T.: Scalable and interactive segmentation and visualization of neural processes in EM datasets. IEEE Trans. Vis. Comput. Graph. **15**(6), 1505–1514 (2009)

Laha, B., Sensharma, K., Schiffbauer, J.D., Bowman, D.A.: Effects of immersion on visual analysis of volume data. IEEE Trans. Vis. Comput. Graph. **18**(4), 597–606 (2012)

Laha, B., Bowman, D.A., Socha, J.J.: Effects of VR system fidelity on analyzing isosurface visualization of volume datasets. IEEE Trans. Vis. Comput. Graph. **20**(4), 513–522 (2014)

Lasserre, S., Hernando, J., Hill, S., Schürmann, F., De Miguel Anasagasti, P., Jaoude, G., Markram, H.: A neuron membrane mesh representation for visualization of electrophysiological simulations. IEEE Trans. Vis. Comput. Graph. **18**(2), 214–227 (2012)

LaTorre, A., Alonso-Nanclares, L., Muelas, S., Peña, J.M., DeFelipe, J.: Segmentation of neuronal nuclei based on clump splitting and a two-step binarization of images. Expert Syst. Appl. **40**(16), 6521–6530 (2013)

Morales, J., Alonso-Nanclares, L., Rodríguez, J.R., DeFelipe, J., Rodríguez, Á., Merchán-Pérez, Á.: Espina: a tool for the automated segmentation and counting of synapses in large stacks of electron microscopy images. Front. Neuroanat. **5**, 18 (2011)

Nordlie, E., Plesser, H.E.: Visualizing neuronal network connectivity with connectivity pattern tables. Front. Neuroinformat. **3**, 39 (2010)

Nowke, C., Schmidt, M., van Albada, S., Eppler, J., Bakker, R., Diesmann, M., Hentschel, B., Kuhlen, T.: VisNEST – Interactive analysis of neural activity data. In: IEEE Symposium on Biological Data Visualization (in Conjunction with IEEE VIS 2013), pp. 65–72 (2013)

Rick, T., von Kapri, A., Caspers, S., Amunts, K., Zilles, K., Kuhlen, T.: Visualization of probabilistic fiber tracts in virtual reality. In: J. Westwood et al. (eds.) Studies in Health Technology and Informatics, vol. 163, pp. 486–492. IOS Press, Amsterdam (2011)

da Silva, M., Zhang, S., Demiralp, C., Laidlaw, D.: Visualizing diffusion tensor volume differences. In: IEEE Visualization Conference (2001)

Roberts, M., Jeong, W., Vazquez-Reina, A., Unger, M., Bischof, H., Lichtman, J., Pfister, H.: Neural process reconstruction from sparse user scribbles. In: IEEE Symposium on Biological Data Visualization (BioVis) (2011)

Schmitt, S., Evers, J.F., Duch, C., Scholz, M., Obermayer, K.: New methods for the computer-assisted 3D Reconstruction of Neurons from Confocal Image Stacks. NeuroImage **23**(4), 1283–1298 (2004)

Weinstein, D.M., Kindlmann, G.L., Lundberg, E.C.: Tensorlines: Advection-diffusion based propagation through diffusion tensor fields. In: IEEE Visualization Conference, pp. 249–253 (1999)

Visualization of Large-Scale Neural Simulations

Juan B. Hernando, Carlos Duelo, and Vicente Martin[✉]

CeSViMa – Centro de Supercomputación Y Visualización de Madrid,
Universidad Politécnica de Madrid, Campus de Montegancedo,
Boadilla Del Monte, 28660 Madrid, Spain
jhernando@fi.upm.es, {cduelo,vicente}@cesvima.upm.es

Abstract. The widespread availability of modern infrastructures able to process large amounts of data and run sophisticated models of complex phenomena, is making simulation-based research a usual technique among the scientific tools. The impact of these techniques is so large, that they have been touted as the new paradigms for scientific discovery: the third, in relation to large-scale simulations, and fourth, in relation to data-intensive computing. In the traditional approach, the results of complex simulations are typically very large data sets that are later mined for knowledge. In a more dynamic approach, the user interacts with the simulation, steering it and visualizing the results in an exploratory way in order to gain knowledge. If this is properly done, it can not only make better use of the available resources, but also produce insight that would not be possible in a static, post-mortem analysis of the results. However, it is not easy to include live visualization and analysis in a workflow that has been designed to fit the available HW&SW infrastructure and to finish with a set of files for off-line study. This traditional process could very well turn into unfeasible if computing continues its way to a future limited by the storage capabilities, thus making impractical the storage for later analysis paradigm typical of today's simulations. In this cases, having a scientist in the loop, aided by a set of analysis and data reduction techniques, will be necessary to understand the results and produce new science. The purpose of the present paper is to outline the main problems that have to be solved to visualize simulation results with an application to the Human Brain Project. The complexity and needs of present day visualization tools in this domain will be exemplified using RTNeuron, a code to represent neural activity in close to real time.

1   Introduction

Visualization is a key technology to understand complex phenomena. Human cognition is very well suited to find patterns and trends in visual presentations. In fact, it is estimated that half of the neurons in the human brain are associated to vision, allowing to comprehend significantly more complexity through visualization than using other techniques. This was realized soon, and visual data representations have been used extensively since very early [1]. It was only much more recently that the need to explore the results of sophisticated simulations

© Springer International Publishing Switzerland 2014
L. Grandinetti et al. (Eds.): BrainComp 2013, LNCS 8603, pp. 184–197, 2014.
DOI: 10.1007/978-3-319-12084-3_15

and experimental data, paired with advances in computer graphics made computer based visualization practical for general use. Powerful computers made possible the exploration of complex models in large parameter space and simulations that were previously unfeasible, became routine. The amount of data to be analyzed grew very rapidly, requiring the development of new techniques to extract useful knowledge. Visualization was born from the idea of taking advantage of the visual capabilities of the brain to help understanding these otherwise intractable data sets. Going one step further, the same capability could also be used to put a human in the simulation loop, allowing to interactively guide the simulation for an active exploration and discovery.

Scientific Visualization as a discipline is relatively modern. It received a large impulse from the seminal 1987 NSF report "Visualization and Scientific Computing" [2], where most of the modern ideas were already present: exploration, steering, communication and even debugging were mentioned. Curiously enough, brain structure and function was highlighted among a dozen scientific research opportunities. Visualization infrastructures were also discussed and, although technology has moved a long way since then, the basic paradigm did not changed that much until a few years ago, when the explosion in available data [31] and distributed computing and storage built another compelling case with information visualization and visual analytics at its core.

In a typical scientific visualization scenario, [3] a large simulation is run in a supercomputer in batch mode. As much data as storage allows is recorded for later off-line analysis. This analysis involves the reduction of data in several orders of magnitude, and it is usually done in a different computer. The data is prepared for visualization, typically in yet another computer or visualization cluster. This is an example of the postprocessing that is nowadays the most usual technique to use visualization in large-scale simulations. It lacks interactivity and there is no possibility to have a scientist in the loop controlling the simulation. It is an effective use of resources only in the sense that supercomputer time allocation is optimal due to the use of a queuing system, but it neither allows for discovery through exploration nor change the simulation parameters on the fly. Both techniques can lead to potential savings, whether because a simulation is not progressing as expected and has to be killed before completion or because preliminary results require to explore different situations from those initially envisioned. Sometimes there exists the possibility of running a simulation and having, at the same time, a visualization cluster that can communicate with the main simulation machine through a high bandwidth network. In this situation, the visualization calculations are done in the visualization cluster using data directly from the simulation. This coprocessing can be done online or offline, depending on the available resources and type of simulation, but it requires a large amount of data movement among machines, and data movement is a major issue in large-scale computing.

The evolution of high performance computers has followed a path that today is dominated by commodity CPUs and subsystems. Whereas in 2001 the Linpack benchmark report [4] listed, in the first page of the ranking of the fastest CPUs in the world, only vector processors specially built for scientific computing, in 2004, only commodity CPUs remained. The cost effectiveness of the big machines was beaten by day to day, ordinary computers with CPUs built for the mass-market of servers and workstations. A SW infrastructure as well as cheap communication HW were also in place by that time and this resulted in clusters becoming the new de facto architecture for HPC. The way to increase its power beyond the usual Moore's Law gains, was then driven by adding more and more processors. Parallelization and scalability were the new mantra while the performance raised from the gigaflop to the teraflop and then to the petaflop. Ultimately, new limits have been hit and while coprocessors are helping to achieve still more performance, the increase in power consumption, the memory wall, the need to scale to millions of cores, etc. are eroding an exponential growth in speed that has been maintained for decades [5]. It is widely believed that exascale levels of performance for a reasonable set of applications and within a reasonable power budget will be much more difficult to achieve than the previous Tera and Peta milestones. We will get there only through the systematic improvement of several key technologies. Even mass-market constraints could also play a role in the how and when we will achieve Exaflop performance. The large-scale simulations panorama is bound to have different constraints, and one of the most likely is linked to data movement. In this new world, FLOPS will be cheap, while I/O and data transfer will be expensive. We are used to gigaflop computers with seberal gigabytes of memory. Petaflop class computers might still have Petabyte memory[1], but an exaflop computer is not expected to have an exabyte memory. Memory bandwidths to different memory levels will scale differently and the energy cost of moving data has to be taken into account. Hence, in planning for the visualization and steering of the simulations in an exaflop capable computer, a key issue will be to limit data movement.

Today, transferring or storing the large amounts of raw data that requires the postprocessing or coprocessing paradigms is costly in time and resources. In a memory and I/O bandwidth constrained world, this could turn these approaches into unfeasible. A better solution would be to avoid data movement altogether by reducing or summarizing the data produced in situ. Only the reduced data will be transferred for storage and offline analysis or for visualization. In situ processing has another advantage as a means to simplify and summarize the data in order to be visualized during the simulation and used by a scientist in the loop, allowing to steer the simulation and help the discovery by exploration. In situ processing is, however, not a very popular approach today. On one hand, current supercomputers are not specifically designed for this and scientists are unwilling to use the scarce supercomputing resources assigned to a project for visualization calculations and, on the other, integrating visualization with calculation demands resources in the form of time or of an specialist in visualization,

---

[1] Main memory (not in the accelerators) in the fastest Top500 machines now in production (early 2014) or soon to be released is 0.6 PB for the 27 Pflop/s Titan at ORNL, USA, and 1PB for the expected 54.9 Pflop/s Tianhe-2, to be installed at NUDT, China. An exaflop computer is expected around 2020.

who is not always available. To respond to its main challenge of not duplicating memory, simulation and visualization codes must share data in memory. Also, it must not compromise on the resiliency of the simulation and the overhead must be small and not spoil its scaling characteristics. Along with keeping the amount of visualization processing low compared with the total load, this means to balance the visualization load together with the simulation. This might be difficult in practice due to the different nature of both processes and that the data or work distribution used by the simulation might be very different than the one used by the visualization. The current lack of specialized graphics hardware and software stack in most supercomputers -something that might change in a possible design of an interactive supercomputer- does not help to keep low the relative load of visualization vs. simulation.

Human brain simulations are expected to proceed in a multiscale way, with molecular scale calculations conveying information to be used at cell scale, from cell to circuit and so on till the higher levels of organization are reached. From a visualization perspective, this means that many different types of data, possibly from different origins and involved in different processes at different scales have the potential to be represented in a interactive session. From a data perspective, the overall situation is not very different from the situation in visual analytics and its general goal of facilitating the exploration and interaction with big and complex data [6]. Visual Analytics is defined on top of three layers: Visualization to provide exploration capabilities and abstractions to allow reasoning on the extracted information; analytics, to provide the data reduction and information extraction capabilities; and data management to store, retrieve and distribute data for visualization and analytics. In the human brain simulation case, an additional interface with the running simulation should be present, and the analytics layer should be prepared to interact also with the simulation. Most existing analytical systems are not prepared for this interaction. In many cases this is because today many exploratory tasks run on much smaller data and analysis and visualization give results fast. On exascale data this will not be the case, however visualizations have to be presented fast even although the underlying calculation has not yet finished. A new breed of algorithms with the ability of quickly present approximate results that can be iteratively refined when needed should be developed [7]. In an in situ paradigm, the resources to run these algorithms and the corresponding visualization have to be shared with the main simulation and meet the requirements for a fluid interaction (i.e.: less than 100ms of reaction time for an interaction and that actions should be completed in less than 10 seconds, depending on the cognitive cost [30]) this leads to problems with the way in which current supercomputers are designed and managed and that have yet to be solved. Likewise, the data management layer to support extremely large data and the needs of visualization still needs to be developed. Smaller scale solutions resort to in-memory databases, an approach that might not be feasible for the envisioned exascale-class machines.

The successful integration of these elements in interactive workflows will be key for the successful exploitation of simulation-based science. Although much work has been done, it is a complex challenge and there is still much to do. To exemplify what is the state of the art today in visualization for the exploration of brain simulations we will present the status of RTNeuron, a real time visualizer for cortical circuit simulations. This is a specific piece in the visualization layer. The description of its requisites, arquitecture and performance will give a hint of the complexity of what will be the future visualization infrastructure for the human brain.

2   Case Study: Cortical Circuit Simulations and RTNeuron

The Blue Brain Project [11] (BBP) started in the École Polytechnique Fédérale de Lausanne in 2005 as the first attempt to build a computational brain model created by unifying the known data in a systematic way. The final goal is to allow neuroscientists to conduct *in silico* research in the human brain function and dysfunction. The first stages have been focused on the detailed modelling of a small piece of tissue of the rat cortex and providing the software tool-chain that allow its simulation on a supercomputer.

The Human Brain Project (HBP), one of the EU FET Flagship initiatives, builds on the BBP, but has a wider scope and is backed by a much larger academic consortium. The HBP extends the BBP's main goal in several areas, a prominent one is to apply the outcomes of brain research in the development of new technology such as neuromorphic computing and brain-inspired robotics.

Although in the context of the HBP many different simulation methods will be integrated in truly multi-scale models of the brain, the two main approaches for large neuron network simulation are based on point neurons on the one hand, and electrical models of detailed neurons on the other. The mathematical tool for the first is the leaky integrate-and-fire model whereas detailed neurons are modeled using cable models and Hodgkin-Huxley equations. NEST [8] is the usual framework of choice for large scale point neuron simulations and NEURON [9] for cable based models. Each method has its own benefits and drawbacks, and they are, in fact, complementary approaches to the ultimate goal of simulating a whole brain.

Visualization and analysis techniques specifically developed for point neuron simulations are as valuable as those devoted to morphologically detailed models, even more when they can be combined to address the problems of the multi-scale scenarios foreseen for the HBP simulation technology. However, for the scope of this paper, we will restrict ourselves to the problems pertaining to the visualization of morphologically detailed simulations only, which is the hardest case. In particular, we will focus on RTNeuron, a custom software tool developed in the context of the BBP for the post-mortem interactive visualization of cortical circuit simulations. We will analyze its shortcomings and requirements in order to adapt it to the paradigm shift that interactive supercomputing entails.

2.1 Circuit Building, Electrical Model Creation and Simulation Running

The simulations carried out currently in the BBP model a piece or cortical tissue that is believed to be the minimal unit of information processing in the neocortex, the *cortical column*. These simulations contain from 10,000 up to several 100,000 neurons, depending on the number of columns and the estimations of neurons per column used. This model is already capable of showing activity patterns that can be found on in vivo specimens [15].

The circuit is created by first reconstructing cells taken from samples of electrophysiology experiments. The geometrical template for the cortical column is an hexagonal prism of 320 nm of radius and 2 mm of height. Multiple instances of representatives of the different cell types are distributed inside this template based on known statistical information about their spatial distributions. Touches between axons and dendrites of different cells are detected and converted into functional connections, i.e. synapses, also based on knowledge from the available literature. More details of these processes are described by Hay et al. [13] and Hill et al. [14].

Electrical modelling of single neurons is based on multi-compartment cable models using Hodgkin-Huxley equations. How the parameters are fit to reproduce the behaviour of the different electrical types is described by Druckmann et al. [12] and Hay et al. [13].

The circuit simulations are performed using a version of NEURON [10]. These simulations are run on a Blue Gene P supercomputer using up to several thousands processors where a second of biological time takes in the order of one hour to be completed. The typical output of a simulation is a record with the spike times of all neurons. Additionally it is possible to generate reports that record the values over time of a single variable for a selected set of electrical compartments.

2.2 Visualization of Detailed Cortical Circuit Simulations

From the point of view of analysis, some users have very specific procedures which are well established and visualization can only help enhance the presentation of these results for communication. However, many other users do not have a clear idea of what to look for and this requires an exploratory analysis tool. In these situations, effective visualization can help in tasks like the navigation of data sets, the selection and identification of circuit elements with features that can be easily identified visually, the comparison of different simulation ensembles, etc. In some other cases, for example in circuit building, visualization can be used to verify the correctness of the model and debug possible issues.

Exploratory analysis tools need to be suited for the application domain and designed using a user-centric approach whenever possible. However, they must provide enough flexibility for the users to configure them for their personal needs. In the analysis of cortical circuits, programmability is a highly desired feature, particularly for the case of computational neuroscientist because most of the analysis is already based on scripting and pipeline design. Another important issue in an interactive scenario is that simulation, analysis and visualization must be able to communicate and exchange information easily and efficiently.

The best domain specificity is provided by custom tailored solutions, specially in this case, because no off-the-shelf solutions are available for complex neuronal network visualization and analysis. However, many software problems are common to other domains and it makes sense to solve them just once. This last statement will become specially true for the frameworks that will be required for interactive supercomputing at the exascale, where it will become totally unpractical to solve the same problems over and over. Currently, implementations of the usual data flow model [16] of visualization and analysis applications—using tools such as VTK [27] and its derivatives—fulfill many of the requirements. However, domain specific techniques for visual mappings and rendering still need to be developed.

In terms of data sizes relevant to a visualization, the reconstruction of cell morphologies consist of polylines connected in a tree structure, where each point is assigned a radius. On average, a morphological skeleton has 4,700 segments, but this figure varies greatly depending on the cell type (excitatory cells are usually large and, in general, those that have long range connections). The network graph has a degree of connectivity that has no equivalent in any other domain. Each cell forms an average number of 30,000 synapses with other cells, which is far beyond the state-of-art in graph visualization. Polygonal meshes that model the cell membrane can be obtained from the skeletal morphologies [19]. These models have 150,000 triangles and 75,000 vertices per neuron on average. So far, the morphological models are instanced several times within a circuit, but in the short term every morphology will be completely unique. The electrical model consist of around 300 electrical compartments per cell, and the output of a simulation where a single scalar value of single float precision (typically the membrane voltage) per electrical compartment is recorded is almost 1.2 GB for 1000 cells, 1 s of biological time reported at 0.1 s intervals. This looks like a small size, but it is just the bare minimum for just one variable of a small circuit in a small simulation. A naive extrapolation of this numbers to the estimated 100 billion of neurons in the human brain amounts to about one hundred exabytes. By way of contrast, all the information in the world in 2007, including movies, etc. optimally compressed would amount to about 300 exabytes [20].

One of the first decisions to take when designing a visualization system is whether to represent the information preserving its geometrical details or to use abstract representations that filter non-relevant information depending on the use case. Abstract representations are appealing as they can reduce the visual complexity and yet be very informative, however this requires a clear idea of what are the user cases. In the RTNeuron case, detailed visualization has been initially pursued for several reasons:

– It was required for media production for dissemination purposes.
– It can be used to gain a better understanding of the circuit structure and function, for example applying rendering techniques that mimic the results

obtained from experimental imaging techniques such as voltage sensitive dyes, but without some of their physical limitations like diffraction limits, accessibility of tissue areas, selectability of cell sub-populations, reuse of samples for different purposes, ...

– Based on user feedback, it can be the starting point for the design of more informative and comprehensible abstract representations.

For detailed visualization, neurons pose very particular geometrical problems, the more so within the context of a whole circuit. Neurons are geometrically intricate objects with very thin branches compared to the overall volume they occupy. Inside a circuit, the branches are strongly entwined, making it difficult to visually follow a single branch in the context of the full circuit. For a detailed visualization of the circuit these characteristics imply a lot of visual clutter, aliasing problems (due to the sub-pixel geometry size) and a computational expensive rendering.

Cluttering can be addressed by allowing interactive selection of objects and modification of the attributes that determine the visual appearance. Configuring the appearance, by manipulation of the color maps, for example, makes possible to highlight important features and cull away unimportant details. One visual property which is interesting is transparency because it can provide a simple mapping from object properties to visual importance in the final image. However, transparency increases the computational complexity because the rendering algorithm has to sort the contribution of each polygon at each pixel. State of the art algorithms to solve this problem rely on sorting at the pixel level [17], so there's no need to do any view-dependent sorting of the polygons. Rendering complexity can be reduced using level of detail representations, however the complexity of large circuits still requires parallel rendering solutions, specially if unique morphologies are used. Aliasing can be solved by brute force if enough compute power is available to do super-sampling.

VTK's rendering back end is relatively inflexible compared to libraries specifically designed for rendering. This makes it necessary to do non trivial modifications which require expert knowledge in order to generate the kind of visualizations we are looking for [18]. This fact is one of the original motivations for developing a custom tool such as RTNeuron. However, for large scale in-situ visualization it will be more sensible to reuse components from a more general software stack. Nonetheless, we still foresee that specific algorithms will be needed for rendering.

2.3 RTNeuron

RTNeuron is a high performance tool for the visualization of the structure and function of detailed cortical circuits in a very straightforward fashion. It can display cells (Fig. 1a), synapses (Fig. 1b) and playback simulation reports consisting of a single scalar variables mapped onto the cell surfaces (Fig. 1c).

The core of RTNeuron is a C++ parallel rendering library based on Equalizer [21], OpenSceneGraph [22] and the data model used in the BBP. OpenSceneGraph is a scene graph library based on OpenGL. The core library provides the

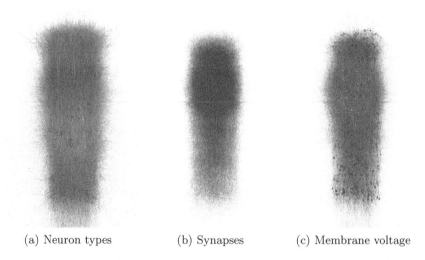

(a) Neuron types   (b) Synapses   (c) Membrane voltage

Fig. 1. Three different data views from a 5,000 neuron circuit. Figure 1a shows the neurons using a different color for each morphological type. Inhibitory neurons are rendered using a palette of blues while excitatory neurons are rendered using red, orange and yellow tones. The transparency value of each branch is computed as a function of the branch width. The middle figure shows all afferent synapses of the 5,000 neuron subset taken from the center of a 10,000 neuron circuit. Inhibitory synapses are blue and excitatory synapses are red. All synapses have an alpha value of 0.1. On the left, a time step of a simulation is presented. The colors show the membrane voltage, using blue to depict hyperpolarization (inhibition), transparent gray for parts at the resting potential, red for depolarization (excitation) and yellow for firing neurons. The alpha value is modulated additionally by multiplying its value from the simulation color map by the width-dependent value computed as in Fig. 1. The image shows intense activity in the upper middle part (Color figure online).

scene management and rendering techniques such as levels of detail, view frustum culling [23], transparency algorithms and the parallel rendering mechanisms [18] needed for high performance and quality.

A Python binding exposes the core API in a more user friendly way. The binding can be used to create custom applications on top of it, like the reference command line tool that features all the options for showing circuits and simulation results. Also, since Python is an interpreted language, the command line tool can spawn an IPython shell that allows full interactive control of the visualization.

Up to now, RTNeuron has mainly covered quality media production and aided in the debugging of circuit building (e.g. touch detection and synapse location). The addition of the Python interface aims to help in scientific discovery.

The current design is based on a series of assumptions:

- The rendering engine is based on hardware accelerated rasterization. Despite the progress made in the recent years in real-time ray-tracing, we consider that the type of scenes to render are not suitable for ray-tracing and that rasterization is a better approach. Rasterization eases the rendering of objects independently and the application of object-wide properties.
- All the scene has to fit in memory. Additionally, the data sets must be available in all nodes at the same location in the directory tree.
- Cell morphologies will be unique, although for the moment there are many circuits which use multiple instances of each cell reconstruction.
- The majority of use cases are post-mortem visualization, but streaming of simulation data from the simulator to RTNeuron is also possible, although there are no steering capabilities.
- In the post-mortem case, data is available on all the nodes, generally as a file in the local filesystem.

The main parallel rendering algorithms supported are sort-last and sort-first [25] and any combination of those. For sort-last, which is an object space decomposition, a kd-tree based spatial partition is used [18]. Each processor is assigned a leaf of the kd-tree and all the leaves contain approximately the same number of triangles. To support transparency, compositing is done in front to back order. The kd-tree partition ensures that there is a total order between the partial images produced by each processor and that for a given camera position, every processor can compute its position in the compositing sequence. The compositing stage only works with the direct-send algorithm [26], because other compositing algorithms that do not have a one-to-all communication step require dynamic changes to the compositing steps, i.e.: which processor sends and receives, and in which order. For circuits with unique morphologies, using sort-last effectively reduces the memory footprint at each node because the geometry can be clipped to the bounding box of each kd-tree leaf.

One of the main problems of the current approach for massive scenes is that weak-scalability is surprisingly bad (Fig. 2a), specially when transparency is enabled. Further analysis has shown that a substantial part of this imbalance comes from the transparency algorithm used in these benchmarks, dual-depth peeling, which is far from being state of the art. In some nodes, the rendering takes much longer because the algorithm has to iterate more times (Fig. 2b). Unfortunately, the rendering time of more recent non approximate algorithms, such as fragment linked lists [17], also depends on the depth complexity of the scene (i.e. the amount of geometry layers that overlap on each pixel), so we do not expect to have optimal weak-scalability even with this algorithm. This shows us that load balancing cannot be predicted by single variable figures, like the typically quoted for graphics performance, such as triangle counts. In general, there are many other factors that affect rendering time.

For future ultra-scale architectures the current post-mortem scenario will not be sustainable, not only due to scalability, but also due to the data movement issues mentioned in the introduction [28]. This is a general problem and applies

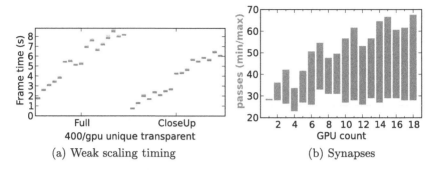

(a) Weak scaling timing   (b) Synapses

Fig. 2. Weak-scaling tests for different circuits sizes and GPU counts in a scene using transparency and two different camera positions (full and closeup). The circuit size is 400 multiplied by the number of GPUs used. Each bar shows the interquartile range and the median of the rendering time of 25 frames. As can be seen, the scalability (left) is much worse than the optimal one. This is because despite the geometry workload is balanced (in terms of triangles per GPU) the depth complexity is not. The higher the depth complexity, the more expensive is the sorting required for a correct transparency. This translates in an unbalanced number of render passes, as shown on the right. The test system was a visualization cluster with Intel Xeon X5690 @3.47 Ghz CPU, 24 GB of RAM and 3 NVidia GTX 580 graphics cards with 3 GB of DRAM per each of the six nodes used, having QDR Inifiniband as the network interconnect. The transparency algorithm chosen was dual-depth peeling [24] because it doesn't place an upper limit on the maximum depth complexity.

not only to visualization, but also to analysis techniques that need to do data aggregation with the whole circuit. In this scenario it seems that in-situ visualization and analysis is the only way to go. The paradigm shift from post-mortem analysis and visualization to in-situ is a challenge for both developers and users. Users will need to resort to exploratory techniques that are either performed during the simulation or, if used after the runs, will have access only to heavily reduced data sets. The co-design of the simulation and visualization and data analysis will be the norm.

Detailed visualization of cortical network simulation shares many problems with other domains, but it also has some particular details:

– The trend for exascale architectures seems to go towards having much more computing power per node, but without a substantial increase in the memory size. At the same time, detailed visualization requires geometrical information that is not needed by the simulation. Since the simulation is already memory bandwidth and size limited, visualization needs to minimize the memory footprint as much as possible. Given the relative low cost of computation compared to memory capacity and bandwidth, the solution to this problem will presumably involve to trade computing for memory and resort to on-the-fly generation of the geometrical models needed for rendering. Avoiding data replications in the host side in the case that there is a graphics hardware accelerator is also important and current graphics SW is not specifically designed for this. For example, for OpenGL based rendering this is mainly under control of the driver. Current drivers do not have support to avoid data replication, although new versions appear to start addressing this issue.

– Rendering large circuits requires sort-last parallelizations because otherwise the memory consumption is too high. For in-situ visualization, this means that the data partition made by the simulation needs to be reused by the visualization. Unfortunately, the data decomposition applied to the circuit by NEURON is unrelated to the spatial partition used for correct transparency and it does not provide a total order between the partial images that each node could generate. This mismatch among simulation and visualization is a potential source of problems that, in general, can be only addressed through co-design. In the present case, a potential solution is to capture all the fragments of a pixel during rendering, and exchange this information between the nodes using direct send, so each processor receives all the information to compose a portion of the screen. Even with a good communications network, this approach may not work without any compression. A similar approach has already been proposed [29], however, the results are difficult to extrapolate to our scenes, resolutions and node counts, testing is needed to ascertain the feasibility of this approach.

3   Conclusions

Very large scale simulations will open new areas to research and, in some cases, it appears as the only way to move forward in the quest for knowledge and technology. The path will not be easy and it is not expected that, as has happened in the past, the sole reliance on an increased circuit integration as the main driver to reach higher computational capability will let us achieve exaflop levels of performance. A clever mixture of techniques will be needed to achieve and successfully exploit this new capacity. A major problem will be to actually extract knowledge from computations that mix data sources and simulations of an unprecedented size. Visualization and data analysis will be key for this purpose. The case of the Human Brain Project could actually be the first major project to be confronted with this new way of doing science.

In this paper we have outlined some of the problems and described them in the context of a state of the art visualization tool for large neural simulations. Currently, the main problems relate to the scaling characteristics of the visualization with respect to the simulation. There is a mismatch between the simulation and the visualization and analysis capabilities. Much of this mismatch comes because in situ visualization for neural simulations is still in its infancy. The next generation of SW and HW for the large scale, will have to tackle a new set of problems and merely evolutionary approaches will not suffice. Simulation codes have received much more attention and scale to hundreds of thousands of processors, whereas visualization is much more limited. It is believed that data movement is going to be a major issue in future exascale architectures and in situ techniques will have to be developed. Simulation, visualization and analysis will have to share a comparatively more reduced memory space using access patterns that will also differ. HW and SW design for the exascale will need to take this into account and balance the different requirements. Otherwise, these problems will move the bottleneck to the visualization and analysis phase.

Acknowledgements. This work has been partially funded by the Spanish Ministry of Education and Science (Cajal Blue Brain project) and the Human Brain Project (FP7-604102-HBP). The authors would also like to thank the Blue Brain Project for the collaboration framework in which this work has been developed.

References

1. Tufte, E.R.: The Visual Display of Quantitative Information. Graphics Press, Cheshire (2001)
2. McCormick, B.H., et al.: Visualization in Scientific Computing. Comput. Graph. **21**(6), 1–14 (1987)
3. Yu, H., Wang, C., Grout, R.W., Chen, J.H., Ma, K.-L.: In situ visualization for large-scale combustion simulations. IEEE Comput. Graph. Appl. **30**(3), 45–57 (2010)
4. Dongarra, J.: Performance of various computers using standard linear equations software (Linpack Benchmark Report), University of Tennessee Computer Science Technical Report, CS-89-85 (2013)
5. www.top500.org
6. Fekete, J.D.: Software and hardware infrastructures for visual analytics. Computer **46**(7), 22–29 (2013)
7. Fisher, D., Popov, I., Drucker, S., Schraefel, M.: Trust me, I'm partially right: incremental visualization lets analysts explore large datasets faster. In: CHI 12, pp. 1673–1682 (2012)
8. Gewaltig, M.-O., Diesmann, M.: NEST (NEural Simulation Tool). Scholarpedia **2**(4), 1430 (2007)
9. Carnevale, N.T., Hines, M.L.: The NEURON Book. Cambridge University Press, Cambridge (2006)
10. Hines, M.L., Eichner, H., Schürmann, F.: Fully implicit parallel simulation of single neurons. J. Comput. Neurosci. **25**(3), 439–448 (2008)
11. Markram, H.: The blue brain project. Nat. Rev. Neurosci. **7**(2), 153–160 (2006)
12. Druckmann, S., Banitt, Y., Gidon, A.A., Schürmann, F., Henry, M., Segev, I.: A novel multiple objective optimization framework for constraining conductance-based neuron models by experimental data. Front. Neurosci. **1**(1), 7–18 (2007)
13. Hay, E., Hill, S., Schürmann, F., Markram, H., Segev, I.: Models of neocortical layer 5b pyramidal cells capturing a wide range of dendritic and perisomatic active properties. PLoS Comput. Biol. **7**(7), e1002107 (2011)
14. Hill, S.L., Wang, Y., Riachi, I., Schürmann, F., Markram, H.: Statistical connectivity provides a sufficient foundation for specific functional connectivity in neocortical neural microcircuits. In: Proceedings of the National Academy of Sciences (2012)
15. Reimann, M.W., Anastassiou, C.A., Perin, R., Hill, S.L., Markram, H., Koch, C.: A biophysically detailed model of neocortical local field potentials predicts the critical role of active membrane currents. Neuron **79**(2), 375–390 (2013)
16. Haber, R.B., McNabb, D.A.: Visualization idioms: a conceptual model for scientific visualization systems. In: Nielson, G.M., Shriver, B., Rosenblum, L.J. (eds.) Visualization in Scientific Computing, pp. 74–93. IEEE Computer Society, Los Alamitos (1990)

17. Gruen, H., Thibieroz, N.: OIT and indirect illumination using DX11 linked lists. In: Proceedings of the 2010 Game Developer Conference (2010)
18. Hernando, J.B., Biddiscombe, J., Bohara, B., Eilemann, S., Schürmann, F.: Practical parallel rendering of detailed neuron simulations. In: Eurographics Symposium on Parallel Graphics and Visualization (2013)
19. Lasserre, S., Hernando, J.B., Schürmann, F., De Miguel Anasagasti, P., Abou-Jaoudé, G., Markram, H.: A neuron membrane mesh representation for visualization of electrophysiological simulations. IEEE Trans. Visualiz. Comput. Graph. **18**(2), 214–227 (2012)
20. Hilbert, M., López, P.: The world's technological capacity to store, communicate, and compute information. Science **332**, 60–65 (2011)
21. Eilemann, S., Makhinya, M., Pajarola, R.: Equalizer: a scalable parallel rendering framework. IEEE Trans. Visualiz. Comput. Graph. **15**, 436–452 (2009)
22. Robert, O., Burns, D., et al.: OpenSceneGraph (2001–2014). http://www.openscenegraph.org
23. Hernando, J.B., Pastor, L., Schürmann, F.: Towards real-time visualization of detailed neural tissue models: view frustum culling for parallel rendering. In: BioVis 2012: 2nd IEEE Symposium on biological data visualization (2012)
24. Bavoil, L., Myers, L.K.: Order independent transparency with dual depth peeling. Technical report, NVIDIA Corporation (2008)
25. Molnar, S., Cox, M., Ellsworth, D., Fuchs, H.: A sorting classification of parallel rendering. IEEE Comput. Graph. Appl. **14**(4), 23–32 (1994)
26. Eilemann, S., Pajarola, R.: Direct send compositing for parallel sort-last rendering. In: Eurographics Symposium on Parallel Graphics and Visualization, pp. 29–36 (2007)
27. Schroeder, W.J., Martin, K., Lorensen, W.E.: The Visualization Toolkit: An Object-Oriented Approach to 3D Graphics, 3rd edn. Kitware Inc. (formerly Prentice-Hall), New York (2003)
28. Dongarra, J., Beckman, P., et al.: The international exascale software roadmap. Int. J. High Perform. Comput. Appl. **25**(1), 3–60 (2011)
29. Kauker, D., Krone, M., Panagiotidis, A., Reina, G., Ertl, T.: Evaluation of per-pixel linked lists for distributed rendering and comparative analysis. Comput. Vis. Sci. **15**(3), 111–121 (2012)
30. Miller, R.B.: Response time in man-computer conversational transactions. In: Proceedings of AFIPS Fall Joint Computer Conference, vol. 33, pp. 267–277 (1968)
31. DOE ASCAC, Data Subcommittee: Synergistic Challenges in Data-Intensive Science and Exascale Computing (2013)

Supercomputing Infrastructure
for Simulations of the Human Brain

Thomas Lippert[1,2]([✉]) and Boris Orth[1,2]

[1] Jülich Supercomputing Centre, Institute for Advanced Simulation,
Forschungszentrum Jülich, 52425 Jülich, Germany
`th.lippert@fz-julich.de`
[2] Jülich Aachen Research Alliance (JARA), Jülich, Germany

Abstract. Decoding the human brain is considered as one of the great-est challenges faced by 21st century science. Advancing brain research by simulating the full human brain promises to provide profound insights into its complex functionality and into what makes us human. These insights will help to understand brain diseases and to develop novel treatments.

Modern high performance computing technology not only allows to bring these goals into focus, it might itself be transformed profoundly being guided towards the exascale and beyond. On the one hand, infor-mation and communication technology (ICT) provides us with a com-pletely new understanding of the brain and its diseases. On the other hand, this understanding of the brain will lead inevitably to *brain inspired*, radical innovation in computing. In particular, the Human Brain Project, one of the two EU Flagship research projects, will require data-intensive HPC at an extreme scale and fully interactive visualization and steering capabilities. Eventually, revolutionary new computing technolo-gies, so-called neuromorphic devices, are expected to become reality.

The following contribution outlines the plans for the HBP's High Per-formance Computing (HPC) platform. A central brain simulation system at Jülich Research Centre, Germany, is planned to be operated as a user facility. It will provide the optimized hardware-software environment run-ning a full virtual human brain model. Neuroscientists will be enabled to carry out in-silico experiments based on this model. The platform will be complemented by a software development system at CSCS in Lugano, Switzerland, and a third system will be running efficient molecular-level simulations at BSC in Barcelona, Spain. Finally, a system adapted to support massive data analytics will be hosted at CINECA in Bologna, Italy. During the ramp-up phase of the project (2013-2916), the HBP will link with PRACE institutions that have expressed their interest in adding in-kind support to the Platform and will try to motivate PRACE to establish programmatic access to PRACE systems, in order to allow peer-reviewed usage of the entire European Tier-0 capability.

1 Introduction

Human Brain Project. In January 2013, the European Commission selected the Human Brain Project (HBP) as one of two large-scale initiatives driven by and

© Springer International Publishing Switzerland 2014
L. Grandinetti et al. (Eds.): BrainComp 2013, LNCS 8603, pp. 198–212, 2014.
DOI: 10.1007/978-3-319-12084-3_16

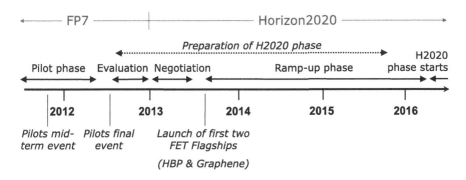

Fig. 1. Timeline of the Human Brain Project until the start of the operational phase.

driving information technology [1]. Six candidates reached the final round in an evaluation process starting out with about 50 expressions of interest, which were further condensed to about 20 proposals [2]. The HBP will receive funding through the EU's new Future and Emerging Technologies (FET) Flagship initiative which will start in October 2013. The HBP marks, for the first time, a deep union of Neuroscience and Computer Science worldwide, fostering a novel methodology to study the brain and creating benefit for both sides. The 2.5-year ramp-up phase of the project (until March 2016), which is embedded in the EU's 7th Framework Programme, will be followed by an operational phase under the upcoming next framework programme, called Horizon 2020, *cf.* Fig. 1. In the ramp-up phase of the HBP, more than 80 European and international research institutions are federated, with more partners supposed to join the consortium through a Competitive Partner Call Programme. The HBP was initiated and is led by the neuroscientist and biologist Henry Markram from the Swiss Ecole Polytechnique Fédérale de Lausanne (EPFL). The entire HBP Flagship project will be subdivided into four phases. The operational phases 2 to 4 will be funded through the EC's Horizon 2020 programme. The HBP is planned to last for ten years with a total budget estimated to reach about one billion Euros.

Scientific Goal. The overall goal of the HBP is to collect all existing knowledge about the human brain in order to reengineer the brain, piece by piece. This process will lead to a sequence of ever more refined multi-scale models of the human brain. The supercomputer-based interactive simulation of these models will enable neuroscientists to implement their hypotheses regarding the functionality of fundamental processes such as the brain's self-healing capabilities, the understanding of higher-level functionality such as 3-d vision, as well as cognition and finally the emergence of consciousness. In this manner, the resulting model, the "virtual human brain", will provide a fundamentally new instrument to investigate complexity and functioning of the brain as well as its diseases and prospects for therapies. It also promises to improve predictions on the outcome of brain surgery.

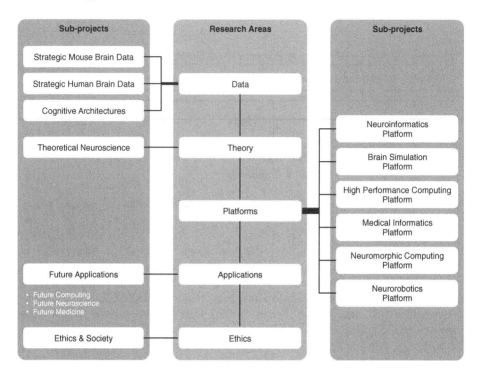

Fig. 2. Organizational structure of the Human Brain Project. The right column shows those sub-projects that are ICT platforms.

Ramp-Up Phase. The primary aim of the coming ramp-up phase of the HBP is to build a new ICT infrastructure for the benefit of future neuroscience, future medicine and future computing, *cf.* Fig. 2. This European research infrastructure is planned to comprise six so-called ICT Platforms. They will be dedicated to Neuroinformatics, Medical Informatics, Brain Simulation, Neuromorphic Computing, Neurorobotics, and finally High-Performance Computing. The neuroinformatics platform will enable the federation of neuroscience data on all levels, from cell to structure, connectome and receptor data up to functional data. Together with medical data gathered in the Medical Informatics Platform, data integration will take place in unifying models created within the Brain Simulation Platform. These models are simulated on the infrastructure provided by the HPC Platform which also creates specific enabling software technologies like environments for interactive steering and visualization on exascale systems. Feedback of the results into HPC development again promises to be a guide towards innovation in ICT and supercomputing.

In a sort of productive loop, the results are validated against empirical data. The HBP's models and simulations will enable neuroscientists to carry out *in silico* experiments on the virtual human brain that cannot be done *in vivo* for practical or ethical reasons. Models of mental processes will be applied in virtual robots through research of the Neurorobotics platform. Finally, in the neuromorphic platform, brain-inspired information processing will be realized by applying these findings on the structure, connectivity and functionality of the brain within "neuromorphic" computing systems, incorporating unique characteristics of the brain such as energy-efficiency, fault-tolerance and the ability to learn.

2   Scientific Challenges

The design of the HPC Platform must primarily follow the requirements of the scientists working in the HBP's subprojects and ICT platforms. On the one hand, it is the multiscale approach to brain simulations as applied in the brain simulation platform that determines the objectives of the HPC platform. On the other hand, it is the truly big data requirements being manifest in the mouse and human brain subprojects, as well as the data federation challenges of the Neuroinformatics and Medical Informatics Platforms, see Fig. 2. Finally, the prospects of feeding back the newly gained knowledge on the information processing capabilities of the human brain into new approaches for supercomputing and big data analytics should be reflected in the orientation of the HPC platform towards R & D, see Sect. 3.1.

2.1   Multiscale Simulations

The multiscale nature of the simulation strategy in the HBP is sketched in Fig. 3. Starting from molecular dynamics simulations on the sub-cellular level—with GROMACS [3] as a representative software package—, the next level is treated by simulating biochemical signaling pathways like ligand-receptor interactions using reaction-diffusion codes—here we cite STEPS [4] as a representative.

Findings from molecular dynamics simulations at the sub-cellular level and reaction diffusion simulations on the synaptic levels will serve as input for a next higher level of abstraction, the simulation of the neuronal network. Neurons of different morphology with their dendrites and axons will form microcircuits with the synapses as contact points. In order to model the functional units properly and in order to compose these units into a kind of "connectome" similar to that of the human brain, extremely detailed investigations of the brain's cellular architecture and the full fiber architecture on a resolution scale approaching $1\,\mu m$ must be carried out, see Sect. 2.2. This defines one step of the iterative brain model building where the available structural, physiological and functional data are brought together creating a unifying brain model. This model will be validated against higher level experimental data and results from simulations, and the refinement will go into the next step.

The HBP will primarily exploit two software packages for the simulation of the human brain, NEST [5,6] and NEURON [7]. The NEURON code allows the use of detailed neuron models, which can take anatomical and biophysical properties of individual neurons into account. NEST is targeted at the simulation

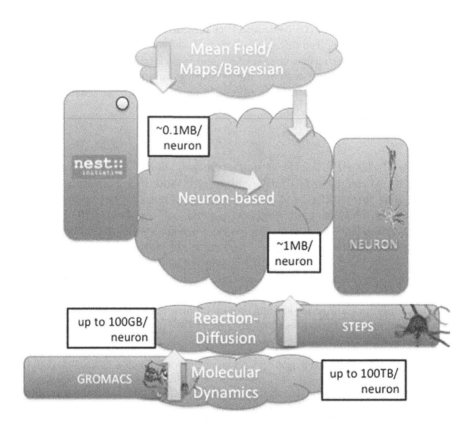

Fig. 3. A multiscale view on brain simulation. The goal is to abstract from level to level catching the essential features on each level in order to gain a simplified representation on the next level (Chart courtesy of Felix Schürmann).

of very large networks and therefore uses a simplified point model. The HBP will also conduct coupled NEST-NEURON simulations in order to bridge the spatial resolution gap.

One major difficulty for the simulations on the sub-cellular and synaptic level is the necessity to bridge time-scales of many orders of magnitude. Speeding up such simulations leads into strong scaling problems, as the system sizes are small compared to the huge distributed memory of multi-petaflop systems, simulating properties and biochemical reactions of proteins. Maybe for some of these investigations novel dedicated computer architectures like ANTON [8] are a solution. There are also promising developments using stochastic methods to tackle very large time scales [9].

It is estimated that about 100 TB per neuron are required for the molecular simulation of all biochemical processes of an entire neuron indicating that state-of-the-art multi-petaflop systems will be well suited and bring us back to weak scaling. It is, however, evident that such a simulation cannot be included into the brain simulation in a dynamical manner, emphasizing again that a multi-scale approach is mandatory. Similarly, reaction-diffusion simulations will require about 100 GB of storage per neuron. Here, we can expect that several thousands of neurons can be treated on large multi-petaflop systems; still this number is far off the scale of a full brain. Also here, a multiscale approach is required.

The simulations of the brain's neuronal network eventually will include the gigantic number of about 100 billion neurons with about 10,000 synapses each. The NEST code needs about 0.1 MB on average per single neuron, leading to a requirement of 10 PB of memory for this simple representation of the full human brain. On today's systems like JUQUEEN at Jülich Supercomputing Centre [10], about 1 % of the human brain can be represented by NEST. On this machine, NEST has been shown to scale up to the full number of 458,752, see the contribution to this volume by Markus Diesmann[1]. For NEURON, at this stage of its evolution, about 1 MB of memory per neuron is required. Both NEST and NEURON, developed on several generations of supercomputers, represent a weak scaling problem, requiring memory far beyond current DRAM capacity.

2.2 Big Data Analytics

A discussed in the previous section, the brain's cellular architecture and the fiber architecture must be known on a resolution scale of about 1 μm in order to understand its functional architecture and its connectome. This field has entered the realm of scientific big data analytics as demonstrated in the contribution to this volume by Katrin Amunts [11]. Figure 4 presents an overview of different length scales and associated methods to analyze aspects of cellular architecture and connectome: Physiological and structural investigations of human brains below 100 μm are carried out in *post mortem* brains. Cell bodies range in size from 1 to 10 μm, the largest cells reach 120 μm in height. Axon diameters cover the range from 1 to 20 μm. They form fiber bundles and compact fiber tracts.

3-dimensional reconstructions of distributions of neurons on the level of entire *post mortem* brains by now have reached a resolution of 20 μm isotropic [12]. One shot imaging of the fiber structure of complete human brain sections by means of Polarized Light Imaging (PLI) is in the range of 60 μm [13]. This spatial resolution could be achieved by combining state-of-the-art scanners and polarimeters with state-of-the-art server-based processing.

However, the limit of resolution for the entire brain is 1 μm for the cellular architecture as achieved by conventional light microscopy and even somewhat beyond by means of confocal laser scanner microscopy (CLSM). Figure 5 clearly demonstrates the need for a resolution on a scale of 1 μm. In practice, sections are cut off the brain by means of a high precision microtome, the microscopical data are taken, and a 3-dimensional reconstruction process is following. The resolution of 1 μm from the CLSM, suitable for single cell analysis, corresponds to about 30 GB of data per slice, *i.e.*, 300 TB for the full brain, based on 16-bit gray value coding. It is evident, that this huge amount of data requires

---

[1] See M. Diesmann, these proceedings [18].

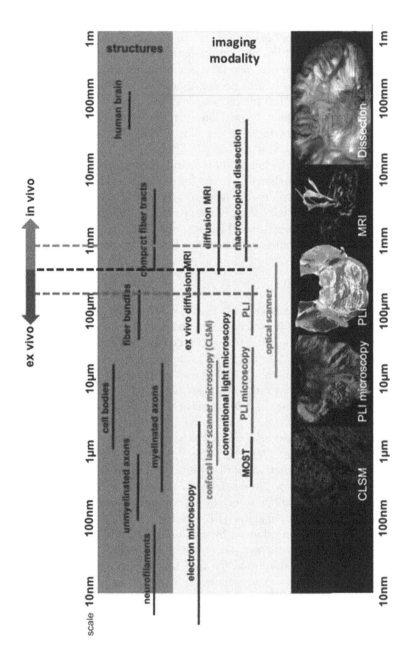

Fig. 4. Dimensions of objects composing cellular architecture and connectome together with corresponding analytics methods (Chart courtesy of Katrin Amunts and Markus Axer).

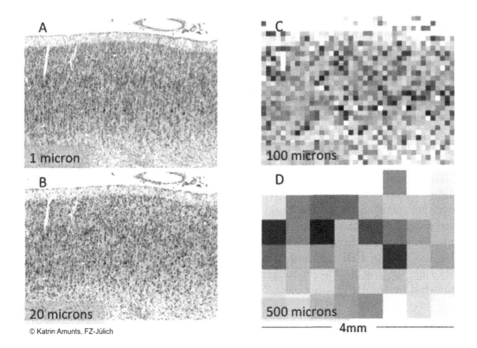

Fig. 5. In order to resolve the smallest cells, a resolution of 1 μm is required (Picture courtesy of Katrin Amunts).

highly advanced HPC technology for both data management and computing, *i.e.*, scientific big data analytics. The 3-dimensional reconstruction process is guided by a partly automatized data processing pipeline with full parallelization of the 3-dimensional reconstruction step on more than 100 nodes of the Jülich cluster JUROPA [14]. In order to assess variability, a representative set of 10 brains will be required eventually, with a total size of the dataset approaching more than 3 PB.

As far as the reconstruction of the connectome is concerned, today's state-of-the-art technologies investigate slices of about 60 μm thickness to determine the vector fields with an in-plane resolution of 60 μm isotropic for the large-area polarimeter, again with server-based processing technology being sufficiently performant.

The method exploits the bi-refringence effect of the myelinated nerve fibers to reconstruct the 3-dimensional vector field of the nerve fibers in a given section. This is achieved by means of the so-called Jones Calculus. By application of an Independent Component Analysis (ICA), dust and damage can be removed from the picture, and by stacking the sections, the full 3-dimensional vector field can be reconstructed through tracking of the vectors from section to section [11]. The workflow for the PLI-processing requires more than 30 distinct processing steps. The steps with Jones Calculus and ICA have been automatized for processing and analysis using the UNICORE parallel and distributed workflow platform [15], developed mainly at the Jülich Supercomputing Centre (JSC).

However, the frontier of resolution of axons is set by PLI microscopy, touching the $1\,\mu m$ level. A $1.5\,\mu m$ resolution of the PLI microscope, as used in Jülich, leads to about $1.5\,TB$ of data per section. With an intended number of 2500 sections per brain, $3.7\,PB$ of data will result from one full brain. These tasks again can only be handled using most advanced scientific big data analytics. It turns out that dealing with representative sets of data will eventually lead to the same orders of magnitude to be managed and analyzed as we have encountered in Sect. 2.1 for the simulation of the full brain.

The examples given are concentrating on the investigation of the human brain structure and connectome. While, in its first five years, the HBP will have a stronger focus on the mouse brain [16], human brain structural data will gain more weight while the project is progressing. In addition, further medical and clinical brain data from all over Europe and worldwide will be gathered and federated by the HBP through its Neuroinformatics and Medical informatics platforms, see Fig. 2. The management and analysis of all these data will be supported by the HPC subproject.

3   HPC Platform

The HPC Platform is the HBP's enabler of multiscale brain simulations on all levels, as well as of scientific big data analytics for mouse and human brain data as discussed in the previous section. It is expected that the understanding of the information processing capabilities of the human brain will inspire ICT and future supercomputing. The R & D efforts as planned for the HPC subproject will reflect all these aspects.

The various types of simulations described in Sect. 2.1 on the sub-cellular and synaptic level will be carried out by several groups in the HBP, mainly supported by the Barcelona Supercomputing Centre (BSC), where the BSC's Tier-0 system will be adapted and upgraded accordingly. In addition, the HBP will rely on machines available in the HPC-ecosystem created by the Partnership for Advanced Computing in Europe (PRACE) [17], subject to the competitive peer-reviewed provision policy of PRACE.

The simulations with NEST and NEURON are a challenge *sui generis*. The sheer amount of cycles required in order to work with the entire virtual brain towards the end of the HBP's last operational phase will need a machine with full exascale capability. A considerable fraction of the capacity of this system will be allocated to the HBP and other neuroscientists, as well as to clinicians, in the manner of a user facility with interactive access. The JSC at Jülich Research Centre is devoted to create the HBP supercomputing facility complemented by a development system located at CSCS in Lugano, the Swiss National Super-computing Centre.

It is the main objective of research and development in the HPC subproject to provide facilities, system software solutions, programming environments, numerical algorithms, interactive steering and visualization sub-systems. The work package structure will allow to meet all these aspects:

WP1 Technology Evaluation (D. Pleiter)
WP2 Mathematical Methods, Programming Models and Tools (J. Labarta)
WP3 Interactive Visualization, Analysis and Control (T. Kuhlen)
WP4 Exascale Data Management (A. Ailamaki)
WP5 Integration and Operations (Th. Schulthess)
WP6 User Support and Community Building (B. Orth)
WP7 Scientific Coordination (Th. Lippert)

In the following subsection, some exemplary activities from the work packages are presented.

3.1 Architecture Evaluation

A primary objective of the HPC subproject is the evaluation and specification of supercomputing and data analytics systems. In the ramp-up phase, we first have to find out what we can learn from benchmarks on available systems. One of the neuron-level network abstractions, NEST, describes the neurons by a relatively simple model and is thus able to scale up to extremely large networks of neurons, dendrites, axons and synapses. Benchmarks [18] have been performed on the Japanese K-Computer [19] as well as on the Jülich JUQUEEN system [10].

The memory capacity of the K-Computer allows to represent 1.73 billion neurons with 10.4 trillion synapses, consuming 1.34 PiBytes of main memory. On JUQUEEN with about 0.45 PiBytes of memory, NEST can still simulate more than 1 billion neurons. The NEST simulation proceeds in intervals. Spikes are delivered through the network from previous intervals and the neuronal states are updated. This implies a short but compute-intensive step. The spikes are exchanged between the processes via MPI, collective communication operations are involved as well. The lesson learned is that NEST requires a large but balanced memory capacity C_{mem} to enable the simulation of large spiking neuronal networks. However, a high memory bandwidth B_{mem} is required as well in order to keep the ratio of simulation time *vs.* simulated time small. It turns out that the relevant metrics is given by

$$R_{\mathrm{mem}} = \frac{C_{\mathrm{mem}}}{B_{\mathrm{mem}}}. \tag{1}$$

Integrating multiple memory technologies, the balance between the different technologies can be optimized with respect to the characteristics of a given simulation code. High-bandwidth memory technologies like GDDR5 and HMC are characterized by $R_{\mathrm{mem}} = \mathcal{O}(10)\,\mathrm{ms}$, standard DDR memory by $R_{\mathrm{mem}} = \mathcal{O}(1)\,\mathrm{s}$, and dense memory technologies like NAND-flash, PCM or STT-MRAM by $R_{\mathrm{mem}} = \mathcal{O}(100)\,\mathrm{s}$.

Creating hierarchical memory models, including novel storage-class memory integrated in the form of network attached memory on a very low latency, highest bandwidth network, and the appropriate middleware solutions are one line

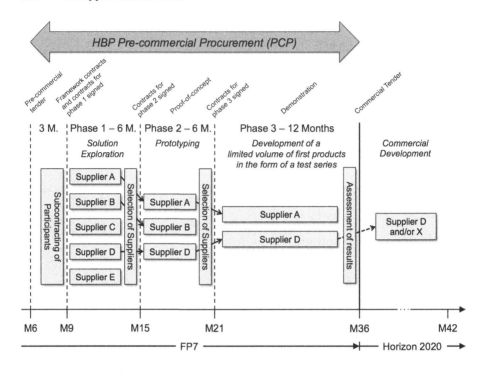

Fig. 6. Stages of the PCP for the HBP in the ramp-up phase.

of investigation carried out in the HPC subproject. Additionally, we have to think about file systems, caches for file systems or the appropriate file system semantics, or offloading pragmas.

3.2   Pre-commercial Procurement

The specific supercomputing requirements for HBP analysis, modeling and simulation are specified in close contact with the simulation subproject. The goal is to drive the development of innovative HPC technology solutions that meet the HBP's specific requirements such as large memory and interactivity. To achieve this goal, the HPC subproject will start an open, transparent and competitive process together with the international HPC industry. The timeline of this Pre-Commercial Procurement (PCP) process is shown in Fig. 6.

The PCP of the HBP will be organized in three phases, with two competing vendors providing prototypes for demonstration and validation in the last phase. In this manner, the most promising HPC technologies meeting the requirements of the HBP will be chosen. These will form the technological basis for the procurement of the HBP's pre-exascale production system with about 50 PF/s performance and about 20 PB of hierarchical memory in the next phase of the project (2016/18).

3.3   Sharpening the Tools

The immense data management and simulation challenges as posed by the HBP, requiring machines by factors larger and more complex than current supercomputing systems, can only be mastered by a holistic strategy including accompanying research. The HPC subproject involves work packages and tasks that will for instance provide new integrative programing models or HPC-adapted numerical algorithms, relevant for brain simulation. Rather than going into details at this stage, let us consider an important element of R & D in the HBP, the field of performance tools.[2]

The goal of the task "performance analysis and tuning" is to support the HBP code teams in analyzing and tuning their simulation codes. The tools have to run on extreme-scale systems and must be enabled to interact with HBP interactive workflows. The partners JSC and BSC are scaling up the tool packages Score-P, Scalasca, CUBE, Extrae, Paraver, and Dimemas.

It is reassuring that the performance analysis package Scalasca 1.4.3 was able to perform on the entire BlueGene/Q at JSC running the NASA NAS benchmark BT-MZ. In fact, the code was tested even on 1,048,704 cores of the system at Argonne National Laboratory. This was the largest successful trace measurement and analysis ever done.

A scaling analysis of the NEST code on BlueGene/Q was performed with varying core numbers on 1, 2, 4, and 8 racks. It was able to automatically determine and classify scaling behavior of each program region. First results showed a significant improvement of the performance in the neural network buildup phase. A low-level analysis with the NEURON neuroscience code is under way. It addresses the integration kernel, with focus on algorithmic density, L2 cache-to- memory bandwidth, stalled cycles, vectorization, and prefetching.

3.4   Making of the HPC Platform

The HBP's HPC Platform subproject is devoted to building the supercomputing and data hard- and software infrastructure required to run cellular brain model simulations up to the scale of a full human brain, and to make this infrastructure available to the consortium and the wider community. Figure 7 shows a sketch of the structure of platform.

A central element of the HPC Platform is the HBP Supercomputer, the project's main production system, which will be built in stages to arrive at the exascale capability needed for cellular simulations of the complete human brain at the beginning of the next decade. It will be the task of the JSC to develop, deploy and operate the HBP Supercomputer.

The interactive supercomputing capabilities that will be developed for the HBP will be invaluable not only for neuroscience but also for a broad range of

---

[2] The fields "programming paradigms" will be presented as a contribution by Jesús Labarta [20], the field "interactive visualization" is found in the contribution of Torsten Kuhlen [21].

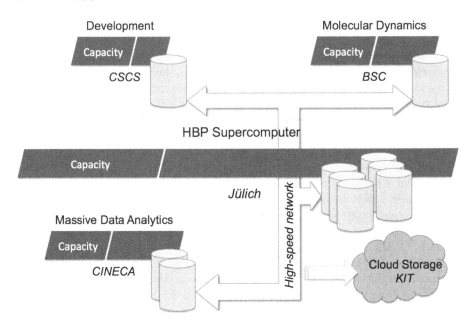

Fig. 7. Supercomputing and data infrastructure for the HBP.

other applications in the life sciences and elsewhere. While the HBP is poised to become a main driver for the future development of high-performance computing, the breadth of applications involved and their requirements will warrant the usability of the HBP Supercomputer for many other fields, too.

Besides the main HBP Supercomputer at Jülich the HBP's HPC Platform will consist of a software development system at CSCS (Lugano, Switzerland), a system for molecular-level simulations at BSC (Barcelona, Spain), and a system for massive data analytics at CINECA (Bologna, Italy). During the ramp-up phase of the project, the HBP will negotiate with further PRACE Tier-0 institutions that have expressed their interest in adding in-kind support to the Platform. A high priority goal is to establish a PRACE community access programme, also to be negotiated in the ramp-up phase. This will allow access to the Tier-0 capability of the HPC Platform, reviewed by the HBP's International Access Board, via PRACE services.

4   Summary and Outlook

The HPC subproject plays a key role in the HBP as it contributes to the project a unique combination of expertise and infrastructure, building the interface between neuroscience and supercomputing. Modern high performance computing technology will not only be essential to bring us closer to the goals regarding future medicine and a deeper understanding of the brain's functions. The HBP has the potential to change the future course of HPC itself. This includes *brain-inspired* computing in the form of algorithms and, furthermore, the radically novel idea of *neuromorphic* computing hardware.

Acknowledgments. In its ramp-up phase, the Human Brain Project is funded primarily by the European Union's Seventh Framework Programme (FP7/2007–2013) under grant agreement $\mathcal{N}^{o.}$ 604102. The Helmholtz Association supports the interdisciplinary collaboration between the Helmholtz programmes "Decoding the Human Brain" and "Supercomputing and Big Data" through funding of the Helmholtz Portfolio "Supercomputing and Modeling for the Human Brain" (SMHB). The SMHB hosts the Simulation Laboratory "Neuroscience" at Jülich Supercomputing Centre, which is partly funded by the Jülich Aachen Research Alliance (JARA) and which is a member of the German National Bernstein Network Computational Neuroscience. We thank Katrin Amunts, Markus Axer, Sonja Grün, Markus Diesmann, Thomas Schulthess and Felix Schürmann for provision of graphical material and for many fruitful and inspiring discussions.

References

1. Markram, H., et al.: Human Brain Project. Web Address, The HBP Consortium. https://www.humanbrainproject.eu/de. Accessed July 2014
2. Markram, H., et al.: The Human Brain Project: A Report to the European Commission. PDF Document, The HBP-PS Consortium (2012). https://www.humanbrainproject.eu/de/news-events
3. Lindahl, E., et al.: GROMACS. Web Address, Stockholm University. http://www.gromacs.org/. Accessed July 2014
4. De Schutter, E., et al.: STEPS: Stochastic Engine for Pathway Simulation. Web Address, Okinawa Institute of Science and Technology (OIST). http://steps.sourceforge.net/STEPS/members.php. Accessed July 2014
5. Gewaltig, M.O., Diesmann, M., Morrison, A., Plesser, H.E.: NEST: NEural Simulation Tool. Web Address, EPFL, FZJ and UMB. http://www.nest-initiative.org/Software:About_NEST. Accessed July 2014
6. Gewaltig, M.O., Diesmann, M.: NEST: NEural Simulation Tool. Scholarpedia **2**, 1430 (2007)
7. Hines, M., et al.: NEURON. Web Address, Yale University. http://www.neuron.yale.edu/neuron/. Accessed July 2014
8. Piana, S., Klepeis, J.L., Shaw, D.E.: Assessing the accuracy of physical models used in protein-folding simulations: quantitative evidence from long molecular dynamics simulations. Curr. Opin. Struct. Biol. **24**, 98–105 (2014)
9. Irbck, A., Mohanty, S.: PROFASI: a Monte Carlo simulation package for protein folding and aggregation. J. Comput. Chem. **27**, 1548–1555 (2006)
10. Stephan, M., et al.: JUQUEEN: The Blue Gene/Q at Jülich Supercomputing Centre. Web Address, FZ-Jülich. http://www.fz-juelich.de/ias/jsc/EN/Expertise/Supercomputers/JUQUEEN/JUQUEEN_node.html. Accessed July 2014
11. Amunts, K., Bücker, O., Axer, M.: Towards a multiscale, high-resolution model of the human brain. In: Grandinetti, L., Lippert, T., Petkov, N. (eds.) BrainComp 2013. LNCS, vol. 8603, pp. 3–14. Springer, Heidelberg (2014)

12. Amunts, K., Lepage, C., Borgeat, L., Mohlberg, H., Dickscheid, T., Rousseau, M.É., Bludau, S., Bazin, P.L., Lewis, L.B., Oros-Peusquens, A.M., Shah, N.J., Lippert, T., Zilles, K., Evans, A.C.: Bigbrain: an ultrahigh-resolution 3d human brain model. Science **340**, 1472–1475 (2013)
13. Axer, M., Gräßel, D., Reckfort, J., Tabbi, G., Amunts, K.: PL: Polarized Light Imaging. Web Address, FZ-Jülich. http://www.fz-juelich.de/inm/inm-1/ EN/Forschung/_docs/PLI/PLI_node.html. Accessed July 2014
14. Detert, U., et al.: JUROPA: Jülich Research on Petaflop Architectures. Web Address, FZ-Jülich. http://www.fz-juelich.de/ias/jsc/EN/Expertise/ Supercomputers/JUROPA/JUROPA_node.html. Accessed July 2014
15. Streit, A., et al.: UNICORE: Uniform Interface to Computing Resources. Web Address, FZ-Jülich and KIT. http://www.unicore.eu. Accessed July 2014
16. Silvestri, L., Sacconi, F., Pavone, L.S.: The connectomics challenge. Funct. Neurol. **28**, 167–173 (2013)
17. Bassini, S., et al.: PRACE: Partnership for Advanced Computing in Europe. Web Address, PRACE AISBL Brussels. http://www.prace-ri.eu/. Accessed July 2014
18. van Albada, S.J., Kunkel, S., Morrison, A., Diesmann, M.: Integrating brain structure and dynamics on supercomputers. In: Grandinetti, L., Lippert, T., Petkov, N. (eds.) BrainComp 2013. LNCS, vol. 8603, pp. 22–32. Springer, Heidelberg (2014)
19. Hirao, K., et al.: K Computer. Web Address, Riken – Advanced Institute for Computational Science. http://www.aics.riken.jp/en/k-computer/about/. Accessed July 2014
20. Lopez, V., Sola, M., Labarta, J.: Performance analysis and parallelization strategies in neuron simulation codes. In: Grandinetti, L., Lippert, T., Petkov, N. (eds.) BrainComp 2013. LNCS, vol. 8603, pp. 143–156. Springer, Heidelberg (2014)
21. Kuhlen, T.W., Hentschel, B.: Towards an explorative visual analysis of cortical neuronal network simulations. In: Grandinetti, L., Lippert, T., Petkov, N. (eds.) BrainComp 2013. LNCS, vol. 8603, pp. 171–183. Springer, Heidelberg (2014)

Author Index

Printed in the United States
By Bookmasters